DUNANT

THE STORY OF THE RED CROSS

HENRI DUNANT

*Sculpture by Ernst Durig, in the National Headquarters
of the American Red Cross, Washington, D.C.*

Dunant

THE STORY OF THE RED CROSS

By MARTIN GUMPERT

New York
OXFORD UNIVERSITY PRESS
1938

Copyright, 1938, by Oxford University Press, New York, Inc.

Printed in the United States of America

10/03

Contents

DUNANT
THE STORY OF THE
RED CROSS

Dunant

THE STORY OF THE RED CROSS

I

Youth in Geneva

THIS is the story of Henri Dunant: a rich banker, whose interest centred in his business, blundered by chance into the inferno of a battlefield. He became obsessed with the idea of doing everything humanly possible against the inhuman horror of war. His passionate struggle, as a private individual, against political powers and bureaucracies ended with the founding of the Red Cross, but meanwhile his reputation and money had been sacrificed. He was one of Europe's outstanding figures, but with his fortune he also lost his bourgeois status. For years he lived as a beggar in misery and concealment. Decades later the old man, whom everyone had long believed dead, was discovered in the alms-house of a Swiss village. He was awarded the Nobel Prize. He died without ever quitting his alms-house. He died—a few years more and the bloody convulsion of the World War overwhelmed the earth.

The few pictures and descriptions we have of Dunant fill in the outline of his life. As a child, he was delicate, pampered, reticent, well-behaved; as a youth, more melancholy, restless and aggressive.

His restlessness was tempered by those pious traditions in which he had been brought up. Soon he was following a predestined career as an upright and successful banker. Wider travel awakened his ambitions, sharpened his perceptions and intensified his natural instinct to give of himself and to take of those whom he chanced to meet. He dressed with an elegance that was a happy mean between the provincial and the adventurer. In summer he affected those white linen suits that make Africa's heat bearable to its colonists. The result was something exotic and singular in his appearance. His glance was at once keen and brooding, vague and decisive. His voice was soft and moving: he was a good listener, which left him free to think of other things. A well-groomed beard of the period and fashion adorned his cheeks and temples. The Swiss banker had become a European gentleman. Then, gradually, traces of grief, of doubt and loneliness appeared on his face. He grew heavier and broader, but more shy and haughty. At the height of his career he seems more childlike than he should have been. This created confidence, but it also led to abuses. He lost his power to command himself or others. He no longer took care of himself. When poverty claimed him his deterioration was rapid. His appearance shocked his acquaintances. It seemed that no good could be expected of him. Gentleman no more, bourgeois no more, he made an indifferent beggar. From the unreliable he descended rapidly to the suspect: he felt that suspicion pursued him and became in turn suspicious and embittered. Then, at the close of his life, we see him again, sitting in his easy-chair, with the long white beard of wisdom, and in all the pride and nobility of old age and the liberated dignity of a heart that has found clarity and peace.

The Red Cross is the first practical manifestation of international law, the first international agreement that mankind has ever—in the main—lived up to. But the history of Henri Dunant, the man who fathered this important achievement, is a hazy and practically unknown legend.

Dunant died in 1910. Only a few years have passed since his death, yet to-day his forgotten name has to be dug out as if from the debris of ages. No comprehensive account exists of his life. His friends have idealized and his enemies maligned it, while, consciously or unconsciously, the well-meaning historians of the Red Cross have drawn a veil over the tragic stages of his extraordinary career. If for long stretches it is dark and perplexing, it had its periods of splendour and European fame as well as its extremes of bitter suffering and sorrow. No one has ever taken the pains to describe or interpret the real meaning of Dunant's life. This difficult attempt must be made.

The Red Cross is one of the few humanitarian ideas in history that has ever become a reality. Above the barbarism of our times it stands out like a tragic monument to the great and dual-natured nineteenth century. Imperfect and faulty, and in an ideological sense scarcely defensible, it is nevertheless a binding and effective pact against the inhuman social and political delusions which are afflicting the peoples of the earth to-day.

The essential thing to be brought out is what any unromanticized account of the Red Cross must show, namely, that the average, unheroic man of ordinary character, strengths and weaknesses, can, on the promptings of reason and conscience, become the truly blessed Leader of any community. This is a democratic idea, and it presupposes that minds and hearts are characteristic of normal human beings— the kind of heart that rebels against suffering and wrong, the kind of mind that seeks refuge from the demonic power of evil in order and in moderation. To-day this is a dangerous, and for all its ingenuousness, revolutionary idea that may cost a man his home and freedom. The great and tragic life of Henri Dunant helps us to understand the great and tragic nineteenth century, the much misjudged, often misunderstood generation of our fathers and grandfathers.

Henri Dunant was born in 1828, at Geneva, of an old, respected and well-to-do family. To all appearances, Geneva was still a patrician republic of whose governing *conseil représentatif* Dunant's father, Jean Jacques, was a member. The new democratic constitution of 1842 first curtailed the privileges of the ruling families.

Dunant's mother, Marie Antoinette, was the daughter of a Councillor Colladon who for several years was the director of the Geneva hospital and Mayor of nearby Avully. The Colladons came originally from La Châtre in Berry. During the Reformation, Germain and Léon Colladon became citizens of Geneva on the same day as Jean Jacques Rousseau.

Their mother's brother was the well-known physicist, Daniel Colladon, to whom we are indebted for important technical improvements in tunnel-driving.

Geneva is a cheerful but fundamentally serious city: it bears one of the most singular imprints of Europe's blood-stained history. Here in the very heart of the Continent, built like a Paradise at the end of the great lake beyond which tower the highest mountains in Europe, it suffers much from rain and fog—dark and gloomy in shadow, radiant and gay in the sunlight. With the austerity of the Alps forever before its eyes, and the fullness and animation of the Latin spirit in its heart, the historical countenance of Geneva is obdurate and stony, energetic, successful and unhappy, and so are its citizens. Rodolf Toepffer, Europe's greatest humorist, Jean Jacques Rousseau, her most decisive revolutionist, Calvin, her gloomiest messenger of God, all created their masterworks in Geneva. Scorn and revolt and pitiless religious zeal saturate the very soil on which the League of Nations now holds the fate of the world in faltering hands.

Calvin's iron rule has never quite relinquished Geneva. The city affords a most thought-provoking example of dictatorship. After he had left Geneva, the martyred citizens begged the pious tyrant on their knees to return to them and complete his work, the gloomy and hopeless doctrine of predestination, the predetermination of good and evil. What would the outcome be? The religion of success, taught and revered to this day, the reward of worldly goods for the repentant sinner, the unworthiness of poverty, the class-divided world of the blessed and the damned.

Calvin's spirit ruled Geneva. And Dunant, destined to be a worthy sinner, a Genevese patrician, grew up in this world of pious wealth—a world which had, however, begun to question and to struggle. For the aristocratic order of the little Genevan republic was beset by radical and democratic ideas wherein the natural law of Rousseau, and the *éclaircissement* of those spiritual fathers of the French Revolution, Voltaire and Diderot, first made their bow in the form of petty social and political squabbles.

Business was flourishing in Geneva. After the brief and bloodless civil strife, Switzerland settled down to its happy role as the neutral centre of gravity in the midst of Europe's convulsions. The little cosmopolitan city, the round of whose everyday life was so peacefully side-tracked, was scarcely aware of being the exact geographic point on which the opposing tendencies of Eastern and Western Europe converged. Yet it was to be the stage for spiritual and political struggles that would usher in the dawn of a new epoch of civilization.

Europe in 1830: the eruption of the French Revolution had long since been followed by Napoleonic reaction. Positive rationalism ruled France, the worship of reason beyond all bounds of reason! This movement, starting from Rousseau, was transformed by Napoleon's grandiose imperialist conception into such practical creations as technical schools to encourage industrial progress, as freedom of trade, or the plan for a Pan-European capitalism, which protected by the 'Continental System' against the competition of England, was to insure the economic power of a united Europe.

Locke, the English predecessor of Rousseau, was the founder of a natural law of English vintage, in which private property held its divinely appointed place beside the freedom of the individual. At the same time, puritanism, which for all its pious strictness was perfectly realistic where mundane interests were concerned, laid the spiritual basis for the capitalist and liberal development of England.

In Germany, however, two powerful tendencies set themselves against western rationalism. The idealistic philosophy of Kant and Hegel narrowed the freedom of the individual and subjected it to the dominion of a metaphysic independent of the human will. And the Romantic movement, originating in Eastern Europe, sought to save the European soul from impending destruction—a struggle of the lonely hearts for the God who was more and more dissolving in the mists of rational doctrine. Hence the last frantic embrace of European tradition and the historic past, the strong bias toward Catholicism and the futile effort to revive the mystic wonders of the Middle Ages.

From the philosophers to the generals runs a long but inevitable road: the fortunate bourgeois of the nineteenth century had to fight only against ideologies, which it remained for the twentieth century to translate into hand-grenades and bombing-planes. Romanticism was the first German spiritual movement since the Reformation whose influence spread throughout Europe. Delicate, precious and dreamy

in its poetic side, nevertheless it was to have a definite
share, as Heinrich Heine shrewdly foretold, in the
coming conflicts. For above all it concealed the germ
of nationalism, a malady inevitable perhaps, but fatal
to the life of Europe.

For a quiet, unsuspecting bourgeois, the period into
which Dunant was born was far from prepossessing.
A dull, provincial style of life, an endless succession
of relatively peaceable and secluded European state-
lets, a political reaction which left to persons not suspect to it a tolerable measure of freedom.

The symptoms of coming unrest were unnoticed:
what business man would look for dynamite in literature? The psychological problem of the Stendhalian
novel, Balzac's sociological acumen, the tender and
yearning lyrics of the Romantics, even the economic
Utopias of the Englishman Robert Owen, or the writings of such early French socialists as Fourier, and
Byron's revolutionary moods—all were at best
drawing-room conversation for the readers of the
Journal des Débats.

The bourgeoisie, blinded by their wealth, did not
see that the very causes of their enrichment would
one day threaten them with annihilation. Capitalism's victorious march was just striking up, and
money was pouring from a thousand sources.

Enrichissez-vous!, the war-cry of Louis Philippe,
the monarch whom a consortium of bankers and generals had brought to power in 1830, was followed with
alacrity and an entire disregard of consequences. Yet
darkly and indefinably was felt the revolutionary collapse of the old society. A restless oscillation began

between liberalism and political reaction. The conservatism of the old feudal caste was by no means identical with reaction. Who was more threatened by the advancing strength of industrial capitalism than the land-holding noble, the man of the world from whose hands the new usurpers, now working their way up from the lower depths, were snatching power?

Only gradually, under the extortionate pressure of capitalism, was the unholy alliance formed between the ruling and the possessing classes. Time and again, the aristocratic caste, bound by tradition and cosmopolitan by culture, had demonstrated a more sensitive instinct and a greater sense of responsibility toward the coming social conflicts than did the upstart middle class. Time and again, it sought, even if unsuccessfully and inadequately, for solutions of the frightful dilemma, and after each attempt became more dependent on the power of capitalism.

The history of nineteenth century humanitarianism, the freeing of the peasants, the abolition of slavery, the founding of the Red Cross, the first pacifist stirrings, questionable but well-intentioned charity—all are evidences of enlightened conservatism's participation in the social problem. Similarly, the American Revolution, with the great figure of Washington, was the rebellion of an agrarian class, which had no bourgeoisie—only five per cent of the population lived in the cities—against the mercantilist exploitation of the English.

But revolutionaries of another sort, to whom the press paid little attention and of whom the masses

were perfectly oblivious, went about their tasks in
the quiet workshops and laboratories of scientific re-
search. All the speculations of the human mind and
feeling, all the basic principles of philosophy, politics
and economics collapsed before the elemental forces
of science, as, developing with unsuspected richness,
it profoundly altered the whole biological picture of
the human race.

That man in all his expressions is a biological object
was never more forcefully demonstrated than by the
scientific discoveries of the nineteenth century. For
it was their amelioration of the discrepancies of man's
lot that first created, as the result of a new kind of
demand for happiness, those very catastrophic spiritual, social and political problems which confront us
to-day. The first machines robbed the worker of his
work, the first steamships narrowed the oceans, the
first locomotives annihilated distance. (The Man-
chester-Liverpool Railway was opened in 1831.) Industrial production began its mad upswing, constantly creating new needs. The explosive development of world trade hastened colonization and the
opening up of the remotest lands, brought in raw materials for ever more complete mechanical utilization,
tore down walls and wove an ever-widening network
of civilized relationships around the world.

In the eighteen thirties, the first gas lamp was
lighted. Between the Observatory and the physics
laboratory at Göttingen, Gauss and Weber exchanged
the first telegraphic signals to come over a wire.
Schleiden and Schwann described plant and animal
cells, Baer isolated the human egg, while in the same

year Wöhler, with his synthesis of urea, founded organic chemistry.

The vast, mysterious prerequisites for the creation of a systematic hygiene and for the struggle of society against disease had been completed. The result was a healthier, securer, more aggressive man, but a mankind more suffering and more filled with hate.

Mortality decreased from year to year while the average life increased from year to year. Almost within the span of the nineteenth century, the population of Europe tripled, growing from 180,000,000 to 470,000,000. The population of the United States increased from 5,300,000 to 76,000,000. This teeming ant-heap had to be fed and clothed, its needs satisfied with work and pleasure. A dizzying and vicious circle resulted: capital and finished goods flowed from the constantly augmenting industrial centres to the raw material and agrarian areas, which exchanged their natural products against new needs and higher standards. With the growing opportunities for easy profits, the desire grew to exploit defenceless and superabundant labour. This privilege of exploitation on the part of the emancipated bourgeoisie was vigorously contested by the nobles. But the magic spell of a money economy lured on ever larger hordes of speculators. The all-but-unlimited need for investments on the part of the adventurous entrepreneurs transformed labour into columns of ciphers and balances. For a period in which slavery still existed, the risky game of the organization of mankind into classes held no terrors.

This outburst of boundless and heady optimism

was increased by a decade of economic advance and
discovery. The influence of philosophy was on the
wane. Act and fact held the centre of the stage. And
so loud and officious was this primitive faith in the
unswerving progress of civilization that the first faint
signals of advance on the part of the disillusioned
working-classes, who were touched only by the drib-
lets of prosperity's deluge, were drowned in the hubbub over Positivism.

There was social misery. In 1831 came the revolt
of the Lyons silk workers with the battle-cry, '*Vivre
en travaillant ou mourir en combattant!*' In 1834 came
the slaughter in the workers' quarters of the Rue
Transnonaine whose agonies live on in the artistic
record of Daumier. Only in England, which was the
first country to experience the shady side of industrial
development when desperate workers wrecked the
machines, were serious practical measures taken
in a law guaranteeing the right of combination
(1825), and the consequent development of the trade
unions.

The rest of Europe fought human misery of all
kinds with the non-political weapons of charity. We
must not ridicule the nineteenth century's humanitarianism. We have no right to. It was a remnant of
the great libertarian teachings of the century's close.
It sprang from an honest feeling for human dignity,
a religious belief in goodness and the inner obligation
to charity, from true generosity, and perhaps also, in
part, from the bad conscience of a privileged and selfish caste.

But there was still a conscience at that time that

could be touched. The naïve and credulous optimism
of the age took a straight and direct path from the
heart of the helper to the heart of the helped. The
naked fact remains that in our times, with their clut-
ter of social theories, not a single new humanitarian
idea has made its appearance. The nineteenth century, with its charitable ladies, pathetic bazaars and
committees, solved the most serious problems of human misery successfully and decently—the abolition
of serfdom, slavery and feudal dependence, the beginnings of protection for the working-class, the freeing of the peasants, provision for and care of the
poor, and last but not least, the attempt to hu-
manize war through the Geneva Convention of the
Red Cross.

Would it be possible to-day to arouse people to a
crusade against wrong through books or appeals, as
was always the case in the nineteenth century, from
Harriet Beecher Stowe's *Uncle Tom's Cabin* and
Victor Hugo's *Les Misérables* to Zola's *J'accuse*? The
heroes of humanitarianism had a better fate then than
they have to-day. During their lifetime, they were
honoured and admired, and even now are accorded
full rites by the motion picture industry. It was felt
that even the shadow of pain and suffering was a last
damnable blot on modern civilization.

Uncle Tom's Cabin played a definite part in precipi-
tating the American Civil War and in furthering the
victory of the emancipators.

With the support of her government, Florence
Nightingale, together with a band of courageous Eng-
lishwomen, went to the actual battlefields—the first

women to perform such Samaritan service. On the Russian side, the Grand Duchess Maria Pavlovna organized the women to care for the wounded.

The English Quakeress, Elizabeth Fry, dedicated her life and fortune to reforming the intolerable conditions of the English prisons. William Booth, with his Christian Mission, began to lay the groundwork for the organization of a Salvation Army against sin and godlessness.

War in the nineteenth century, despite all the terror and horror that technical, organizational and inadequate sanitation entailed, was conducted with a chivalry that the barbarism of our time cannot conceive. Blasphemous as it may sound, there was a pacifism of the generals: the will to destroy admitted limits dictated by conscience.

The Austrian General, Prince Schwarzenberg, writes to his wife from Russia in 1812: 'War is a hateful thing. What horrible sights it shows us daily, distress, misery, suffering and depravity of all kinds, misfortune's scornful sneer, inhuman cruelty; in short, an honest man's heart is revolted ten times a day . . .' And a few weeks later: 'Of course, it will be thought a weakness, but the fact is that war revolts me for all the incalculable suffering it spreads in every conceivable form among mankind.'

Alexander II signed the peace in the Crimean War after being horrified by the suffering he had seen in the hospitals. After the battle of Montebello, Napoleon III issued an order that all the enemy wounded were to be returned to their homes forthwith in order, he said, 'to mitigate, in so far as I am

able, the sufferings of the war, and to set an example
in checking its avoidable harshnesses.'

But the most exemplary in this connection was the
Swiss General Dufour who played so significant a part
in the founding of the Red Cross.

It may be said that the organized murder of human
beings is so monstrous as to preclude any concept of
humanity, but that does not change the fact that
there are kinds and degrees of wars. The wars of our
century are all the more frightful, evil and anarchic
because they deny humanity itself as something
Utopian. To some of the men of the nineteenth century, however, social evil seemed avoidable and possible of correction. They believed in the end of injustice and the upward evolution of humanity: we
must now give up this belief.

. . .

In this atmosphere Dunant, proclaiming the praises
of the good and successful man, grew up. Geneva, as
we know, was a focus of countless disquieting symptoms, which, however, its citizens with their piety
and confirmed satisfaction with the world, managed
to keep in harmonious balance.

Henri Dunant was a man without a childhood. In
no passage of the rambling recollections of his old age
do we find any reference to his earliest years. Inevitably, his training in the spell of that environment
fashioned him into a worthy and aspiring bourgeois.
After the victory of the democracy, the patricians
withdrew grumblingly from public affairs, which did
not in the least impair their spiritual hegemony and

left them free to dedicate themselves the more zealously to their moral obligations.

Dunant's father was for years the head of an institution for orphans; his mother 'permitted Geneva's
orphan girls the use of her estate so that they might
from time to time, under the supervision of their
head-mistress, spend a few happy hours among its
flowers and shrubs.' Such touching examples of a well-
meaning, if patronizing and remote benevolence, were
constantly before young Henri's eyes. Soon he was
himself a member of a benevolent society, was seeking
out invalid and dying old ladies to offer them comfort. The sickly and infirm young man spent his Sun-
day afternoons in prison, where he read to the prisoners from travel-books or other works of an educational
nature. During the week he studied banking with
Messrs. Lullin and Sautter.

But amidst this philistine solicitude for misfortune
a new note was presently to sound. Wafted from
pietistic England, the religious movement known as
the *Réveil* was to permeate the Christian world in the
first half of the century. It stressed the importance of
the Bible and of conduct as living and creative factors
in history. Genevese society was stirred to its depths.
The work of Pastor Louis Gaussen especially, which
appeared between 1839 and 1849 in three fat volumes,
and which explained universal history in the light of
scriptural prophecy, immediately caused a religious
sensation.

There is no doubt but that the voice of the *Réveil*
had a decisive influence on the youthful and impres-
sionable Henri Dunant. The apostolic frenzy which

was to characterize all his work, the prophetic and non-intellectual formulation of his demands, in which extreme and daring fantasy is constantly found side by side with a sure instinct for the practical and expedient, is entirely in the spirit of the *Réveil*.

Dunant was one of the first propagandists of a modern dimension. He was master of the technique of moulding public opinion with the methods of an inspired business man—only what he had to sell was a great and noble idea. He 'upped' the sales of humanity.

It is no accident that a Swiss business man of Calvinist Protestant persuasion should have initiated the greatest and most successful of humanitarian enterprises. Nor is it an accident that the circles which he tried to enlist for his idea, and which were prepared for vigorous co-operation, belonged to a social category that we should call reactionary. At the time it was the only category capable of acting.

There is some comfort in the thought that a supra-political idea dictated by dignity and decency could thrive even on reactionary soil. Considered historically, it explains the peculiar feudal note in the Red Cross, even to-day, especially in the countries of its origin.

There was a moment at the beginning of the century, when the idealism of the Scriptures and the ideas of human freedom typical of the *éclaircissement* seemed about to merge under the happiest auspices— humanism and conservatism joining hands. Witness the almost revolutionary freedom and lack of prejudice of the early Romantics, and the true spirit of progress evinced by the Brothers Humboldt and Minister Hardenberg who came from the tradition-bound hierarchy of Prussian officialdom. The conservative character of the American Revolution has already been cited.

But the tempo of technical development proved too headlong, the social conflicts engendered by every new discovery too pressing. The life went out of humanity. The old society with its age-enfeebled optimism was unequal to the task of organizing itself anew out of its own resources. With the downfall of Napoleonic rule at the Congress of Vienna, that unholy prototype of the League of Nations, the European system fell into a web of political intrigue and ambition in which every idea of the peaceful evolution of progress was doomed to perish. Enemies of progress and of reform, like Metternich and Gentz, or Frederick William IV, the 'Royal Romantic,' were in the saddle.

But at the moment of industrial expansion, old Europe felt the strong pulse of youthful vigour. The whole grandiose prospect of the capitalist world in construction was unfolding. The family, the church, the schools were as yet undisturbed laboratories of bourgeois culture, forging its moral and spiritual support. The adventurous upsurge in a world expanded by technology and science gave free initiative for good or evil, and large scope for action.

And Dunant, developing concurrently, and well stocked with all the bourgeois virtues, gathered about him a small band of comrades for long walks over the hills of the Geneva countryside—sons of business men like himself, whom his strange unrest astonished and inspired. They met in the evenings for discussion in Dunant's home. Soon there were more than a hundred, even a few ministers among them. One of the group, Max Perrot, was later to recall: 'I hardly knew him, he was not one of my friends, but I admired his active piety.'

Perrot, inspired by Dunant, became the first president of the still flourishing Young Men's Christian Association—*Union chrétienne de jeunes Gens*. Even in building up this first international youth organization, which has since become so important, Dunant played his characteristic role as minister of propaganda.

The soft seats of office were never for him. He was a weak and almost timid speaker. Crowds frightened him. His great successes came as the result of private conversations. His art consisted in holding these conversations at the right time with the right people. They were carefully prepared in advance with all the finesse of an astonishing diplomatic instinct. His calculations nearly always justified themselves. With admirable adaptability he found the right tone for every situation. For him Europe's insurmountable boundaries did not exist. Internationalism was his constant goal.

For several years Dunant travelled in France, Alsace, Belgium and Holland as the official representative of the Association. For the first time he discovered the thriving cities of Western Europe and felt the breath of the great adventurous world. Wherever he went he was successful, and the little Genevese society soon grew into a federation of many branches.

A circular which Dunant, then in his twenty-fourth year, addressed at this time (1852) to the French Protestant ministry is very characteristic:

DEAR FRIENDS AND BROTHERS,

A group of Christian young men has met together in Geneva to do reverence and worship to the Lord Jesus Whom they wish to serve and praise. They have heard that among you, too, there are brothers in Christ, young like themselves, who love their Redeemer and gather together that under His guidance, and through the reading of the Holy Scriptures, they may instruct themselves further. Being deeply edified thereby, they wish to unite with you in Christian friendship. Therefore, we hasten, dear brothers in Christ, although we do not have the happiness of knowing you personally, to assure you of our deep fraternal affection. We beg you to exchange correspondence with us in order to keep intact this Christian affection among the children of the same Father, that some of us may be profited to the greater glory of the Lord. We approach you, too, as a witness to the world that all the disciples of Jesus, who acknowledge and love Him before God as their sole refuge and sole righteousness, are no other than one great spiritual family whose members love one another sincerely, even though they be strangers, in the sign of the Dearly Beloved Who is their Guide, their Friend, their God and their Lord . . .

Extraordinary language from youth to youth! And even if we ascribe much of its exuberant lack of ideas, behind which perhaps some authentic religious emotion lurks, to an inverted and exaggerated rhetoric, we still have to ask ourselves with alarm what could have been in the minds of the Genevese bourgeois youth of the year 1851. Had they heard nothing of the Chartist outbreaks in England, which had summoned the English industrial proletariat to its first organized struggle with capitalism? Nothing of the first general strike or the demand for a shorter working day? Had they never heard of Carlyle whose social conservatism should have lifted up their youthful hearts? 'The spirit of evil rules. Mammonism, self-seeking, whence unmindfulness of duty. This spirit needs to be changed! Instead of scepticism faith, instead of Mammonism idealism, instead of individualism social feeling must be restored to the hearts of men!' (*Past and Present*, 1843.)

Did they know nothing of the Christian socialists, like Charles Kingsley, Theodore Hughes, J.D.Maurice, who strove to legitimatize the new social spirit with the fundamental Christian truths? Did they not know that only recently at nearby Yverdon, in their own Switzerland, Pestalozzi and Froebel had prepared a revolution in pedagogy, while the simple and rebellious soul of Weitling, the Magdeburg tailor, had proclaimed a communism of the heart before hospitable Switzerland had him arrested and packed him off to New York and the hardships of an early emigrant's life? Had they heard nothing of the outbreaks among the Silesian weavers in 1844, when a household industry, reduced to the last crust of bread, uttered its cry of desperation? At this time Karl Marx was already an *emigré* in London after founding the Communist League in Brussels. In *The Communist*

Manifesto, the slogan, 'Proletarians of the world, unite!' had already fallen on a deaf world. The demand for socialization of the means of production through class struggle as the road towards a socialist society—had this menacing new idea never penetrated Geneva? Then, too, bourgeois revolution (in reality the rebellion of industry against the increasingly oppressive power of finance) spread in the next few years: in February 1848, in Paris, with the workers' representatives, Louis Blanc and Alexandre Albert, in the government. The collapse of the Austro-Italian towns before the assault of the 'Young Italians,' Mazzini's *Carbonari* and the adventurer Garibaldi; the March Revolution in front of the Royal Palace in Berlin; the sudden rise of Napoleon III; even the brief war with the Sonderbund in their own Switzerland, which was to give their fatherland its definitive form as a united federal state—were these not the dramatic stages of an overturn which one would expect to have agitated young men who read the newspapers and heard the hum of the telegraph, in other and in deeper ways?

We who have a hundred experiences of the restriction of political outlook and opinion in a much more accessible world need scarcely be surprised at the vagueness and ignorance of Genevese youth in the year 1851. One tends to under-rate out of all historical perspective the caste spirit of a given historical moment.

By 1851 the revolutions had run their course. The socialist tocsin, also inspired at the beginning with the optimism of progress, had been silenced. ('We wish to be as free as the birds of the air, and like them to pass care-free through life, in happy flight and sweet harmony.'—Weitling.) Darkest reaction and the political negation of freedom were in control. The social spirit, of which Carlyle had dreamed, and whose moral force was to tame both capitalism and socialism, had been laid low for a long time to come.

England, it is true, was to have an era of social peace under the paternalistic government of Victoria, but only because it could, with a moderation that was at once reasonable and shrewd business, offer the proletariat improved conditions under the capitalist system. The development of the trade unions in England had met with little opposition. It was not even especially difficult. For literally overnight a new Golden Age had set in.

It is one of the great ironies of history that at the very moment when the French proletariat was drenching the pavements of Paris with its blood, only to be compelled for a long time to come to renounce all hope of extending its rights, the tremendous California gold strike was drenching humanity with a fabulous rain of gold. The enormous increase of capital through the apparently limitless production of gold benefited England above all, for she guided the riches of the world into the channels of her already prepared and rapidly developing commerce. In 1851 the first International Exposition was held in London. England's monopolistic position in the world market was firmly established.

Not only in England, but throughout the civilized world the intoxication of a splendid era of prosperity was felt. The demoralizing influence of great wealth quickly and easily acquired brushed aside all the checks and warnings of an awakened social conscience, postponing conflicts for a later crisis. Gambler and speculator, successful gambler and successful speculator, robbed the bourgeoisie of its intelligence and sense.

The sums which were swindled at this time in railroad stocks, in the questionable bond issues of exotic states, in founding new and fantastic colonies can hardly be calculated even by our contemporary standards.

The London Exposition, which was opened in the new Crystal Palace at the instigation of Prince Albert, Queen Victoria's German husband, made an enormous impression on the world. With a blare of trumpets and the intoning of choirs, a new and fortunate Europe was proclaimed, a Europe which had vanquished destructive and barbarous war, so harmful, too, to business; a Europe of the toiling and acquisitive intelligence, a world of the business men, of the factory barons, bankers and barristers.

Nothing travels faster or penetrates farther than the smell of money. And its effect is anaesthetic: the awareness of pain comes only on awakening.

Even to an idyllic spot like Geneva, where much savoury capital was heaped together, the gold fever penetrated and did not spare the aspiring bourgeois youth despite their evangelical preoccupation with the word of God. Indeed, it would have required an unusual degree of doctrinaire obstinacy and contempt of the world not to profit by the heyday of business.

Besides, was not Dunant a trained and ambitious young banker?

Accordingly, in 1854 he entered the service of the *Compagnie des Colonies Suisses de Sétif*, which had extensive interests in North Africa and in whose employ he travelled for five years, until 1858, in Algiers, Kabylia, Tunis and Sicily. Contact with the old corsair romanticism, still living on the splendours of the Islamic world conquest, must have been a decisive adventure for the young Dunant.

On the coasts of the most inaccessible of the continents, soon to be partitioned with much effort, into spheres of European influence, the final struggle between the Middle Ages and modern times was being fought out in its most tangible form in the middle of the nineteenth century. The Mediterranean, whose European shore, because of the lack of political unity as in Italy or because of political convulsions as in France, saw the rise of no centralized power, was the domain of professional pirates. Whoever ventured into the Sultan's sphere of influence unarmed could expect the sad lot of slavery unless special treaties guaranteed his life and property.

Until late into the nineteenth century, hordes of Christians—chiefly Corsicans, Ragusans and Neapolitans—were held in Africa in a sort of concentration camp, called Fondouk. As late as 1741, the Bey Ali Pasha had his son Hussein depopulate and enslave the entire island of Tabara, which had been taken over by France for the Royal Africa Company. Slavery was a sad fate, but not monstrous. Voltaire, for example, invested 5,000 francs in a negro slaver. He boasted himself that it was '*une bonne affaire et une bonne action*'—the genius of the French language leaving it unclear whether he thought it a good action or good business.

Only by degrees was the premise of man's right to freedom, which had long been recognized in practical affairs, reversed. In 1814, Lady William Bentinck, the wife of an admiral, landed in Tunis and out of her own pocket purchased the freedom of thirty Italian slaves, at 300 piastres for the lot. During Easter-week, 1816, a mission which Queen Caroline had entrusted to Lord Exmouth, succeeded in abolishing Christian slavery through Mahmoud Bey, the ruler of Tunis. In Algiers, the French occupation of 1830 first began the destruction of the slave trade. In the British Empire, 800,000 slaves were given their freedom on 1 August 1834, £20,000,000 being promised the owners in compensation. Slavery in Europe was finally abolished on 19 May 1861, by an edict of Alexander II of Russia which liberated some 20,000,000 serfs.

In 1858 Fick of Geneva published an account of Dunant's travel experiences—*Notice sur la Régence de Tunis*. It was a modest and reliable report full of sound observation on the geographic and ethnologic conditions, and probably brought him some recognition. As a result, in 1859 he was named a corresponding member of the Paris *Société d'Ethnographie*.

But even at one point in this book his apostolic zeal broke the impartiality of the traveller and amateur explorer with astonishing vehemence. It is the chapter on slavery which later, during the American

Civil War in 1863, was published separately under the title: *L'Esclavage chez les Musulmans et aux États-Unis d'Amerique*. Fortified with a mass of quotations from the Koran and the Bible, Dunant sought to prove that the Mohammedan form of slavery could be called harmless and philanthropic compared with the inhumanity of the American slave states. His facts were extremely impressive. He supported them with accounts taken from such newspapers as the *Richmond Examiner*, the *Daily Orleanian*, the *Dadeville Banner*, the *Memphis Eagle*, and the *Pensacola Democrat*, describing slave auctions, hair-raising mock trials of lynchers, man-hunts with bloodhounds, and so forth. He showed the complete lack of rights for the negro under the state laws of Virginia, South Carolina, Alabama and Georgia. He quoted a law passed on 12 February 1853 by Illinois, a state hostile to slavery, brutally forbidding the immigration, or even the transit, of freed negroes or mulattoes, with the provision that every one caught would be sold at public auction: a mulatto was further defined as any person having a quarter strain of negro blood.

Thus, on the eve of the Civil War, he drew a truly appalling picture of human callousness and closed with a prophetic outburst which was informed by now with somewhat more substance than the moving tirades of his youth:

Cursed be those who trample underfoot the spirit of Christianity, who transgress the elementary principles of humanity and modern civilization. Do they think to postpone their awakening until one day their slavery goes down in a clap of thunder . . . 'I tremble for my country when I remember that God is just,' said Thomas Jefferson, President of the United States in 1801, in a speech on slavery. 'Vengeance is mine,' saith the Lord, 'and I shall repay.'

This is the spirit—mixed with all the ingredients of Genevese piety and puritan humanity—of Harriet Beecher Stowe, whom Dunant had met during her brief stay in Geneva.

But in addition to the deepening of his humanitarian impulse, Dunant gained something else from his African sojourn. For the first time he met some of the real rulers of contemporary Europe. Through a friend of his family, *comte* Budé, who lived at Ferney, near Geneva, he was brought into close association with his nephew, General de Beaufort. As Napoleon's Chief-of-Staff, the General held one of the most important posts in the army. De Beaufort in turn gave him an impressive introduction to General Mac-Mahon, then Governor of Algiers.

The next developments in this story are of the greatest importance for Dunant's life, since by an extraordinary twist of fate they lead directly to the founding of the Red Cross. At the same time they are at the root of the tragic turn his life took soon after his work was completed.

In his earlier years, Dunant had sufficient available capital to rate as a serious financier. The dangerously Utopian aura surrounding his plans at a time when Utopias were daily becoming realities attracted rather than frightened people away. Now, however, he was to conceive a plan that overstepped by far the limits set for a young business man—he made himself Director and President of the 'Financial and Industrial Company of the Mons-Gemila Mills in Algiers,' which with a capital of one million francs sought to exploit seven hectares of land.

It was a risky and fantastic venture, one of many which were turning up every day, but there was no reason to see why, with Dunant's Swiss tenacity, his good connections in the government, his Genevese money and his thorough knowledge of the locale, it should not succeed. In 1858 he became a naturalized French subject without losing his Swiss citizenship. In his endless petty struggle with the bureaucracy and money-lenders, he composed petition after petition, pulling out all the stops of that organ of personal diplomacy that he understood so well.

His successive business failures can be explained only psychologically—his capacity and his willingness to suffer. With a heart so easily touched, so easily stirred, one does not become a successful speculator in millions. The spirit of the prophets, which was reborn in the soul of this Genevan business man to be the battle-ground of its ecstatic and demonic struggles, destroyed the speculator, and saved the pure human soul. Dunant lapsed into the contemptible ranks of those who make plans and have constructive ideas, but who lack the ruthlessness and selfishness to turn them into money. Almost against his will, Dunant was a Samaritan. That face which so willingly pondered all earthly vanities remained turned toward the shadow of this earth, undergoing all vicissitudes and all the afflictions of misfortune.

II

Europe: 1850-1859

THE fanfares of the London Exposition proved deceptive. Two years later the great powers of Europe were at each other's throats. Eternal peace had not as yet settled down upon a continent torn with passion and the thirst for power. War simplified decisions which less sanguinary diplomacy was unable to enforce.

Tsar Nicholas I had dreams of a Pan-Slavic Empire. He hoped to wrest the Romanian provinces of Moldavia and Walachia from Turkey, bring the Balkan Slavs, the Bulgars and the Serbs under Russian influence and establish a protectorate over the Greek Christians within the Turkish Empire. Turkey rejected an ultimatum. In July 1853 Gortshakov invaded the Danubian Principalities and Turkey declared war.

The position of the Turks grew quickly critical. But the western powers would not tolerate Russia in the Mediterranean. In March 1854 therefore, France and England went to the assistance of Turkey. The allied fleets transported great masses of troops, some 175,000 men, who then lay starving and wasting with disease by the thousand in the fields of the Dobrudja. It was decided to invade the Crimea; the fleets advanced across the Black Sea. In the autumn of 1854 began the siege of Sevastopol. The Russians scuttled their warships and blocked the harbour. But their troops were beaten in a bloody engagement at Inkerman. In the autumn of 1855, Sevastopol fell to the armies of Marshal Niel. During the closing months of the campaign, a couple of Piedmontese regiments, sent by Cavour, fought on the Turkish side, and the reason for this sudden Russophobia on the part of the Italians was presently to be made clear.

It was a barbarous war in which disease was more deadly than cannon—disease against which even the helping hand of Miss Nightingale, who took up the struggle against death with military discipline in the hospitals of Scutari, was powerless. In November 1854, in compliance with a request of the Secretary for War, Lord Herbert, she arrived in Constantinople with thirty-seven assistants. Though in a short time the mortality fell from forty-two to two per cent, 16,000 men died in vain of disease. But the name of the first woman Samaritan became an almost sacred symbol to the world. She was the second Queen of England.

To avoid further sacrifices, Alexander II, who succeeded his father shortly before the end of the war, consented to a peace that reduced Russian influence in Europe practically to zero.

England's relations with France developed more and more in the spirit of an *entente cordiale*: Victoria and Albert made their visit to Paris. They were charmed and succumbed to the spell of the city which was turned into a dazzling pyrotechnic display of welfare and culture. Musset, Gautier, Sainte-Beuve, Gavarni, Guys, sat on the terraces of the Café Tortoni. The architect Haussmann tore down whole blocks of houses as light flooded a ring of broad new boulevards.

On 30 March 1856 the Peace of Paris was signed, neutralizing the Black Sea. Again a brilliantly illuminated and tumultuous spectacle of European brotherhood took place with an international exposition and bright beacons of progress. Amidst the festivities an heir to the throne, the little Lou, was born. The Emperor was victor and hero—the nineteenth century's most adventurous, ambiguous and fascinating sovereign.

In 1815 the seven-year-old Prince had arrived with his mother, Hortense, at Geneva, a hunted and banished member of the Napoleon family. He attended school at Augsburg, then lived in the Swiss Thurgau where he acquired citizenship. At twenty-two he participated with his brother in a revolt in the Romagna: his brother died. Napoleon returned to Switzerland and studied under the artillery captain Dufour. After the death of the Duke of Reichstadt he saw himself as the Napoleonic Pretender. A heart filled with hate and an excess of ambition in his brain, he made his first *coup d'état* at Strasbourg in 1836. He was captured and shipped off to America. Presently, he was in Switzerland again. France sought his expulsion. He fled to London, wrote romantic political books, edited a newspaper, *L'Idée Napoléonienne*. In 1840

his second *coup d'état* failed at Boulogne. This time
he was sentenced to life imprisonment in the fortress
of Ham. In 1848 his book, *De l'Extinction du Pau-
périsme* appeared—a singular farrago of ideas of
state socialism and national imperialism. In the tattered clothes of the mason Badinguet, he made his
escape in 1846 and reached London. He did not have
much longer to wait. The February Revolution compelled Louis Philippe, King of the *juste milieu,* to
abdicate. The nation wanted to carry out Napoleon's
ideas of the nationalization of work at once, for as
Lamartine said: 'France is bored.' National workshops were founded, to be quickly suppressed when
the June uprising was put down with an iron hand
by General Cavaignac. There was a presidential election and Louis Napoleon Bonaparte defeated Cavaignac. In December 1851 he suspended the electoral
laws by a *coup d'état,* had Cavaignac and Thiers arrested, obtained for himself by a national referendum
the powers of an absolute monarch, and on 2 December 1852 he was Emperor of the French.

The violent activity, and probably the bad conscience of the usurper, never forsook Napoleon III.
He never lost a sense of insecurity from his years of
emigration. He wanted to be a super-Napoleon. New
political exigencies were arising constantly, constantly he faced the need of demonstrating his legiti-
macy by new miracles before the nation and the
world. He travelled up and down the country making
speeches—half an emperor and half a political scrib-
bler. He had to give up his political liberalism early.
He fell into dependency on the French clericals. In

1849 he sent Oudinot to Rome to save Pope Pius IX from the republican Garibaldi. No royal house wanted him for a son-in-law, so, in 1853, he married the beautiful Spanish Countess, Eugénie de Montijo.

The fortunate outcome of the Crimean War raised his prestige and the power of France tremendously. In the background the colonies were growing. Algeria and Senegambia were expanded. The Annamese War created a French Indo-China.

Prussia had fallen under the rigid pietism of Frederick William IV, whose mental illness was developing apace: for example, such *opéra bouffe* as the three-day Neuenburger War, in which the Swiss Canton of Neuchâtel had to defend itself from 2 September to 4 September 1856 against becoming a part of Prussia on the basis of an old hereditary pact. Napoleon saved Switzerland and saved Prussia by an authoritative pronouncement. Small wonder if ambition began to dangle before his eyes the outlines of Napoleonic Empire, fast becoming a reality—of an endless succession of famous deeds. Fate intervened.

On 14 January 1858 the Italian, Felix Orsini, and three confederates, threw a bomb at the coach in which the imperial couple were driving to the *Opéra*, a few minutes before the curtain went up on *William Tell*. A revolution in France would help precipitate the struggle for Italian liberation. Eugénie and the Emperor were unhurt, but ten people among the crowd were killed and a hundred and fifty injured.

Orsini was executed, but his testament, which Napoleon himself sent to the defence attorney, Jules Favre, was published. In his last letter from prison, the condemned Orsini implored the Emperor to liberate the fatherland. 'The blessings of 25,000,000 Italians will follow Your Majesty into eternity.'

Whether Napoleon's belief in his destiny was great or small, one thing is certain, that from that moment on he took an active interest in developments in Italy, and in a quite opposite sense than before. Cavour's game was prospering. With Metternich, Disraeli and Bismarck, he belongs to the inspired diplomats of the century.

Squat, bespectacled, professional Cavour, the uncontested leader of the *Risorgimento*, of the national unification of Italy, was from 1852 one of the leading Piedmontese statesmen under Victor Immanuel II, King of Sardinia. A few years previously, Immanuel's father, Carl Albert, had been easily defeated by the Austrian, Radetzky. The defeat was a heavy blow to a united Italy, which, as Metternich cynically remarked, was 'only a geographical expression.' Now the right moment seemed to have arrived for Cavour to win a powerful ally.

Through his participation in the Crimean War, he had gained admission to the peace conference at Paris. At a secret meeting with Napoleon, at Plombières, in July 1858, they concluded an offensive alliance against Austria by the terms of which Napoleon was to receive Savoy and Nice as compensation. Little Piedmont began to arm against the Habsburg giant. In April 1859 a reluctant ultimatum was dispatched from Vienna, demanding immediate disarmament and, when Cavour refused, Austria declared war: the occasion had been given.

The short but unusually bloody war which now blazed up in the heart of Europe has its own historical importance. Apart from revolutions, punitive political expeditions and colonial struggles, among which the Crimean War in 'far-away Turkey' may be included, the clash of arms had been stilled for half a century in Europe. This was the first modern war, with railroads, telegraphs and war correspondents, and public opinion hourly participating. It was, in fact, one of the most dilettante wars ever fought.

In France, until the day it broke out, there was only one man who ever dreamed of such a war—Napoleon. But 'enthusiasm' was created with astonishing rapidity. The cartoonists who caricatured the Austrian enemy, and a fiery appeal of the Emperor played their part: 'Soldiers, I am placing myself at your head to lead you into battle. We are aiding the struggle for freedom of a nation which demands its independence. We shall rescue it from foreign oppression. We are fighting in a sacred cause which has the sympathy of the whole world . . .'

Mérimée writes that the soldiers went off 'as if to a ball: on the coaches they painted, "Excursion to Italy and Vienna." As they marched to the station, the crowds loaded them with flowers, brought them wine, embraced them and entreated them to kill as many Austrians as possible.'

Thus 130,000 men plunged with time-honoured psychosis into a war which, had the enemy been more competent, would have turned into a disaster.

Said Randon, Minister of War, 'We lack everything but courage.'

But the Austrian Commander Gyulai lacked even courage. During the uprising in Hungary in 1849, he had shown a talent for shooting down defenceless peasants, but he could not lead an army. Invaluable weeks were wasted while his only tactic was to avoid the enemy. By the time he was superseded by the twenty-eight-year-old Emperor Francis Joseph and more experienced generals, it was already too late. The junction of the French with the Italians had been effected and they drove the Austrians before them. The Austrians were clogging their single line of track from Milan to Verona and were exhausted by the long marches and by hunger.

Near Montebello, they suffered their first great defeat. Then, on 4 June there was a battle near Magenta —a Don Quixote battle, arranged by chance, without strategy and without commanders. Only when the Austrians abandoned Lombardy and retired on their line of Venetian forts did the allies realize that they had won. Napoleon made a triumphal entry into liberated Milan.

'In 1859, the French won a victory by using the methods of 1809 against an opponent with the strategic ideas of 1757,' writes Phillip Guedalla. A few weeks later, on 24 June there was another unpremeditated battle, the bloody catastrophe of Solferino, the most murderous blood-bath of the century. Napoleon sat on his white horse in Castiglione and smoked more than fifty cigarettes: his nerves were cracking. 'The poor people, the poor people, this horrible war!' Disquieting news was coming from France, the Prussians were mobilizing on the Rhine.

On 11 July Napoleon met Francis Joseph at Villa-franca. A hasty preliminary peace was concluded by which the Austrians kept Venezia. After the victorious campaign, Cavour was left half in the lurch. He finished the unification of Italy with his own resources.

III

Solferino

ON the battlefield of Solferino, Dunant suddenly re-
appears. What had brought this banker and industrialist to share the perils of war? He himself always
maintained later that he was simply a tourist caught
by chance in the maelstrom, but existing documents
prove something else. The mills of Mons-Gémila, the
million franc project on which his ambition had been
toiling for years, constantly thwarted by bureau-
cratic obstruction, lay behind his extraordinary idea
of explaining his financial difficulties to the Emperor
in a hail of bullets. Dunant's presumptuousness, his
utter ignorance of the actual horror of death is only
an aspect of the arch simplicity and egocentric blindness of the capitalist mind.

And, like the wrath of God, the horrors of the
battlefield of Solferino shocked his bourgeois soul out
of its golden day-dream, and left its owner on his
knees among the blood and carrion.

When he arrived on 20 June at the little Apennine
village of Pontremoli, he had in his portmanteau
two highly extraordinary volumes, elegantly em-

bossed with the imperial arms and recently from the presses of the Genevese publisher, Fick, who had printed his first book so handsomely. One high-flown title read: *The Empire of Charlemagne Restored, or the Holy Roman Empire Renewed by His Majesty the Emperor Napoleon III, by J.Henri Dunant, Director and President of the Financial and Industrial Company of the Mills of Mons-Gemila (Algiers), Member of the Asiatic Society of Paris, of the French Oriental Society, of the Geographic Society of Paris and Geneva, of the Historical Society of Algiers etc.* The other, of which a single copy had been printed, was entitled: *Memorandum on the Financial and Industrial Company of the Mills of Mons-Gemila in Algeria, Capital One Million, by J.Henri Dunant, President of the Company: a Report of Steps which have been taken uninterruptedly from 1853 to 1859 to Maintain an Area of more than Seven Hectares of Land in Algeria.*

In Pontremoli he ran into his somewhat astonished patron, General de Beaufort, in front of the *Casa Dante* on the piazza. Dunant disclosed his intention to the General, who as we know was familiar with his affairs, and who did not appear to be especially surprised at this mixture of war and business. They spoke of the horrors of the times. ' What do you expect,' was the soldier's point of view, 'you can't make an omelette without breaking some eggs. If you want to see a real battle, you should cross the Apennines at once.'

Dunant did not lose a moment. Armed with a fresh introduction to MacMahon, he travelled day and night by diligence and was presently in Brescia. He could hear the cannon thundering in the distance. The bridges had been blown up, he waded the stream. All coaches were commandeered; he found an old cart and a young Mantuan who had deserted the Austrians and who knew the country. On 24 June, the day of Solferino, Dunant reached Castiglione: he was in the very heart of the battle.

. . .

Napoleon had left Brescia two days before. Victor Immanuel II, King of Sardinia, had started from Desenzano. Marshal Baraguay d'Hilliers was before Solferino. MacMahon, the victor of Magenta, was advancing on Cavriana. The Imperial Guard occupied Castiglione. The allied armies numbered 150,000 men with 400 cannon.

The Emperor Francis Joseph had rallied nine army corps, 170,000 men with 500 cannon. The Austrians advanced across the Muncio and occupied the heights of Pozzolengo as far as Guidizzolo. The artillery was protected by earthworks between the two armies commanded by Counts Wimpffen and Schlick. Their position seemed impregnable.

No one had foreseen so sudden and dramatic a turn of event. Each had completed his deployment almost unobserved by the other, and as day dawned, more than 300,000 men faced each other on a front ten miles long, waiting for the signal to join battle. The Austrians marched in close formation, in battle array, with the imperial eagles flying. The motley colours of the French uniforms, cuirassiers, lancers and dragoons, shone in the sun. Trumpet signals and the roll of drums rent the air; the sharp crack of musketry and hollow pounding of cannon; white puffs of smoke from bursting projectiles; dust-whirls from the galloping squadrons. It all looked good-natured, not to say joyous, like the gay pictures in the history books of our youth. A gigantic game of soldiers, an unconscious outburst of exuberant life, a festive splendour unfolded itself, robbing destruction, in whose name all this was done, of its terrors. Dunant's heart was deeply thrilled by the fascinating din and magic power, the hundreds of thousands of men moving forward as if to embrace each other.

The French, who had been up since daybreak, had nothing but a few swallows of wretched coffee. For the Austrians, exhausted by forced night marching, there had been a double ration of schnapps.

The heat became unbearable from minute to minute: the earth seemed to steam. As if in a magnetic-field, hunger was driven against hunger.

They threw away their knapsacks with their pitiable possessions and iron rations. They pushed on, on to fixed bayonets between their ribs. Horses' hoofs and the wheels of the gun-carriages mangled the limbs of the helplessly wounded. When ammunition gave out and gun-barrels burst, the fight went on with fists, stones and knives. Every farmyard became a fort, every sand-heap a prize fertilized with rivers of blood. The military formation, which had been so puppet-like and pictorial in its precision, had lost all order: at staff headquarters, it was strategy; on the battlefield, it was slaughter.

Again and again, the French tried to storm the heights and silence the cannon. The Austrians were entrenched behind the houses and churches of Medole, Solferino and Cavriana, and an iron rain drove the attackers back. The hill of Roccolo, *Madonna della Scoperta*, was taken six times and lost six times by the Italians.

The Austrians fought like maddened animals. Heavy fire was directed on their reserves. Whole companies were smashed to pieces. But each time they closed their ranks again, while a surplus of victims kept thrusting themselves out of the herd, freed from the frightful suspense of waiting, and eager to rush forward and to die.

Toward noon, the sky was overcast and presently a dreadful thunderstorm broke. The lightning licked through the dark and gruesome landscape, cries and oaths rang out above the smoking heaps of shattered and burning villages and woods.

Napoleon ordered the Guard to storm Solferino and the fort of San Cassano simultaneously. Under a cloud-burst, Marshal Baraguay's troops forced their way into the town. The Austrian front was broken, the retreat began. The Emperor Francis Joseph moved his staff to Volta. Guidizzolo was held until ten o'clock that night. On improvised bridges the fleeing Austrians streamed to the rear. The roads were blocked with shattered wagons, cannon and dead horses. The first wounded, ragged and bleeding, began to reach Villafranca. The Battle of Solferino had been fought.

From holes and cellars the blackened faces of peasants began to appear. Like sick rats, they sat, not knowing what to do, hunched over their ruined pos-

sessions. They did not recognize the same world,
their native earth, which they had left flourishing
and in order fifteen hours before, and which now,
after the catastrophe, looked like one great sup-
purating wound.

Even during the battle, field-hospitals, distinguished by pennants had been hastily set up in elevated places. But as each nation used different
colours for this purpose, the hospitals were not recognized and were bombarded. Doctors, wounded, and
irreplaceable supplies were destroyed.

Water became more and more precious. Pickets with
guns stood around every drying spring and guarded
every drop. Men laid their faces in the filthy and infected puddles, lapping up the moisture like cattle.

Groups of soldiers and Lombard peasants collected
the wounded, made a note of the number stamped
on the uniform of each and piled the bodies in rows
one on another in a common grave. No one stopped
long to ask if the heart in some unconscious body was
still beating. The rotting, stinking refuse had to
disappear.

By degrees, a certain order appeared out of the
chaos: Castiglione became a concentration point for
the wounded. Soon the little city was filled to overflowing with 6,000 wounded and other sufferers
amidst whom stood two doctors not knowing what to
do. Long caravans of ox-carts and mules endlessly
brought in their groaning loads.

Long columns of prisoners, marching in formation,
led to the rumour that the Austrians were coming
back. In a trice the houses were barricaded, tricolors

and Sardinian flags were torn down, drivers unharnessed their horses and dashed off with the traces dangling. Gradually the tumult subsided. Every house had become a hospital. People did not know where to put the wounded in order to get them out of their houses.

The small infirmary, the cloister, the barracks of San Luigi, the church of the Capuchins were all but attacked by cursing, wailing soldiers. Whoever could still use his fists fought his way in to his heap of straw. Everyone was mercilessly defending his threatened life. The worst fate was that of the prisoners who, herded together, disarmed and defenceless, were abandoned like lepers.

Armed with a pass, Dunant hastened to the quarter of the town where the suffering seemed the greatest. Five hundred men had taken shelter in the *Chiesa Maggiore*. Untold others were lying on the stone steps and on the grass-plot in front. Dunant arrived just as two prisoners, who had been discovered in the church and who could not stand on their feet, were being thrown down the steps with curses.

'Stop!' he cried, 'don't do that! *Sono fratelli!* We are all brothers!'

Fists released their victims. The soldiers hesitated. They regarded incredulously this gentleman in white who seemed to have sprung out of the ground and who uttered his humane command in a calm and clear voice.

Sono fratelli! The new watch-word spread through the town like wildfire. A trace of smiling happiness and goodness appeared in the comfortless gloom and demoralization which threatened to engulf all souls.

A bustling activity began, an endless pilgrimage to the *Chiesa Maggiore*. The women brought big white bundles of lint on their heads. Boys fetched buckets of water and jugs of soup. Dunant sent his cart to Brescia, giving his Italian a well-filled purse. The man returned bringing sponges, linen, tobacco, mallows, camomile, sugar, oranges and lemons.

The straw pallets lay in rows. In the sacristy a bandaging-room was established. The wounded could wash and the bandages be changed. Four Austrian doctors hurried tirelessly from pallet to pallet, together with a German doctor whom chance had brought there, and a couple of Italian students. The band of assistants grew. An extraordinary old naval officer appeared, with the decorations of forgotten battles on his coat, and a Monsieur Suchard from Neuchâtel, an Italian priest, a French journalist and a pair of inquisitive Englishmen who forced their way into the church and were practically made prisoners, but were soon voluntarily helping with the rest. The most zealous proved to be a bearded corporal, wounded at Magenta, whose wounds had hardly closed. He followed every step Dunant made with a touching mixture of grumbling and admiration.

A consignment of chloroform, the miraculous new drug for killing pain, was received from Brescia. But as too many of the wounded never came out of the anaesthetic (there was no one with any experience in administering it) the doctors had to go to work again with saw and knife without the drug, while piercing shrieks from the little room where operations were performed sent shudders through the church.

Dunant toiled for three days and nights as if in a dream. It was a nightmare of Dantesque and infernal power peopled with the grotesque and depraved fantasies of Bosch. What a fearful awakening from the dream-world of his bourgeois existence, lapped in money and in piety, to the horrors of reality! There was no end. Where one wound closed another broke open. The flow of blood simply could not be staunched. While he rallied one poor soul back to life, another sank unsuccoured into the arms of death. His helping hands were as blind and unjust in their efforts as fate itself, and the power of one man over his brothers seemed to him sinister.

The moment of exhaustion and recollection brought a remarkable reflex. Did Dunant remember the original purpose of his journey? Or did his own energetic nature oblige him to undertake any activity in order to shake off the unbearable lethargy of horror into which he was threatening to sink?

It was six o'clock in the evening. He ordered the driver to get the cart ready. At the last moment the bearded corporal insisted on going with him. Dunant drove off into the night. By nine they were in Cavriana. The town had been stripped bare by the Austrians and the inhabitants had to be fed from the regimental kitchens.

In order to inquire about Marshal MacMahon's headquarters, Dunant halted before the house that the Emperor had occupied since Friday. The arrival of the cart attracted considerable attention and

several officers questioned the corporal curiously. He
gave respectful but vague answers. Dunant's order
to drive on to Borghetto to the Duke of Magenta
impressed them with the portentous and mysterious
mission of this civilian.

It was a pitch-black night. The Italian, who did not
know the country, lost his way until a sign-post informed them that they were on the road to Volta
and must soon run headlong into the Austrians.

At this the driver was seized with panic. At every
turn of the road he expected to come upon the enemy.
A shot close by sent him entirely out of his mind and
Dunant had to turn the reins over to the corporal.
The wreckage on all sides, the croaking of flocks of
crows that were gorging on the refuse of the battle,
the *ignis fatuus*, all increased the Mantuan's fears.
All the spirits were abroad. As a black monster
loomed up in front of them, he gave one terrified cry.
It was a *vivandière's* big umbrella, shot through with
holes and torn by the wind. They went farther. An
outpost commanded them to halt. 'Corporal of the
First Engineers Corps, Seventh Company.' 'Pass!'
They galloped. The cart was threatening to fall to
pieces. Shortly before midnight the dark houses of
Borghetto appeared. They stopped by a feeble light.
It was Marshal MacMahon's headquarters.

This nocturnal visitation of the extraordinary cart
caused the greatest astonishment. But a friendly orderly fetched a bag of straw for Dunant. The corporal and the driver found sleeping quarters in the
cart.

At six o'clock the next morning, Dunant was standing before MacMahon. The bare room reminded Dunant of his bank in Geneva. Papers lay in piles. On the walls were maps and charts covered with figures. The Marshal was seated at a writing-table, reckoning, a pince-nez on his nose. Several buttons of his coat were unfastened. He looked like a banker in uniform. In fact, this was the clearing-house of war, where human life was reckoned and assigned.

'For God's sake, Monsieur Dunant,' said Mac-Mahon, 'how did you get here?' Dunant described his conversation afterwards. 'I reported to the famous general in a few words what I had seen in my three days at Castiglione, and the lack of aid for the enormous number of wounded. Among other things, I mentioned the appalling condition in which I had found the Austrian wounded, and the immediate necessity of pressing the captured doctors into service. I made the Duke of Magenta swear in the name of humanity to obtain for me a suitable opportunity of discussing the deplorable conditions with the Emperor.'

MacMahon took Dunant seriously. He sent him on to Cavriana to General Headquarters with a brief note to the Emperor's civilian attaché, Charles Robert. Dunant called about noon. He did not see the Emperor. He stated his business. An order issued shortly after, liberating the captured doctors, was presumably the result of his intercession.

He also delivered his book. He had consistently said nothing about it, which was a mistake. There is a letter dated from General Headquarters, 29 June 1859:

DEAR SIR:

The Emperor has considered the book which you propose publishing under the title 'The Roman Empire.' His Majesty commands me to inform you that while he is grateful to you for submitting it, you may not make use of the dedication, and has further expressed the wish that out of regard for present political circumstances you abstain from a publication which might cause inconveniences.

The Deputy for Petitions in the Cabinet of the Emperor,

CHARLES ROBERT

An unmistakable annoyance breathes through these lines. Napoleon, while as a rule extremely susceptible to any glorification of his mission, was about to end the war by making peace. At the moment, Dunant's Genevese prophecies, extolling him as the only legitimate successor of the Roman Emperors and Charlemagne, and just to round out the lunacy, Nebuchadnezzar, seemed highly inopportune to him.

What an extraordinary mixture the Dunant of that day was! Naïve obsessionism, Bible mania, Byzantinism, a banker's spirit, an almost arrogant audacity, officiousness and a capacity for passionate sympathy. This extinct type of early capitalist would be a riddle to-day, a character psychologically incomprehensible if we did not know the historical circumstances that moulded him. How like his prototype he was: Napoleon III also united on a larger scale the mind of a speculator, a feeling for civilization and mysticism. Both men were carried to the very pinnacle of their times and then reduced to nothing. And

time would have discarded them entirely did not
their greatness first force itself upon our consciousness at the moment when we, too, are face to face
with our misfortunes.

Dunant was vain. Who is not? He was naïve, essentially non-intellectual. Even when he is silent or
hates, he is an honest, egoistic sinner. This makes it
easy for his enemies to attack and condemn him. But
his genuine piety never forsook him. From childhood
to his Biblical old age he went his courageous way
with its superabundance of trials. He was a speculator, and was not afraid of bankruptcy. He was rich,
and was not afraid of poverty. If he was vain, he was
not afraid of complete oblivion. If he was conventional and prejudiced, he did not draw back from the
most radical departures. God dealt harshly with this
man plagued by all earthly errors. But He helped
him to a great work and a true purgation of his tormented heart.

IV

A New Art of War

THE short war of 1859 has a significance in world history that has never been properly appraised. As the first modern war, it revealed the inadequacy of the previous strategic methods and the unsuspected possibilities that progress had to offer the leadership of armies.

Observant eye-witnesses detected the causes of the disorganization that was apparent on both sides in this campaign. Mass movement and mass battles set aside all prior military experience. A new organization had to be created for the conduct of war.

In Prussia, William I had been ruling since 1858. The threefold constellation of Bismarck, Moltke and Roon had appeared on the horizon—men who thought like soldiers and acted as diplomats. The rise of Prussia as a world power was beginning. Prussia had discovered the value of technique for the destructive act of war, while the German mobilization on the Rhine had revealed the unsatisfactory state of the German arms. A new army had to be created. It was created.

Austria was weakened and ripe to surrender the

overlordship of Germany to Prussia. France was victorious and all too powerful, but its military vanity prevented a bitter though necessary insight into its own weaknesses.

The rise of Italian nationalism had given the signal for national stirrings among other European peoples. Soon the Poles were calling for futile insurrection. National movements began among the Balkan peoples. The day of German unity was at hand.

But the problematic and tragic Napoleon, at the zenith of his career and crowned with the bays of victory, felt no intimations of the fall that lay before him. Napoleon III was a dictator in a democracy, who himself conjured up the foe that was to be his undoing. He wavered, as William II would do later, between Caesarian delusions and social-political reformism. He was a rebel but an oppressor, a diplomatic intriguer but a constitutional monarch, a speculator but a Utopian where civilization was concerned: in reality, a lively and intelligent bourgeois of his century in whose brain converged all the existing and the future elements of European development. He discovered nationalism, brought it out into the light of day, sacrificed important political advantages to it. He had a passion for conferences and plebiscites. Even during his last days, the fallen monarch sketched a fantastic plan to a visitor from London—the abolition of war. An international council would regulate the world's affairs at regular sessions and an assembly of the nations would arrive at decisions on the basis of international law. In 1872 this was the delusion of a mortally sick and exiled dictator in whose ears was still ringing his own cry of horror at Sedan: 'The firing must positively stop! The firing must stop! It shall stop . . . too much blood has flowed!'

The banker Dunant was simply an individual without position or power. He lived his egoistic, meaningless, supernumerary existence on the edge of events—until blood—the blood of Solferino, awakened him, too, to responsibility.

The men of the twentieth century are in greater danger, more threatened, more vulnerable than their forbears. Among the catastrophes of a sick society, wars, economic crises and insane ideologies, they suffer more directly and more universally. Everyone of us alive to-day has been caught once, or will be caught, in the terrible grasp of a fate which shakes and imperils his existence. Each of us to-day has his direct share in the public misfortune. It is no longer a question of chance whom the tragic lightning will strike. The chance is whom it will not strike. To combat and avert catastrophe is a public concern, the right and duty of every living creature—we have gained that knowledge. But there is a dreadful intermediate period in political change when the individual surrenders his responsibility for human happiness to the community, that is to say, the masses. And the masses, who are careless toward responsibility, unaccustomed to thinking and tired of feeling, let adventurers, fanatics and politicians snatch their responsibility from them. Uncontrollable and drunk with their own propaganda, these sinister forces are driving humanity to disaster. Well-meaning and de-cent human behaviour is caught in the barbed wire of its own powerless and effete organization. Anarchy and national insanity are permitted to parade unpunished as practical politics. A biologically and ethically established humanitarianism, all of whose premises are clear, is rendered contemptible and hateful. After the nineteenth century, in an access of nobility, had declared life sacred, and the task was clearly indicated to transform life that was worthless into life of value and capacity, the criminal catch-phrase 'wishy-washy humanitarianism' was coined. And with this slogan the right of the individual to life and freedom was unscrupulously and shamelessly destroyed as if it were a malignant growth.

We must face this state of affairs without illusions before we presume to find the benevolence of the nineteenth century absurd or repugnant. Certainly, charity is repugnant to us, it is too much like giving away a bit of an assured existence as a bribe for the repose of one's own soul. But man's imagination will never suffice to visualize suffering that he has not himself experienced. More effective is his fear of the contagion of suffering, the wish to keep it at arm's length, the knowledge that the unbearable can and must lead to dangerous outbreaks. The nineteenth century, which invented hygiene, was also in a fair way to invent a successful hygiene for the diseases of society. The taming of the apocalyptic horsemen appeared imminent. There were human rights whose inviolability seemed a prerequisite for the security of all, and to uphold which money and labour were voluntarily given. Only the Anglo-Saxon countries and France to-day retain a traditional remnant of all this. Poverty is a danger but by scientific methods it could be uprooted. Humanitarianism is not a sentimental overflowing of the heart, nor a religious conviction, but a demand of the intelligence. How terribly old-fashioned and primitive these words sound, as if they sprang from the positive materialism of the end of the century. And, indeed, that is the intention. Surely life is too complex, too bound up with the spirit, for its conflicts to be approached with such simplified formulae. The shaping of the individual destiny will forever be a mystery. But how avoidable suffering is to be prevented and the fate of mankind kept out of the hands of criminals is a technical question. The decline of the nineteenth century began at the moment when it made of a technical problem an article of ideological conviction.

The case of Dunant is an example. Dunant was inwardly prepared by the influence of Genevan piety when he appeared on the battlefield of Solferino. Until that moment he had been one of innumerable other aimless alms-givers. Inevitably, his experience of horror converted him into an active apostle of a vast humanitarian plan. It is sufficiently important to follow the stages of this conversion.

Immediately after the outbreak of hostilities, a plan of action was proposed in the worldly and pietistic circles of Geneva. On the initiative of Mme Adrien Naville-Rigaud, a committee was formed which requested Dunant's assistance. Actually, this committee was no different from other spawning-grounds of bourgeois vanity and ambition which

under the patronage of honourable presidents, vice-
presidents and secretaries put social feeling at the
service of social careerism. Probably it remained
more or less an affair of the Geneva *salons*. Dunant
bluntly refused to co-operate, asking: 'Why talk
about shredding lint before a single man has been
wounded?' His experience was soon to answer his
arrogant question.

On 28 June, the day of exhaustion, after his return
from General Headquarters to the church of suffering
at Castiglione, Dunant addressed an appeal for help
to the *comtesse* de Gasparin:

HONOURED *COMTESSE*,

Permit me to turn to you in the extraordinary circumstances in which I find myself. For three days, I have
been caring for the wounded of Solferino, and I have
more than a thousand of these unfortunates in my
charge. We have 40,000 wounded, Austrians and Allies,
from this dreadful event. There are not enough doctors
and I have to supplement them, for better or for worse,
with a few peasant women and prisoners. At the beginning of the struggle, I hastened from Brescia to the battlefield. Nothing can describe the frightful consequences
of this battle. One must recall the great battles of the
First Empire to find anything comparable. The Crimean
War was nothing in comparison. (This is the opinion of
generals, officers and men who went through the campaigns in Africa and the Crimea.)

I cannot begin to describe the things I have seen. But
emboldened by the blessings of the unfortunate wounded
and dying, to whom I must say a few words of comfort,
I turn to you with the request that you supply our troops
with tobacco and cigarettes as you did in the Crimean

War. Time is lacking for me to amplify my proposal, but
if I could convey to you all the eloquence of a heart that
has lived through what I have lived through, then you
would not hesitate even for a moment to organize a great
meeting in France for this truly Christian work. There
are soldiers who would rather go without something to
eat and drink if only they have something to smoke . . .

I am writing from the battlefield. There one cannot
choose his impressions. The battlefield with its heaps of
dead and dying is nothing compared with a church in
which five hundred wounded are lying one on top of the
other . . . Every fifteen minutes for three days, I have
seen a human being die in unimaginable agonies. A glass
of water, a cigar, a friendly smile—and they become
changed natures who suffer the hour of death bravely
and calmly. Pardon, but I am weeping continuously as I
write. I must close. They are calling me.

P.S. We have to try to find even the most elementary
necessities in Brescia. Here we have nothing except lint.
The Lombard tobacco is poor, but even that is lacking
here. A hundred cigarettes in a church in which hundreds
of wounded are lying, purify the air and lessen the horrible stenches.

Step by step we can follow the change in Dunant.
Now nothing stood between him and the horror of
the experiences that shook his heart. He cries out—
and it is a cry for tobacco. Still he saw no way out,
only a compulsion to satisfy indescribable needs with
the most necessary things. He saw the soldiers throw
themselves like wild beasts on the cigars which two
English travellers offered them. Tobacco smoke was
supposed to be sanitive and disinfectant.

Dunant appealed to the *comtesse* Gasparin, a

Genevese by birth, the wife of a pious French aristocrat, because at the time of the Crimean War she had
successfully organized a similar meeting. His appeal
was heard. Soon excerpts from his letter appeared in
L'Illustration and the *Journal de Genève*.

A few days previously, the President of the *Société
Évangélique*, Merle d'Aubigné, had, under the chest-
nut-trees of Monchoisy, described to Genevese society the cruel agonies of Frenchmen, Italians and
Germans, bleeding to death without so much as a
comforting word. Lint was not enough. 'A better
lint is needed: hearts that love the unfortunate . . .
Who will whisper to them the name of the Lord? Is
there no tongue in which to utter to them the word
of the great Comforter? Prayers are needed, people
are needed, money is needed.'

To the peaceful Genevese in their shady park by
the lake, prayers glowed brighter than tobacco. A
few thousand francs were immediately collected and
young people announced themselves ready for the
mission. Several days later, Dunant's letter appeared.
The energetic *comtesse* de Gasparin, whose piety
bore a somewhat more realistic stamp, effected a
compromise which united both trends, the spiritual
and the material. On 9 July Dunant received a letter
from Mme Adrien Naville, informing him that 'three
young students from the *Oratoire*'—as the free the-
ological faculty of the *Société Évangélique* was called
—'had started for Italy under the direction of Pastor
Charpiot after receiving brief instruction in bandaging.' They were to work in the hospitals where help
was lacking.

Dunant was never to see this expedition which may be regarded as the practical beginning of Genevese sanitary activity. The young people met a rather adventurous fate. They arrived in Italy on 11 July and visited all the important hospitals, assisted in bandaging the wounded, distributed oranges, peppermints, sugar, lemons, cigarettes and religious tracts. But it was precisely these religious writings that displeased the authorities. They questioned the young men, arrested them as spies and anarchists, and finally threw them into prison, from which the Milanese banker, Brot, had the greatest difficulty in releasing them. Still another Genevese, the physician Dr. Appia, who was later to play a significant part in the founding of the Red Cross, had been in Italy since the beginning of the campaign. He had placed himself at the disposal of the 'Turin Ladies' Committee for the Collection of Bandages and Lint for the Wounded.' There will be more to say concerning him.

Meanwhile, on the thirtieth, Dunant had gone to Brescia to continue his activities in the hospitals there. From this period we possess another document, another step in the evolution from alms-giver to advocate of humanity. On 3 July he wrote to his patron, General de Beaufort:

MONSIEUR LE GÉNÉRAL,

Permit me to thank you for the kindnesses you have shown me and to relate to you briefly the incidents of my journey.

I arrived at Solferino at the moment of the battle.

This caused me to forget my book and my letter for two whole days. I took care, as far as I was able, of the wounded who are lying almost without any help in the church, and with the assistance of the women of Castiglione have given impetus to a kind of organized aid for these poor unfortunates.

In Brescia I have collected linen and shirts, which were wholly lacking, camomile for washing the wounds, lemons, sugar, tobacco etc. I have made my headquarters in two churches that were more forsaken than the others. Then I have organized assistance for myself: tourists, even Englishmen, Austrian prisoners, slightly-wounded soldiers, and thanks to the wonderful and kind-hearted women of Castiglione, we have rescued some unfortunates from certain death.

Never shall I be able to forget the eyes of these victims who wished to kiss my hand. It was shocking. The poor French soldier, so brave in danger, so patient in suffering, and so grateful for a glass of water!

The appearance of the battlefield is nothing compared with the despair of the poor wretches who lay in heaps one, two, even three days without care, without help, believing themselves abandoned. I have seen old soldiers, brave *zouaves*, who cried like children. It would break your heart. In the corners of the churches I found many who had simply been forgotten, others who for days had been brought nothing to eat or drink. Many, despite their terrible wounds, had never been bandaged, men whom a little quicker assistance might have saved. Still others remained for days without having their bandages changed because nobody gave them a thought. Almost all were naked, still covered with blood and swarming with flies and maggots. There they lay on the stones or on straw, pieces of which stuck in their wounds, surrounded by a hideous filth and horrible stench. And day after day.

The doctors have done what they could. But there are not enough of them, and many sound men who wanted to help could not bear the terrible sights in the church . . .

Here ends the fragment of letter as far as we know it, but Dunant wrote in his *Recollections* that in closing he besought the General to use all his influence with the Emperor to prevent the repetition of such frightful disorganization.

His conscience was now almost crystallized. A man who would dare to describe to a general who had advanced his business interests, the failure of his own army, and in such matter-of-fact and unsparing terms, can never know peace again.

The almost deliberate way in which Dunant completed his reaction from horror, and changed from the pathetic and affected muddle-head to the inexorable and sober accuser, is extremely important for an understanding of this extraordinary man and his life.

From his childhood, Dunant had been trained to examine suffering. He must have anticipated horror from actual war. But the horrors of the reality he found so far exceeded anything he could have imagined that they shook him to the core, scattered all his scheme of well-ordered piety to the winds and reduced him for the first time in his life to that state of helplessness and the need for help, which he was accustomed to find in the miserable objects of his charitable practices. This state of bewilderment in which all the props and traditions of his existence failed him, this mortification of the egoism at the heart of a Genevese business man was bound to prove unendurable. He was too religious to seek any other way out than that of protest and indictment. It meant too much for his own life to have the shattered and disfigured image of a degenerate humanity restored.

Thus this affair became his affair, this wrong, this evil, in which he was involved by chance as a spectator, was added unto him and he became a partner in guilt, a defenceless accessory coerced into every crime of that battlefield. His guilt must be expiated. The cry of the victims must be silenced. Dunant took it up, he cried out with them, cried louder, until society was ready to redeem him by an act . . .

After Solferino, Dunant went to Brescia, and from there to Milan. Owing to the intense heat, the transport of wounded was effected almost exclusively at night. Before the station in Milan stood black, silent human masses, waiting to receive the thousands of maimed and wounded on whom, still shouting and rejoicing, they had showered flowers a few weeks before. Under the flickering pine torches the exhausted soldiers were loaded into the sumptuous coaches of the Milanese patricians. The nobility had thrown open the doors of its palaces. The Borromeo family alone took in three hundred invalids. The cloister of the Ursulines was converted into a hospital. The *Marchesa Pallavicini* conducted the central collection bureau for gifts and supplies. Little bands of slightly-wounded Frenchmen staggered along the streets in tattered uniforms on their way home. The ladies of Milan had replaced their blood-stained shirts with splendid linens. The town was profoundly shocked by this great European misfortune which had struck it with the unforseen suddenness of an earthquake. No one was prepared for such a deluge of blood and misery. In the *salons* it was excitedly discussed.

Dunant lent a hand where he was needed. But here, too, he missed no opportunity to make social connections. In Milanese society, in the *salon* of the *comtesse* Verri-Borromeo, he discussed the necessity of distinguishing the doctors and hospitals in war by some emblem which would be respected by all parties. The ladies were for it, but the gentlemen considered such a plan Utopian and impossible.

At the time of the Peace of Villafranca, in the middle of July, Dunant returned to Switzerland. 'I had to breathe the air of the high mountains again in order to restore my health, which was shattered by the painful excitements at Castiglione.'

After his return from the wars, in the peace and quiet of his home, Dunant reacted like the ordinary citizen—he wanted to forget, to forget quickly. The brief heroic episode—unintentional, we may say—of his life seemed finished.

Have we not observed a thousand men undergo the most frightful experiences and then quietly and decently resume their private lives? The heroism of the soldier, which is able for a time to drive the characterless bourgeois to superhuman exertions, to the closeness of death, contempt for life and human murder, does not endure. The gulf is too great between the anarchy of war and the life of the ordered world.

With a weird precision, the weather-worn and mud-stained heroes of the trenches once more turn into harmless shoe-makers and tailors. Once the mass tocsin to lawlessness is stilled, their excited hearts feel again, as in a fairy-tale, the blessings of sleep and of forgetfulness. Only after long years of dormancy does the picture of atrocity and horror come to mind again, but as a purged and very altered memory. Then war is recollected as the manly, gay, alluring adventure which so unforgettably broke the round of their little lives, and of which their children now dream until they, too, awaken one day as heroes, bleeding and tattered, to the inconceivable reality.

Only the very few, adventurers, criminals or saints, are unable to forget the frightful face of war and never can find peace. The dualism of a humanity that ploughs the fields and wastes the fields gives them no rest. The death that is blessed and the death that is condemned finds no equation in their consciences. They must continue to murder or they must curse war.

Dunant was no longer a bourgeois and not yet a prophet. The duality in his mind is clear from one little episode. After his return to Geneva he heaped reproaches on the *comtesse* Gasparin because she had published his letter from the battlefield. He had written it 'in a moment of complete self-forgetfulness.' Finally he asked for the return of his correspondence. And when Madame de Gasparin, who had been entirely without personal motives in the matter, and was now deeply offended, pointed out to him that he himself had expressly asked for publication, he replied a few days later contritely:

' My only excuse lies in my shattered nervous condition, which caused me to forget what I had written to you, and which has brought me to such a state of confusion and painful agitation that I hardly expect to recover. In the terrible moments through which I have lived, I was unable to understand the full significance of my actions.'

Dunant wished to recover, he did not wish to be reminded any further of himself. In sober Geneva, he felt only shame at the behaviour of a banker who set out to transact big business and then lost himself in the spectacle of the depravity of war almost to the point of exaltation.

Once more the business man came uppermost. Dunant recovered. He went to Paris on business.

V

The Splendour of Paris

'PARIS is the great cosmopolitan centre from which ideas radiate to all the points of the compass. The fact that something has originated in Paris is a perpetual endorsement of it,' wrote Dunant.

He was bewitched by the city which was to be his destiny. The Swiss banker, who while old beyond his years at thirty-one, would never in his life throw off a certain provincial infantilism, rightly sensed that Paris had something which he lacked. As yet he knew nothing of the perfidy of success or the mock earnestness of a society that feels a hardening of its financial arteries.

The sound of the marching Italian troops had scarcely died away on the boulevards where, crowned with bays and much trumpeted, they had paraded their gratitude for victorious assistance. Paris, actually at a turning-point in its destiny, seemed at the height of its power. It was incredible that the glorious upward course of France, over which once more hovered the suggestive insignia of a Napoleon, might some day end. The silent man in the Tuilleries, with

his waxed moustaches, and his long pale face ending
in the rather scrubby imperial, with the eternal
cigarette and the weary eyes turned inward, concentrated in his brain definite and peculiar ideas about
the future map of Europe. Anxiously or confidently,
the governments were gazing at this mild and mysterious sphinx in his gray trousers, white vest, modest
black coat and high top-hat, who was taking fantastic
modern ideologies and with uncanny energy making
world history of them. Only, in Prussia's Paris em-
bassy sat Bismarck—a cool, a colossal observer—
whose head was never affected by wine and who enjoyed the music of Offenbach with a sort of distant
pleasure. Bismarck made this note: 'France has two
amusing women, the Empress, the most beautiful
woman I know, and La Walewska but no man.'
One terse line exhausted the subject of the Emperor's
face: 'From a distance it looks like something: close
up, it is nothing.'

The romantic realism of Napoleon III was essentially nothing more than an anticipation of the Treaty
of Versailles and the era of European conferences. He
would have fitted marvellously into the League of
Nations at Geneva. But in 1860 it was too soon and
in 1938 too late. The diplomats who had grown great
in the tradition of the Treaty of Vienna of 1815
could not conceive of the rights of minorities:
Austria would have been reduced to nothing. Even
reforming Alexander II, although prepared for the
liberation of the serfs, grew constantly more reactionary under the pressure of Polish nationalism.
Lord Palmerston could not imagine that nations

'which had held their lands with good right for half a century would be much interested in discussing with good-natured neighbours all their wishes with respect to correcting the frontiers.' Italy, where Napoleon's troops were protecting the Pope against Napoleon's allies, the Piedmontese nationalists, was a continual source of worry. It was the tragedy of untimely liberalism that it should represent rights whose realization meant its own destruction.

When Napoleon proposed a conference to carry out a 'limitation of the excessive European armaments caused by mutual distrust,' and began to agitate for it at a moment when political tensions were visibly intensifying, he lost his reputation as a practical statesman with friend and foe.

Napoleon III stood as the lone European of a forlorn hope. For he speculated on a European consciousness. To-day, almost eighty years later, it would still be a forlorn hope. He sat in his always overheated room in the Palais Bourbon, poring over the preliminary studies for his great work on Julius Caesar. He had Mérimée instruct him in the religion of the ancient Romans and sent archaeological experts to Germany, while in Berlin the generals were poring over the staff maps of the French frontier. In 1860 it was easier to pursue a Prussian than a European policy. Beyond the Alps, the German *Risorgimento* was preparing in Prussian style along the lines of a masterly and inexorable political design.

Napoleon, the enemy of the Habsburgs and advocate of the principle of nationality, viewed the preparations with distinct and unconcealed goodwill.

He was entirely unsuspicious that the cap-stone of the new structure of Empire was to be his downfall.

Paris had experienced four political systems in thirty years. There were Bourbonists, Orléanists, Bonapartists and Republicans of the most varied hues. In addition, there was the tremendous power of the clericals who exploited the diversity of political opinion in the interest of Rome. Everywhere were groups whose sentiments and material interests were tied up with the past or linked with the future. Napoleon, who no longer wished to be a dictator, could no longer be one, since he must base his liberal foreign policy on a liberal domestic policy, was in a mood for compromise—and spoiled his chances with everyone.

He alienated the clericals who blamed him for the Pope's loss of temporal power; and the Bourbons who were vainly defending their last political foothold in Naples against Garibaldi's revolutionists; and the Orléanist Thiers, nostalgic for the vanished days of Louis Philippe; and the Republicans who had never forgiven the *coup d'état*. And the industrialists who blamed him for the free trade agreement which Fould, Minister of Commerce, and the Englishman, Cobden, had concluded without even consulting the Parliament at St. Cloud.

Still there were opportunities to feed French public opinion with successes. Nice and Savoy were annexed accordingly to the terms of the treaty with Cavour. There was a colonial war in Syria, and a march in common with the English against Peking where European rifles enjoyed a brilliant triumph over the bows and arrows of Asia. But then, what next?

The Emperor's advisers were third rate and they fought with an insane censorship against an intellectual opposition that was growing by leaps and bounds. The youth of England had a dangerous penchant for defending the rights of other people to freedom. Emigré Victor Hugo, from his exile in the island of Jersey, kept wafting strophes of intense hate across the Channel and *Napoleon the Little* was published. It began a literary vogue of epidemic proportion, and the struggle against Napoleon was preached between Byron-adoration and Rossetti-worship. The Liberator of Italy emerged a traitor from the verses of Italophile Browning and Mazzini-phile Swinburne, and a whole string of also-rans joined in—Bowen, Odger, Baxter. In France, the Republicans from Ollivier (at the beginning of wisdom) to bull-necked Gambetta (at the beginning of his career) were more and more gaining ground. Daudet, the royalist, and Zola, the liberal, wrote their political travesties. Flaubert's *Madame Bovary* was prosecuted. Napoleon lost a battle against the Café Procopé. On 24 November 1860 a decree was signed which promised the introduction of parliamentarism on an almost English scale.

Paris did not become less interesting with the turn to the left. The Emperor seemed almost relieved, for the usurper who could never quite free himself from his past was surrendering more and more to wishful dreams of democracy. Ollivier, whose star was on the rise, was a son-in-law of Liszt. In March 1861 the *Opéra*, The Temple of Berlioz, Rossini and Meyerbeer, seethed with the barbaric discords of Richard

Wagner's *Tannhäuser*. The Emperor applauded. The Princess Metternich broke her fan in her enthusiasm. The public rioted. But Paris was and remained the centre of the world.

Paris becomes difficult for a stranger when he first tries to live and succeed there. Dunant, the recently naturalized Frenchman, was to feel this. He had resumed his struggle for the mills at Mons-Gemila. But he was no match for the labyrinth of ante-rooms and *salons* whose mirrors suspiciously reflect the suppliants from several sides. There is nothing more opaque than the mechanism of a ruling class which feels itself threatened and in which everybody is everybody else's enemy. The higher powers cancel out. Secretaries and subalterns rule. Decisions are retracted before they are given.

Dunant did his best. He became a devout student of those indirect methods which were the mysterious ways to success in the Second Empire. He never missed a dinner, a name, a party, and had good relations with Catholics, intellectuals and Jews, with clubs and learned societies. On 7 November 1859, at the *Société d'Ethnographie*, he described the case of a young Austrian prisoner whose hair had turned grey during the Battle of Solferino, and this improbable fact was immediately used by the geographer Cortembert in his monograph on characteristics of the hair of various nations.

Yet all these ambitious exertions helped but little. He was refused the construction of those waterfalls without which his grist mills could not turn. In fact a rival suddenly appeared who threatened to snatch

the whole plan away from him. In November 1859
he sent the Emperor a new memorandum. But the
Emperor in Paris seemed to be more inaccessible than
in Solferino.

Why did Dunant get no farther? He was cleverer
than others, younger, calmer, more energetic. But
when he sat at lunch with important persons in the
warm gas-heat and plush of one of those boulevard
restaurants where red Chambertin sheds its blessings
on business, all too often, through the fumes of wine
and piping-hot food, would peer the hungry and
thirsty faces from the church of Castiglione. And
instead of Mons-Gemila, he would talk about Solferino. And the red faces of the commissary officers
whose meal he had disturbed in Castiglione with
appeals for help would grow clearer. At such moments
Dunant would say very unfriendly and disagreeable
things. The patriotic hearts of the gentlemen sitting
opposite would be shocked at the irrationality of
this young man who was so violently attacking the
very authorities from whom he wanted assistance.
The conversation would run on politely and non-
committally, but Dunant's market value began to
fall.

Disappointed, Dunant returned to Geneva. He
did not as yet see the deep gulf over which only rebels
can leap, which divides the men who make history
from the men whom history afflicts. Who loves a
cripple who displays his wounds? He dragged his experience around with him like leprosy. 'He exag-
gerates,' thought the generous. 'Dangerous atrocity
stories,' said the malicious. But the appalling truth

of Solferino became a nervous affliction, a product of the mind of young Monsieur Dunant.

He fought with all his strength against the forces which were driving him farther and farther, like a ship-wrecked sailor, from the safe shore of the bourgeois existence which had been his birthright and which he had transgressed. To his own world, which could never see nor understand what he had been through, he became alien and suspect. He could not forget. Yet as he did not want to give up completely, he must attempt to make himself understood. He decided to write down his horrible experiences.

Dunant set to work as if by means of this confession he would ease his conscience. He shut himself away. He guarded his plan like a secret. 'I hesitated a long time before I determined to write a brief account of those scenes of desperation which it had been my sad privilege to witness.' At first, it had not been his intention to 'initiate the public into those frightful scenes, those horrible sufferings which he had witnessed after the terrible battle of Solferino.' Even now he had no thought of making himself an instrument of mass propaganda. The book was to be printed privately for his 'family and his numerous friends.' He wanted to account for the event that seemed to be becoming a disaster in his own life. The task outgrew him.

While I was secretly writing my *Recollections of Solferino*, I seemed to be lifted out of myself, governed by a higher power, inspired by a divine breath. In the suppressed excitement with which my heart was filled, I was overcome by a feeling of indefinite and yet elemental intuition, transforming my work into the instrument of a higher will. I should help to accomplish a sacred work, which in the future would have an incalculable development for the benefit of mankind. This presentiment drove me on as though I were compelled . . . This energy came from heaven, for, truly, I no longer thought of myself. These *Recollections* had to be written. I cannot express it in any other way. The deep and pain-filled shock of Solferino must be transmitted in this brief account, which would truthfully record what my own eyes had seen. Others must share it so that the humanitarian idea, which was filling me with enthusiasm, might bear fruit and develop of its own strength.

When one reads the *Recollections of Solferino*, especially when one compares it with Dunant's previous literary efforts, one is compelled to accept as authentic his feeling that he wrote it under divine inspiration. There is no more wordiness, no dubious pathos. The book is an honest, concise document covering the events of the battle. It has three distinct parts: a description of the strategy, Dunant's personal experiences, and his demands for the future.

Dunant is an appalling realist. Three long years lay between the reality and the recollection. But the hell of Solferino was indelibly etched on his brain. The countless forms of grief, the long-silent cries of despair are brought to life again by his inexorable pen. He strove for the maximum accuracy and assembled a wealth of material. He had Captain Benjamin Mueller, a Swiss, prepare a map of the vicinity of Solferino on which the positions of the three armies were expertly indicated. Lieutenant Lecomte gave

him his tactical data. He made use of the published
articles of the doctors, Bertherand and Poplimont.
But his contact with Dr.Louis Appia especially
helped him.

Appia came of a Piedmontese family. His father
was a minister. He himself was born at Frankfurt-on-
Main, and left Germany at the time of the 1848
Revolution to settle at Geneva and become a Genevese citizen. He belonged to the *Société Évangélique*.
This German-Italian Protestant was a singular blend
of militant Samaritanism. As a physician and former
Prussian, the soldierly and craftsmanly sides of war
were not so foreign to him as to Dunant. When the
war broke out, he was engaged in composing his work,
*The Ambulance Doctor or Practical Studies of the
Wounds Inflicted by Firearms*. With the proof-sheets
of his book and an apparatus invented by him for
transporting the wounded, he hastened at once to
Solferino and the theatre of war. There he worked as
a medical observer and humanitarian helper. In the
hospitals of Piedmont and Lombardy he distributed
2,000 kilos of bandage-linen that was sent to him
from Geneva. In Desenzano, he presented his apparatus to the French Surgeon-General, the famous
Larrey. He seems to have been the first neutral civilian doctor to offer his services to the army of a
foreign country. In countless letters to his friend, the
Genevese physician, Dr.Maunoir, and in articles for
the *Journal de Genève*, he describes his impressions.
They are essentially a doctor's observations—on
amputations, on the tetanus of wounds, on the new
drugs, chloride of iron, curare and chloroform, whose

practicability for military surgery was having its first tests in this campaign. He lacked Dunant's sensibility and his human feeling, but his testimony gains strength from the superiority of his expert knowledge. But both the experienced surgeon and the inexperienced civilian were filled with a sense of inadequacy and helplessness. In 1859 Appia closes a letter to Dr. Maunoir with the words of the great sixteenth century surgeon Ambroise Paré: '*Je le pansai, Dieu le guérit.*'

Dunant and Appia apparently did not meet in Italy. In January 1860 Victor Immanuel awarded both men the Order of Saints Moritz and Lazarus for their services. On their return they could exchange experiences in Geneva.

But whereas Appia would never seriously question war as a fact ordained by fate, Dunant was a war-hater. His service does not lie in the fact that he first advanced the idea of neutralized aid for the wounded. Its technical urgency and simple human necessity made it inevitable that the idea should be in the air. The Italian Palasciano and the Frenchman Arrault advanced it simultaneously, probably independently of Dunant. Dunant's service is the *Recollections of Solferino*, whose deep impressiveness and spiritual power revealed to an indifferent humanity the real face of war, and left Dunant, the reluctant business man, the one alternative of dedicating the rest of his life to the struggle against the horrors of war.

What had become of the love of glory which, at the opening of the campaign and on the day of Solferino, filled this brave soldier, so that despising his own life, he heroically destroyed his fellow-men's and heedlessly shed their blood? Where is the courage of the early fights, when irresistible and infectious enthusiasm, intensified by the smell of powder, the blaring of trumpets, the crash of military marches, the thunder of cannon and the whistle of bullets, made him oblivious to danger, suffering and death? In the many hospitals of Lombardy one could see what price had been paid for all that, what men mean by the proud word 'glory,' and how dear this glory comes.

But what is the use of reviving the memory of so many scenes of agony and grief, or awakening such painful feelings? What good does it do so complacently to describe such frightful details and unroll such pictures of despair before the reader?

This quite natural question must be answered by another.

Is it not possible to found relief societies in all countries in peace-time with a view to having the wounded, without distinction of nationality, cared for in war-time by volunteers who are well prepared for such work? Since in the future men will continue to kill one another without hating themselves, and as the greatest military glory will consist in destroying as many human lives as possible, and as men will always dare assert with Joseph de Maistre that war is something godlike, as men every day, with a perseverance worthy of a better cause, are contriving more frightful means of destruction, and the inventors of these instruments of murder will be incited still more by the armaments competition of the European states, why should not advantage be taken of a period of comparative peace and quiet to solve this question raised by us, and which is of the greatest significance from the standpoint of humanity as well as Christianity? . . .

That is the object of this book.

Societies of this sort, if they were once permanently established, would be completely ready at the moment war was declared. In every country they must include the most respected and distinguished men as members of their leading committees. They would issue an appeal to everyone who, impelled by a feeling of true humanity, might be willing to devote himself at once to this welfare work. It would consist in giving first aid and care on the battlefield as soon as war broke out, in cordial agreement with the military authorities and under their direction, and, in the rear, to care for the wounded in the hospitals until their recovery . . .

For this we need volunteer nurses, trained in advance and familiar with their task, who will be publicly recognized by the commanders of the belligerent armies, and supported by them in every way in their duty . . .

An appeal must be issued, a plea to the people of all countries and all classes, to the great ones of the world and to the humblest labourer, urging each of them in his way, each in his sphere, and according to his ability, to participate in this good work. Such an appeal should be addressed to both men and women, to the powerful princess on her throne, and to the faithful servant, to the poor solitary widow, to everyone who will devote his last ounce of strength to alleviating the sufferings of his fellow-man. It should be addressed to the general, to the field-marshal, to the philanthropist, to the writer who by his writings can serve a cause which touches all mankind, every nation, every country, every family. For no one can know with any assurance that he will always be protected from the vicissitudes of war.

A congress must be held, to lay down an international, stipulated and sacred principle, which, once accepted and ratified, can serve as the basis for the leagues for relief of the wounded in the different countries of Europe.

Humanity and civilization imperiously demand such a work as this. What prince, what ruler would deny his support to these leagues . . . A country cannot look on indifferently when its sons are fighting in its defence . . .

These leagues could also, once they were permanently established, perform great services in case of epidemics, floods, fires and other unforeseen catastrophes. The same main-spring of brotherly love, which will make possible their creation, will also cause them to respond whenever the need arises.

Even if the frightful destructive means which the nations now possess seem likely to shorten the wars of the future, the battles will be all the more murderous. In our century, in which the unforeseen plays so great a role, will not such wars break out suddenly and unexpectedly?

Do not such considerations give more than enough grounds for not permitting ourselves to be surprised by the event?

Seldom has any Utopia been realized with such astonishing rapidity as the dream of Henri Dunant. It is the privilege of harmless idealists to address appeals to humanity and call for the founding of leagues to combat hereditary evil. But for a private citizen to grasp the wheels of the great war-machine, the most tangible embodiment of the bloody reality of state power, seemed unbelievably daring.

The masterly part of the *Recollections*, which the natural ability of its author made uniquely signifi-

cant, is the wisdom with which no demand is made
that the average man cannot see to be perfectly possible of accomplishment. It was an unfanciful Utopia
open to the imagination of everyone. Dunant's
diplomatic skill sought to work with realities. Both
the enemies of war and the militarists had to agree
on these practical proposals. Indeed, all the basic
ideas of the Red Cross are covered in a few points—
the idea of preparation in advance, the neutralization of doctors and nurses, the uniform emblem, the
extension of its activities to include natural catastrophes. Time and again the effort has been made to
contest the fact, but in vain—in the *Recollections of
Solferino* Dunant was the spiritual father of the Red
Cross.

The success of his book exceeded all expectations.
Even while he was writing it, it was clear to Dunant
that the circle of relatives and friends for whom he
had originally intended it was too narrow. He sent
the completed manuscript to General Dufour, and
that same day, the distinguished and influential
Swiss wrote him the letter which was used as the
preface to the first edition.

It is from examples as appalling as yours that people
must learn what the glory of the battlefield costs in suffering and tears. Men are but too inclined to see only the
radiant side of war and to close their eyes to its tragic
consequences . . .

It is well to direct attention to this humanitarian question. These pages, it seems to me, are to a conspicuous
degree fitted to do this. A painstaking and thorough perusal of them can lead to a solution through the collab-

oration of the humanitarians of all countries. (19 October 1862.)

In November 1862 the *Recollections* appeared in an edition of sixteen hundred copies, again printed at Dunant's expense by J.G.Fick in Geneva. In Paris, Turin, St.Petersburg and Leipzig, there was a mad rush for the book. A month later it was necessary to print another thousand copies, and in March 1863 appeared a third edition of three thousand copies.

Dunant knew how to get his book into the right hands—a further evidence of his talent for propaganda. The book found its way to the desks of ministers of war, to the editorial offices of the leading newspapers, and into the boudoirs of queens.

Dunant's appeal became overnight a European sensation. German, English, Italian and Swedish translations were prepared. On 15 February 1863 there appeared in the *Journal des Débats*, which was still the official journal of European society, a long article of Professor Saint-Marc Girardin that impressed even the Queen of Prussia. Suddenly, Dunant had become a subject of conversation in the *salons*.

The Brothers Goncourt, those pedantically intelligent chroniclers of contemporary events in Paris, noted in their *Journal* of 8 June 1863, 'One finishes this book by damning war.' Victor Hugo wrote later in a letter to Dunant, 'I have read your book with the greatest interest. You are arming humanity and are serving freedom . . . I endorse your noble efforts with enthusiasm, and I send you my heartiest good wishes.' At a gathering at the *Institut*, Dunant met Ernest Renan, and the famous philosopher, whose

Life of Jesus the whole world was discussing, greeted him with the words: 'You have created the greatest work of the century. Europe will probably stand only too much in need of it.' Ferdinand de Lesseps, the inspired builder of the Suez Canal, met Dunant at a time when his own vast and still-uncompleted work was undergoing the sharpest crises and hostility. 'Your success,' he said, 'about which I know a great deal, has been an encouragement to me too to persevere.' Early in 1863 Charles Dickens published in his weekly journal '*All the Year Round*,' which was devoutly read by the English-speaking world, a detailed analysis of the book of the 'travelling amateur' and his difficult and courageous attempt to alleviate the misery of war. He called his essay 'The Man in White.'

Only the French military authorities, who for a long time had regarded young Monsieur Dunant with suspicion, were not at all enthusiastic. When Admiral Fourichon gave a copy of the *Recollections of Solferino* to Marshal Randon, Minister of War, Randon handed it back indignantly. 'That book,' he said, 'was written against France!'

When Marshal Vaillant, the *grand maréchal du Palais*, was asked to endorse Dunant's efforts he answered officially that he did not wish to hear anything about the matter, he regretted that the day was gone by when captured cities were burned, captive garrisons killed and the wounded slaughtered to a man. And he liked to repeat this opinion which he thought did him great credit. At least it was a sincere statement of the soldier's credo, and the old

General's brutal frankness stands in refreshing contrast to the hypocrisy of sentimental military politicians. The Surgeon-General Legouest, in a lecture on the sanitary service in the field, said of Dunant's proposals that they were based on exaggerations which would be equally injurious to the services of all the military powers.

VI

Dunant Captures the Salons

IT cannot be said that a popular movement arose to carry out Dunant's demands. War is too unreal in time of peace for it to become a subject of propaganda for the masses. Only the munitions merchants, the diplomats and a handful of intellectuals have a clear understanding of the evil which they are helping along or struggling to prevent. The dual aspect of Dunant's proposals must have been as welcome to those who saw in them a means for raising an army's effectiveness and striking force as to those who loathed the horrors of war. A practical means had been found for the easing of consciences, and it was a varied assortment of priests, soldiers, politicians, social lionesses, and sincere friends of peace who instinctively grasped the implications of the *Recollections of Solferino*.

In the Orléanist circles of the Faubourg, in the *salons* of the Second Empire, at the *Institut* and the *Académie*, there was much discussion of Dunant. There were cardinals and bishops, senators and ministers, the *duc* de Bassano, the *duc* de Fezensac, the

duc de Rohan, the *duc* de Crillon, the *duc* de Broglie
and such influential ladies as the *comtesse* St.Aulaire,
the 'first lady' of the Orléanists, and the *baronne*
de Staël, grand-daughter of the famous Madame de
Staël. Intoxicated by these fairy-like and illustrious
names which meant so much to him, Dunant staggered up the step-ladder of this earthly hierarchy.
Every democracy develops an unfailing weakness for
social exclusiveness: the Genevese patrician of the
1860's became a proper European via the circuitous
by-paths of Paris.

But events in Geneva were more important for
Dunant's cause. The Dunant-fad in Paris would have
passed quickly and noiselessly into oblivion had not
several bold but matter-of-fact citizens come to his
assistance.

Shortly after the appearance of his book—toward
the end of 1862—Monsieur Gustave Moynier appeared in Dunant's ante-room, a man whom he had
known only casually before. 'As soon as I read the
Recollections of Solferino,' declared Monsieur Moynier,
'I hastened to Monsieur Dunant to congratulate him.'

It was a fateful meeting, for in Moynier appeared
an opponent for whose rational brain Dunant never
would be a match. Both men accomplished tremendous things for the cause of the Red Cross, but deep-
seated and instinctive antipathy must have developed
between them from the first moment: they belonged
to opposite poles.

'I surprised Dunant at a moment when, as he
assured me, he had not the ghost of a plan for turning
his inspiration into fact.'

Moynier was a lawyer, an attorney, an official. He was a pious Protestant, the author of a biography of the Apostle Paul, but from the 'enlightened' circle of the *Réveil* he was far removed indeed. 'Good works' were in his eyes a social science. Intuition and imagination were hostile concepts. The *haut monde* was alien to him. Not diplomats or the cobwebs of human frailty governed Moynier's world, but logical laws and the morality of reason. An idea without organization had no existence for him. He thought in resolutions. He was strong in the conviction that catastrophe can be fought only in unsentimental ways. Excess of feeling, the pathetic appeal to the heart of the masses seemed positively harmful to him. He was President of the Geneva Society for Public Welfare, which he had represented at international congresses in Brussels (1856), Frankfurt (1857) and in London (1862). In London he had heard Florence Nightingale's memorable address on 'The Sanitary Service in the Army and its Reform under Lord Herbert.' The problem was familiar to him. In Dunant's book he discovered the possibility of a constructive solution. He, the man of congresses, conferences and resolutions, found it difficult to understand that this powerful plan bore only the simple signature, Henri Dunant. That already bordered on the visionary.

Moynier promised Dunant the support of his society, which met on 7 February 1863. Everything was still very vague. Passages from the *Recollections of Solferino* were reported on. A Monsieur Raum doubted that an organization for helping the wounded could 'arouse the energy or the enthusiasm of the people.' The opinion seemed to be that the coming Philanthropic Congress in Berlin should occupy itself with the question. Finally, it was unanimously resolved to entrust a commission with further study of the matter.

Ten days later this commission met. It consisted of five men: General Dufour, the physicians, Dr. Maunoir and Dr. Appia, Gustave Moynier and Henri Dunant.

The five realized Dunant's great plan. They founded the Red Cross.

Even at the first meetings, differences of viewpoint between Dunant and Moynier were clearly apparent. Moynier insisted on a legalistic course—the Berlin congress in September should rule on the expediency of societies for helping the wounded.

Dunant wanted much more, as the society's minutes for 17 February 1863 testify:

The public must be made to understand that in the work we are contemplating it is not only a question of sending volunteer nurses to the battlefields. Dunant wanted the public to understand that our plan went much farther. It included the improvement of methods of transport for the wounded, the improvement of service in the hospitals, the universal introduction of necessary innovations for the treatment of sick and wounded soldiers, the creation of a real museum for this work (which would also be useful to the civil population). According to his suggestion, the Committee must be permanent and it must be constantly inspired by a genuine spirit of international *caritas*. It must facilitate the sending of supplies of all kinds, set aside customs duties, prevent the wasting of goods, etc. It would be desirable if sovereigns everywhere became its patrons. Finally, Monsieur Dunant especially insisted on the demand he had raised in his book—that the civilized powers must recognize an international and sacred principle to be determined and guaranteed by a kind of covenant among the governments. It would serve, furthermore, as a protection for every official or unofficial person who devoted himself to the war service.

Moynier hated hyperbole. This program would exceed the powers of any national cabinet. He could not help smiling at his youthful compatriot to whom everything was so simple. But the commission, with no more backing than the one hundred and eighty members of the Geneva Society for Public Welfare thought otherwise. The venerable General Dufour, who can probably be called the most humane warmaker in history, was of the opinion that the memorial must 'above all stress the necessity of obtaining the unanimous agreement of the princes and nations of Europe.' Appia, the military doctor in mufti, wished 'to have all documents procured that may be of use to us, and to establish relations at once with the highest military authorities of the various countries.' Dr. Maunoir, the least-defined of all, whose personality was largely a reflection of the esteem in which he was held by his colleagues, proposed 'that an agitation, if one may so express it, be begun, which will further the recognition of our point of view throughout the world, among high and low, with the sovereigns of Europe and the masses of the population.'

Suddenly, all of them seemed gripped by the mission which had fallen to them. Moynier himself proposed that 'the commission constitute itself a "Permanent International Committee,"' and this self-nomination was unanimously resolved. Still none of the participants quite foresaw the colossal proportions that their scarcely-begun work was to assume. General Dufour stated at the second meeting: 'We must lay out the bounds, then others will come and make a path.' But the original resolution, which to a sceptical observer might easily have seemed like delusions of grandeur, laid down the three important fundamentals—the internationalism of the movement, its centralization in Geneva, and its freedom from partisan or religious tie-ups.

That five private persons, without office or authority, could initiate an undertaking of world-historical importance, that they could carry it through successfully, without immediately becoming entangled in a web of political tendency or governmental encroachment will forever remain one of the strongest evidences of the nineteenth century's greatness. The League of Nations of the year 1918, that huge, muddled, costly authority, has never done anything to compare with this humane civilian act.

VII

The Civil War in America

DR. MAUNOIR's proposal about agitation must have
struck Dunant like a bolt of lightning. From that
moment he entered upon the almost ecstatic state of
restless activity that drove him from one end of
Europe to the other. The essentially timid, and in
public almost helpless man lost all sense of restraint.
There was no door that would not open to him, no
threshold he did not cross and no great one of this
earth who could escape the vehemence of his em-
bassy. He was, there is no question about it, a man
with an obsession. The little man's face was framed
by its black beard leaving the chin clean, as the
style was. His mild but piercing eyes never left their
object. In his black frock-coat with the crossed silk
cravat, the stiff shirt-front, the long and respectable
watch-chain across his vest and the ribbon of his order in his button-hole, he looked like a provincial
French schoolmaster. It was not a face on which
thought or suffering or fate had etched their lines. It
was an open and childlike face, with the conciliatory
expressions of a clever merchant. It was a genial face.

And only very slowly would a penetrating observer suspect that it was also a lonely face. There was no joy in Dunant. He who was forever on the hunt for people, who tracked connections with a true collector's passion, and knew how to manage them, was without any real confidant. He did not know the cordial closeness and intimacy of friendship. He was not loved: he did not love, or so it seems. In his reminiscences, written with the loquacity of old age, scores of names are mentioned, but there is no attachment known which had deeply moved him, no irrevocable separation, no unforgettable happiness.

He possessed all the elements for happiness, but he never succeeded in combining them. After Solferino, he could no longer distinguish the dividing lines between his own life and that of the world. He wanted happiness for the world, no longer for himself. He felt the world's need, not his own suffering. So he became a visionary and a reformer, whom some sense of insufficiency drove to more and more intense dreams. His vanity was of no common kind. It was an almost desperate attempt to save and prove himself as a person, since his own life was more and more overwhelmed, more and more extinguished by his concern for the world without.

In those days his optimism swept everything before it, but it swept him away too, and as he wished the future to be, so he construed the present. Speculative and imaginative, dependent on no one, hardly even on himself, he shaped and coloured facts to his desire and experienced the miracle that they conformed to his will. Money played a tremendously important and a tremendously unimportant role in his mind. In Geneva, piety and profits were inseparable, wealth being the reward of God. But like all bankers, he lost his standards for the stuff. The more his Cause prospered, the worse went his business affairs. Profits meant converts for the Cause. He poured money into his plan, profligately and senselessly. The enterprise flourished mightily under his hands. He no longer knew that earthly and heavenly interest have different market ratings and that charity must not disturb the well-balanced ledger.

On the day after the first meeting, Dunant made one of his frequent trips to Paris. He took with him the article on his book which had appeared in the *Journal des Débats*. At last he hoped to capture Paris, and above all to scale the invisible walls that since Solferino had separated him from Napoleon. It was half a failure. He did not see the Emperor. But he found new influential friends and enthusiastic followers, especially the Swiss Colonel, Huber-Saladin, who was to become one of the most zealous proselytizers, and the *comte* Adolphe de Circourt. He began an extended correspondence with Dunant and on 23 November 1863 wrote him this noble and prophetic letter:

The present situation in both hemispheres justifies your efforts only too well. After a long period, during which the nations, at least outwardly, seemed to have attained a common degree of civilization, a will to submit the settlement of their differences to peaceful negotiations, and to employ weapons only for the subjugation of less advanced races, after this period, which deceived so many distinguished minds with the phantom of eternal peace, we once more face a general appeal to arms, which may bring about those decisions that neither law nor diplomacy are able to effect. It is all too probable that a series of gigantic wars will break out, and in all parts of both continents, take over the solution of these problems with that might which according to the dictates of human nature, is ever the faithful companion of right. So you have come at just the right moment. There is no country which does not owe you attention and endorsement. I trust that your name may forever belong among those few who have deserved well of mankind.

Napoleon was not to speak. He sat in his newly-erected Palace at Vichy, designing tropical uniforms for his soldiers, who were dying of malaria and yellow fever. He had begun the most frivolous war of his career—the campaign in Mexico. It was an adventurous speculation with a tragic and gruesome end. Once more the *juste milieu* of the Second Empire was to show its face, but it was a golden mean between visionary delusion and frivolous conspiracy. This time it bore more resemblance to an act of desperation on the part of the aging man who would more and more seek political ways out. Since the days of his emigration in the Hotel Washington on Broadway, American problems had engrossed him. While he was sitting in the Fortress of Ham, he sketched plans for a *Canale Napoléon*, a prophetic anticipation of Panama. A new Romanization of the continent, where the Anglo-Saxons were more and more crowding out the French influence, was swimming darkly before him. At the same time, he sensed an opportunity to conciliate his old opponent, Francis Joseph, by the creation of a new Habsburg monarchy. Fresh laurels seemed easy to win and would help to cover up his inner political conflicts. So he was only too willing to let a band of conspirators, agents and bankers, who were trembling for the value of Mexican government bonds, lead him into this tropical excess.

Corruption seems to manage well under any political system. There was the dark figure of the banker Jecker, who was earning his pennies by the new half-light of monarchical democracy. The powerful minister De Morny was interested to the extent of a third of the profits which usurer Jecker expected from a 'liberated' Mexico. Spain and England came along, for on their 'changes too Mexican paper was a big item. And so, in the winter of 1861, the unclean expedition set forth on that road at the end of which stood a firing-squad for misled and betrayed Maximilian and a madhouse for poor expelled Carlotta.

At the roadstead of Vera Cruz the hospitals were filling. Greedy Jecker wanted to see his money. The interest of the allies, who quickly perceived that the venture would be difficult and unprofitable, soon cooled. They sailed away and left the French alone. The Mexican President, Benito Juarez, prepared for a long guerilla war. The French had to keep sending new troops. After General Prim came General Lorencez. He was very severely beaten at Puebla, and General Forey replaced him.

Puebla sustained a nine weeks' siege. The hundred miles from the coast to the capital were a long, excruciating road. By the beginning of June, Bazaine's advance guard reached Mexico City. Forey was able to report to Paris, 'the nation is hungering for order, justice and real freedom.' A National Assembly was summoned and its two hundred members offered the imperial crown to the Archduke Maximilian who meanwhile was tending his flowers at Castle Miramare near Trieste. The first act of the drama had ended.

It could not have been played at all if the United States had raised an energetic objection. But America declined to interfere. The great and bloody reckoning of the Civil War had begun, which was to decide the destiny of the entire continent. The fate of John Brown, who was hanged in Charleston in 1859 after a futile rebellion at Harpers Ferry, was the beacon by whose glare the rebellion began.

In 1860 the southern states were in a roughly fascist state of mind. The question of slavery, which threatened their economic security, was the outward cause of a confused racial delusion that had deeper backgrounds. With the annexation of New Mexico and California in 1848, the territorial development of the United States was virtually completed. The settlement of the west coast proceeded rapidly. The main axis of the country ran from north to west. The South, losing its place in the intellectual and economic life of the country, felt itself more and more isolated. All the symptoms of an isolationist psychosis were developing unchecked.

In the North the factories were increasing and the railroads bit deep into the land. After 1848 an uninterrupted stream of emigrants fled from Europe's

oppressors. Even before they landed they were enthusiastic adherents of the freest constitution in the
world, which meant more to them than their shattered lives and which they took more seriously than
the native Americans.

In contrast with these revolutionary invaders, the
cotton planters of the South more and more considered themselves an aristocracy. 'The Cavaliers,
Jacobites and Huguenots who settled the South, by
their very natures, hate, condemn and despise the
Puritans who settled the North. The former are
noble races. The others are slave races, the offspring
of Saxon thralls.' The blood of the Norman conqueror
flowed in the veins of the South. 'The rest of Christendom is in league against us.' Is this not the Na-
tional-Socialist tone of 1938 which also springs in the
last analysis from the fear of isolation?

The presidential election of 1860 was more violent
than ever before. And when the candidate of the six-
year-old Republican Party, which demanded the
abolition of slavery, was elected, the catastrophe
could no longer be deferred. Abraham Lincoln meant
ruin. A Richmond newspaper wrote: 'With Lincoln
comes something worse than slang, rowdyism, brutal-
ity and moral filth; something worse than the rag-tag
of the whiskey saloons of the west and Yankee factories. . . . Along with this comes the insolent and
unbridled leader of the Abolitionists.'

South Carolina started the secession in 1860. Mississippi, Florida, Alabama, Georgia, Louisiana, Texas
followed Virginia, North Carolina, Arkansas and
Tennessee. They united as the Confederate States of

America, elected Jefferson Davis as their President, hoisted the palmetto flag in place of the star-spangled banner and had their own White House at Montgomery, Alabama. Meanwhile, Major Anderson was holding Fort Sumter with eighty-four soldiers loyal to the government, and he refused to surrender. On 19 April 1861, after a bombardment, Fort Sumter fell. The war had begun.

For four long years the armies of the Confederacy and the Union fought with varying success and growing bitterness. Lee, the leader of the South, and Grant, Commander for the North, were strategists of genius. The battle at Gettysburg on 3 July 1863 was to prove decisive. On 1 January 1863 Lincoln proclaimed the slaves free, and two years later emancipation was embodied in a constitutional amendment. Lincoln was re-elected in 1864. On 9 April 1865 the war ended with Lee's surrender to Grant at Appomattox Court House. Five days later Lincoln was assassinated in Washington.

The Civil War in the United States freed a whole continent, perhaps forever, from the plague of national hatred and political rivalry. In addition it produced two things which are of lasting importance in American history: The United States Sanitary Commission and Clara Barton.

It is astonishing how infallibly, again and again in different parts of the world, things for which the right moment has come are realized simultaneously and independently.

In the Civil War which broke like a terrible storm over a country that seemed made for eternal peace, the Sanitary Commission accomplished unheard-of triumphs. Even under the difficult circumstances resulting from the duration of the struggle, the climate, the enormous masses of men, the deficient military apparatus, it made the first attempt uniformly to organize the care of the sick and wounded on hygienic principles. Much that seemed Utopian in Dunant's proposals for Europe was translated into fact on the battlefields of the South without his knowledge. Nearly two thousand women served as nurses in the Civil War. They contributed substantially toward the victory by their Samaritanism, which had until then been a privilege of the Catholic Church, but which was foreign to Protestantism. In Germany, since 1836, there had been the Deaconesses; in England, the Protestant Sisters of Charity had been organized since 1840; in 1848, the Sisters of Mercy; in 1851, the Sisterhood of All Saints; in 1854, St. Margaret's. In 1860 Florence Nightingale founded the school for sisters at St. Thomas Hospital in London. But all these organizations still bore essentially the character of religious orders.

Florence Nightingale was the first civil Samaritan on a field of battle. Dunant followed at Solferino. And Clara Barton, who at the outbreak of the Civil War was a clerk in the Patent Office at Washington, was the third in this spiritual league which brought about the humanitarian movement of the century.

She was born on Christmas Day 1821 on a farm near Oxford, Massachusetts, a genuine product of puritan tradition. Her forbears were colonists and soldiers. She knew that the effectiveness of all help depends on order and obedience. She began to visit the hospitals in Washington. But when, after the first Battle of Bull Run, the transport of the wounded began to break down, and men with masses of gangrene on their limbs were brought in, for whom all help was too late, she decided that her place was at the front. She made a trip through New England, collecting money and donations. In Worcester and Bordentown, where she had once founded a school for street children, she found groups of women who gave her a feeble support against the hesitancy of the authorities. From then on she was found wherever need and danger were the greatest. She compelled aid and support for herself. She submitted to every legitimate order, but she rebelled against negligence and thoughtlessness. Countless soldiers owed their lives to her swift intercession. 'Follow the cannon' was her motto.

At Fredericksburg she crossed the Rappahannock with the troops in the face of a withering fire. Balls tore her clothes to ribbons. She rode to Washington to lodge complaints against the officers who refused to turn over the elegant mansions of Fredericksburg to the wounded. She got what she wanted. She became a legendary figure in the army. 'Here comes the stormy petrel,' the soldiers would call to her as through wind and rain she made her way to the front ranks. At Antietam a man was killed in her arms. The bullet passed through her sleeve.

In Washington her name was mentioned with an increasing respect. Shortly before his death, Lincoln proposed that she be officially entrusted with the scarch for all wounded and prisoners. Immediately after the end of the War, she went to the Confederate prison at Andersonville, identified graves, traced the missing and organized an information service. Then she travelled for her shattered health to Europe, never suspecting that there in the meantime a work had been begun that would henceforth fill her whole life, and to which many years later, through the founding of the American Red Cross, she was to render immortal services.

VIII

Prussia Before the Rise

THOUSANDS of copies of the *Recollections of Solferino* were passing from hand to hand. For particularly high-placed personages they were splendidly bound (in Berlin, Privy Councillor Dubois was commissioned by Dunant to deliver such volumes to the King of Prussia). At the Geneva office countless letters of endorsement were being received—a very cool one from Florence Nightingale, a very warm and cordial one from the Grand-Duke of Baden, from Prince Alexander of Hesse, from the King of Holland. But Dunant was off on one of those innumerable excursions on which with unquenchable optimism he pursued the phantom of the mills of Mons-Gemila. First, however, he had handed in the memorandum which was to be given as a report at the Philanthropic Congress in Berlin in the autumn.

The commission had much trouble with it. At this point, involving the formulation of a treaty conformable to international law, Dunant's diction broke down. When after innumerable conferences a more suitable outline was adopted, clearly showing by now the expert collaboration of Moynier, it was suddenly

announced that the congress on which such high
hopes had been founded was not to take place. All the
political plans of the Five were shattered.

The bearer of this news was the Dutch military
physician, Dr.S.H.C.Basting, who from the day that
Mme Micheli of Geneva had sent him a copy of the
Recollections had been an ardent admirer and friend of
Dunant. Basting was that rare creature, a sensitive
and emotional practitioner. He went to work at once
to translate Dunant's book into Dutch. 'I really believe that in this cause you are carrying out God's
work,' he wrote on 3 March 1863.

A long correspondence ensued, in the course of
which Dunant appeared more and more to the enthusiastic Dutchman as a kind of Messiah. His
friendship suffered no lapse when Dunant offered him
shares of Mons-Gemila. But Basting had a shrewd
wife. On 18 February 1864 she wrote Dunant, 'I cannot help observing that you are not at all insensitive
to worldly honours.' Dunant was not alone in the
weakness for orders and honours to which she alluded.
Almost all the members of the Geneva committee had
fallen ill of this democratic sickness whose propagandist value is not to be disputed. The Genevese historian,
Alexis François, writes: 'In Geneva, and particularly
in the Red Cross, there has always been a great weakness for the red ribbon and all kinds of decorations.
Who does not recall the appearance of the eighty-
year-old Gustave Moynier at the Geneva Congress of
1906? With his white beard against a bosom sown with
medals, he resembled an oriental demi-god over whom
had been shaken the treasures of Golconda.'

Basting, who reported that in Berlin 'absolutely nothing was known of any such congress' no doubt proposed to Dunant to visit the International Statistical Congress instead. It was being held in Berlin from the sixth to the twelfth of September.

At the meeting of the committee on 25 August 1863, Dunant informed them that he wished to go to Berlin 'to interest this congress in our work and at the same time do everything possible to arouse the sympathy of the German public'—in which connection he intended to visit Vienna, Dresden, Munich, etc. At the same meeting a resolution was adopted on Moynier's motion, calling for an international conference in Geneva. Moynier and Dunant were to send out the invitations.

Moynier, the friend of congresses, thought that his moment had come. Dunant could do good preliminary work in Berlin. The step into the world was planned. The committee whose 'sessions had the character of family conversations rather than deliberative conferences' was about to go before the forum of Europe.

A few days later, Dunant and Dr. Basting met in Berlin at the Hotel Toepfer, on the Karlsplatz. The hotel still boasted the old traditional Prussian mixture of frugality and comfort. Between the state infirmary, the *Charité*, and Unter den Linden with its ministries, it stood at the focal-point of a new and to him still very unknown world.

Dunant brought with him the invitation dated 1 September:

The Public Welfare Society of Geneva, in accord with a desire expressed by Monsieur Dunant in his book *Re-*

collections of Solferino, has set up a Committee which is authorized to strive for the realization of this desire.

This Committee believes that the ideas of Monsieur Dunant can best be transferred from the field of theory to the field of practice by a convention of those men in the various countries to whose hearts this humanitarian work is close. Only in that way can we explore the extent to which this plan is practicable and the way in which it can be carried out.

After the Geneva Committee had assured itself that its proposal would find a response in the most diverse circles, it decided to call an international conference for the coming twenty-sixth of October, and hopes that Monsieur . . . will do it the honour to attend.

It is especially desirable that the governments shall permit themselves to be represented here, as their co-operation is indispensible for the success of the work.

The Committee has arranged in the form of a convention the proposals which it would like to submit to the conference. You will find the text inclosed.

We urgently request Monsieur . . . that you inform us promptly whether we may count upon your co-operation. In case you are unable to come to Geneva, we shall be greatly indebted to you if you will write us your opinions and comment on the proposed plan.

With the assurance of our distinguished respect, the members of the Geneva Committee for Aid to Wounded Soldiers. Geneva, 1 September 1863,

> General Dufour, Chairman
> Gustave Moynier, Chairman of the Geneva
> Dr. Maunoir   [Public Welfare Society
> Dr. Appia
> Henri Dunant, Secretary

In 1863 Berlin had just entered the period of Bismarckian dictatorship which was to last twenty-eight years and so decisively change the face of Europe. After a series of failures, a legacy from the wavering reign of Frederick William IV, the Regent, William I, came to the throne as King of Prussia. The sixty-three-year-old Hohenzollern, a loyal soldier, permeated with ideas of the God-given rights and duties of a monarch, had been preparing long enough for his office to know what was needful. In Bismarck he found a servant whose Prussian national consciousness and boundless devotion to the dynasty would cold-bloodedly and ruthlessly carry out the most daring political conception of the century. Bismarck possessed that Prussian devotion which justified any treachery as long as it served his cause. His policies were not encumbered with emotion as were those of his opponent, Napoleon III. For him, Europe was a chess-board. He invented combinations and played them as he needed. Friends of to-day were enemies of to-morrow. The greatness of Prussia was the one idea motivating his whole game. And he always knew the right moment at which to exchange brutal force for cautious psychology. As Ambassador to St. Petersburg and Paris he had learned to see through the extremes of European civilization between which lay Prussia.

William I needed to increase his army by more than fifty per cent. The hair rose on the scalps of the worthy deputies of the Progressive Party which, since the elections of 1861, was the strongest party in the *Landtag*, when they saw the 9,500,000 *Taler* item for

army reforms. The budget was refused. They had yet
to learn on what a flight the Prussian eagle had
started. On 6 March 1862 the *Landtag* was dissolved.
New elections in May were a still greater victory for
the Progressives. In September all the army appro-
priations were stricken off. A dangerous situation had
arisen: the King thought of abdicating. Then, on the
advice of his War Minister, Roon, he summoned Bismarck to head the government.

Bismarck's first official business was the *coup d'état*
of 1862. He denied the right of parliament to meddle
with questions of national defence, which were a
prerogative of the throne, and with the help of the
junkers of the Upper Chamber he gained everything
the burghers had refused him. Meanwhile Roon and
Moltke, Chief of General Staff, built up the best and
strongest army on the Continent.

Once the basis for a future policy of force had been
laid in this way, the blows of Bismarckian diplomacy
fell like the sabre strokes of an accomplished duellist.
Soon Europe saw the defeat of Denmark and the in-
timidation of England, the friendship with Russia,
the exclusion of Austria from the Reich, the ever
greater stabilization of Prussia as the central economic and military power in Germany, the isolation
of France and her terrible defeat.

Franco-Russian relations since the end of the
Crimean War had been more than cordial as was
evidenced on several occasions. But here too Napoleon
began to experience grave difficulties because of his
European ideology. In 1863, after long smouldering
underground, serious uprisings occurred in Poland

and Lithuania. The struggle of the Poles for freedom aroused sympathy throughout Europe. The Poles counted especially on help from Napoleon. Until 1860 the French Foreign Minister had been Count Walewski, the illegitimate son of Napoleon I and a Polish countess. The rights of national minorities had been one of the most brilliant principles of Napoleonic policy.

But as usual, demonstrations of sympathy without cannon to back them up are an unfavourable omen for the oppressed. Prussia, which was afraid of its own Polish subjects, sided with Russia from the beginning. A joint request of France, Austria and England that Russia give the Poles their freedom was wrecked on the close alliance between Bismarck and Alexander II. Napoleon could no longer afford an armed intervention. Prussia was too strong. In April 1864 the revolt of the Poles was broken by the Russians with the bloodiest terrorism. Bismarck had his first important triumph.

The atmosphere Dunant found in Berlin was quite similar to that in which important foreign visitors are received there to-day. The new Prussian consciousness was felt in everything. There was a heightened activity with technical achievements. Friendships abroad were promoted because hostile relationships abroad were impending. There was the mixture of cordiality and inaccessibility which is usually so impressive.

Statistics, that new invention of the nineteenth century, in which man and his destiny functioned as ciphers, that science of abstract order which with the help of the laws of probability illumined the mysteries of measure, found fertile soil in Prussia. The Statistical Congress received the full support of the authorities.

Opportunely, the fourth section, which was concerned with comparative health and mortality statistics, and which consisted overwhelmingly of civilian and military doctors, had Dr. Basting as its reporter.

Basting and Dunant sat in the Hotel Toepfer and zealously conferred. Dunant had prepared a talk which Basting translated into German and would deliver. Basting, as a military doctor, was especially fascinated with the idea of neutralizing the physicians, which Dunant had proposed in the *Recollections* but which had not been taken up by the committee who thought it went too far.

On the morning of 8 September they drove to the House of Peers together in an open carriage. As they crossed the Spree, a sudden gust of wind blew the precious papers, which the passengers had placed carefully beside them on the seat, about the bridge. They jumped out of the moving carriage and with difficulty recovered their manuscript before it disappeared beneath the waves.

Four days later, on 12 September Basting addressed the general meeting and exhorted the members 'in the name of the Geneva Committee and on the part of his honoured friend Dunant' to attend the Congress. The chairman replied that in the nature of the matter, there would be no vote on this proposal. 'The Congress must content itself with taking cognizance of Herr Dunant's efforts and ex-

pressing its appreciation of them, while hoping that
the proposed conference in Geneva may contribute
to lessening those sacrifices of life and health which
battles entail.'

What did Dunant's imaginative brain make of this
stiff and almost sceptical endorsement? 'With tears
of joy,' as Basting would remember a decade later,
he left the House of Peers. ' Without losing a moment
or waiting for the end of the session, I hurried to the
court printing-shop to have a circular printed whose
contents had been discussed between Basting and me
with the approval of our Berlin friends.'

Dunant's propaganda magnified the grudging endorsement of the Congress to a stupendous success.
Once more he was right in the end, as against Moynier, in believing that speeches at congresses mean
nothing and are so much table-talk. He scarcely attended the sessions and did not even use the letters
of introduction from Geneva. But he refused no dinners official or unofficial. He met the court preachers
who had access to the conscience of the princes and
princesses. With the Russian Baron von Kruedener,
the grandson of the mystical woman friend of Alexander I, he held conversations on the prophets in
the Bible, a field in which he was much at home. On
14 September there was a great gala dinner at Potsdam where Dunant was presented to the Crown
Prince Frederick and his wife, who had been moved
by his book. The next day there was a dinner at the
home of the Minister of the Interior, Count Eulenburg. Dunant sat between a Spanish senator and a
Bavarian state councillor. Opposite him sat a Saxon

and a Russian dignitary. A Swede and a Norwegian could take part in the conversation.

These were Dunant's great moments. Between the fish and the roast he knew how to move the hearts of his table-companions and to make them enthusiastic for his Cause. All promised him to use their influence with their governments for the Geneva Conference, and they all kept their promises. He knew how to give the whole undertaking an official gloss and international value which lured everyone into joining, made each one fear he might be too late, and even brought some life into the tight faces of the Prussian officers.

The taciturn Roon asked Dr. Basting, 'What does this Herr Dunant really want? What has war to do with this kind of philanthropy?' 'The gentleman is working,' said Dr. Basting, 'to neutralize the wounded on the battlefield.' 'That is another matter, I shall tell the King about it. It will interest him.'

Dunant was received by Roon. The court and military physicians Boeger and Loeffler were present. 'His Majesty took so lively an interest in the whole matter, especially in the question of neutralization, that he sent one of his adjutants to The Hotel Toepfer in order to be informed . . . The adjutant repeated to me again and again in French, "The Minister is body and soul for your ideas. The Minister is downright enthusiastic for your idea!"'

Order amidst the chaos of the battlefield, that at any rate was something over which a Prussian soldier's heart could grow enthusiastic. Even before his departure from Berlin, Dunant had gathered a list

of names for the founding of a Prussian Central
Committee which exceeded his wildest expectations.
There was Prince Henry XIII of Reuss, who in 1865
relinquished his patronage to King William and
Queen Augusta. There was Minister Eulenburg.
There was the celebrated surgeon Von Langenbeck
and the Jewish commercial adviser Mendelssohn,
who represented the banking aristocracy.

But Dunant, intoxicated by his success and supported by Basting, followed one of his sudden im-
pulses and had his famous circular printed on his own
authority, facing the unsuspecting Geneva committee
with an accomplished fact, and expanding the tasks
of the conference far beyond the cautiously planned
objective. It contained a demand for the fullest
neutralization.

International Conference in Geneva, 26 October 1863,
International and Permanent Relief Societies for
Wounded Military Personnel in time of war.

. . . as a result of the favourable reception of its plan at
the Statistical Congress, the Geneva Committee makes
these further proposals beyond those already outlined in
the convention:

1. Every European government shall give the National Committee, which shall be organized in every
European capital and consist of the most respected persons of the country, its very special protection and
patronage.

2. These same governments shall declare that in future the military sanitary personnel, and the persons
connected with it, including the recognized volunteer
helpers, will be considered as neutral persons by the
belligerent powers.

3. In time of war the governments shall undertake to facilitate the dispatch of materials for the personnel, and the donations which the Societies will send to the war-stricken countries.

Finally, the Geneva Committee desires that the International Conference shall study the means whereby this conspicuously humanitarian and benevolent work may be realized with due regard for the laws, customs and usages of the various European nations. Similarly, the Conference would like to investigate how, in a war between the great powers, the most effective aid can be rendered to the personnel of either army, within the theatre of war, while avoiding any suspicion of espionage or intention other than the purely charitable and Christian object of their work.

The Geneva Conference cherishes the hope that the European governments will give their delegates to this Conference the necessary instructions relative to these various points.

Secretary of the Geneva Conference,
J. HENRI DUNANT
Berlin, 15 September 1863

At one stroke an entirely new content had been created for the conference beside which the statutes for relief societies for the wounded, that Moynier had worked out, must play a completely secondary role. Dunant's proposal was a diplomatic matter of a kind and spirit such as until then the world had never seen. A new joint international convention was to be agreed to which interfered with the elementary rights of nations, and which, if it should ever be realized, required for its fulfilment a general understanding of, and subordination to, a humanitarian principle such as could scarcely be hoped for in the current state of political affairs.

Dunant was perfectly clear about the incorrectness of taking so important a step without the consent of his colleagues. But without this bold act of insubordination the Red Cross would probably never have achieved its world importance. To have transformed an organizational affair into a Covenant of world-historical importance—that is Dunant's service.

The commission could not believe their eyes when they first saw the Berlin circular whose countless copies were meanwhile fluttering into the dispatch-boxes of diplomats of all countries. They considered that their painstaking and prudent plan was ruined.

When Dunant, on his return from Berlin, met his friends with the question, 'Well, what did you think of my Berlin circular on neutralization?' Moynier replied bluntly, 'We thought that you were asking the impossible.' General Dufour enveloped himself in silence. But as matters had gone so far and it seemed impossible to disavow Dunant, the official ambassador from Geneva, it was decided to let things take their course for better or for worse.

There is no doubt that the first significant support for Dunant came from Berlin. Not that they were pacifist—quite the contrary. Rather, they were 'war-loving' in the truest sense of the word. The representatives of armed force wanted a 'civilized' war which, as a political instrument, could be invoked or set aside as needed. The 'legitimate' war-machine feared nothing more than the unbridled anarchy which could wrest the 'command of war' from their hands.

In a certain sense the nineteenth century was able to conduct its wars in this spirit of moderation. They were in fact 'humane' and 'expert' wars if one compares them with the barbarism of the World War and all the horrors that resulted and will still result from it. It remained for the twentieth century to dig up a primordial form—the war of total annihilation, the war without declaration or legal basis, without sparing the civilian population or restricting the instruments of destruction, a pitiless bestial raging of the apocalyptic horsemen, pestilence and famine intensified through all the excesses of a devilish technique of destruction. This is the war that in its preparation, its leadership and its actual operations execrates humanity as something hostile and treasonable, and makes mankind through many generations of peace infected and unfit to live.

Dunant did well to take advantage of the readiness of the Prussians to co-operate. The best army and the best organizers must carry the other nations with them. For he felt clearly that henceforth political prestige or political resentment would create support for his plan: in this connection he thought especially of France. He could never have founded the Red Cross with pacifists.

But his mission was not ended with his visit to Berlin. On 11 October he arrived at the Hotel de France in Dresden for an audience with King John of Saxony, which was to take place at half past nine the next morning.

When I got out at the Royal Palace, a flunkey who was waiting at one of the entrances conducted me to the good old court chamberlain. He in turn took me by the hand and led me through a part of the palace until we came to a small, very simple and unadorned room in which, if I remember rightly, there was not even an easy-chair. Before Herr von Gersdorff withdrew, he said to me, 'The King will enter by the opposite door, you will bow three times to him in salutation and wait till he addresses you.' I did not need these well-meant instructions in order to observe the etiquette, and followed the ceremonial point for point when the King appeared. With the greatest kindliness the King inquired as to my wishes. I stated them and concluded, among several other urgent points, 'I shall be endlessly grateful to Your Majesty if you will deign to give your protection to this work in your states, and will send a representative to the Conference which is to be held on the twenty-sixth of this month in Geneva.'

The King smiled as he observed my enthusiasm, but in a very kindly way in order not to intimidate me.

'I shall gladly give my protection to so distinguished an undertaking,' he said, 'but the sending of a delegate is something about which I must consult my Chamber.'

I replied at once with the same respectful zeal, 'Majesty, in a work so exclusively humanitarian, Your Majesty may be sure that your Chamber will concede everything that it pleases the King to decide.'

The King smiled again and concluded the audience. 'I shall do everything within my power, for surely any nation which does not participate in this humanitarian work will be outlawed by European opinion.'

It is touching to observe with what unembarrassed enjoyment Dunant repeats the courtly involutions of his conversation with the King. What a man of the world he could become in the palace of a lesser German princeling! No bow was omitted, and the heart of the old king, to whom an aged court chamberlain led him by the hand was—as in a fairy-tale—generous and touched. There was still a politics of the heart in those days! How would it look to-day?

'I spent the rest of the day and the whole night writing letters to people in most of the European capitals to whom I mentioned the cordial sympathy that the revered Prince evinced for the work. These letters had a telling effect for the Nestor among the kings stood high in the estimation of all European governments and courts.'

In particular, Dunant wrote to the Commissary-General, Baron Darricau, in Paris, who had long since expressed his enthusiasm for Dunant's 'apostolic work,' as he called it. Dunant informed him of the dazzling reception in Berlin and did not forget the King of Saxony's remark about 'European opinion.'

The letter to Darricau arrived just as he was leaving the Ministry of War to go to the Tuileries whither Napoleon had summoned him. The letter, which he read in his carriage on the way, made a deep impression on him. He submitted it to Napoleon at once. The Emperor read it and handed it back, saying, 'You shall go to Geneva, my dear Darricau, to represent France at the Conference.' In this unexpected way, and in spite of the hostility of the then Minister of War and the greater part of his entourage, France was won to the Cause.

Dunant had chosen the right moment to play off the antagonism between Paris and Berlin. Was he not like one of our contemporary flying diplomats, who with the nuances of one hostile speech fresh in his ears, is already sitting with his next adversary, striving to explore states of mind and take advantage of secret combinations?

He did not allow himself a moment to cast a glance at the ancient city on the Elbe and its green-roofed churches. He was an unromantic bustling traveller, with no time left for transient reflection. It was only three weeks before the congress opened.

His next stop was Vienna. The Emperor Francis Joseph was hunting at Ischl at the moment. Still, with the help of the Swiss Ambassador Steiger, Dunant managed to convey his wishes to an archduke. Together with the Swiss Ambassador, he went to the Hofburg to explain in his practiced way to the Archduke Rainer his plan for the conference in Geneva. Vienna at this time was unquestionably the most conventional and conservative spot in Europe. Here they were still living in the past with the Congress of 1815, and were convinced with difficulty and not without astonishment, by the actualities of world history, that the times had changed. The decisive struggle which was hanging over the head of the honourable Habsburg monarchy was simply not believed in the offices of the bureaucracy.

'His Imperial Highness deigned to pronounce three times in emphatic, cordial and kindly tones the approving words, "What a splendid idea!"'

That was certainly not very much, and anyone familiar with the conventional forms of court diplomacy might almost have taken it for a kindly way of

rejecting a fantastic notion. But Dunant was in that
happy state which fanatics achieve and was deaf to
the intonations of irony. He stopped with the literal
words, which in this case too assumed vast proportions, and filled his heart with enthusiasm and de-
light. For himself and his circle he created the illusion
of a Europe led by wise and benevolent princes and
humanitarian ministers, and the simple and trusting
power of his heart knew how to transform this illusion
into a reality. In his hands the non-committal state-
ments of the diplomats, who could always disclaim his
plans with incredible bluntness, became irrevocable
commitments; it was impossible to repudiate them
unless one wanted the reputation of a cynic.

The headlong journey continued:

When I reached Munich, King Maximilian had just
gone to Italy. But Councillor von Herman had informed
the King of the Geneva plans, and he had declared that
he was in fundamental agreement with them. He had left
instructions for me to visit his Minister of War, General Frank, for further discussion. We had great difficulty
in understanding one another. I must confess that I was
painfully impressed by His Excellency's hostility.

'What, sir?' he said rather roughly, 'at your request
you expect me to send a Bavarian representative to
Geneva to a gathering called together by you and some
other unknown individuals!'

'But Herr Minister,' I replied, 'I am not asking for
anything. I have simply felt it my duty to inform you of
something which it is certainly worth your while to hear.
What we are doing in Geneva is being done in the interest
of humanitarianism, that is to say, in the interests of

Bavaria as well as the other countries of Europe. What is involved is an international question of neighbourly love which has already found powerful supporters and exalted patrons.'

But even the coarse Bavarian warrior was vanquished at last by Dunant's persistence so far as to send a delegate.

Meanwhile the letters from Dresden had worked their wonders. The Spanish Count Ripalda, whom Dunant had met in Berlin, founded a committee in Madrid in the name of Queen Isabella who had already read Dunant's book. And the English Secretary for War, Lord Grey, appointed the Inspector-General of Hospitals, Dr.Rutherford, to represent Great Britain at Geneva.

The crusade against history's doormen, who deny the uninitiate access to the diplomatic mystery-plays, had succeeded. For the first time, a private citizen without office or position had effected a political action which brought the nations of Europe beyond self-interest and national lunacy to a common work in the service of humanity.

IX

The Conference of 1863

New work was awaiting Dunant when he returned on
20 October, five days before the opening of the congress. In the meantime, Dufour and Moynier had
gone to Berne to effect the sending of Swiss representatives. Italy had sent no official representative
and Dunant succeeded in having the Italian Consul
in Geneva appointed. Above all, there was a mass of
organizational questions to be settled. They wanted
strictly to avoid giving the meeting a too public character. Geneva was about to elect its council and the
waves of local political passion were rolling high.
They did not want, as Moynier wrote, a 'superficial
crowd who are unsuited to basic work and who will
waste their time in humanitarian talk.' The citizens
of Geneva 'should be kept out on principle to prevent
the meeting from becoming a collection of curiosity-
seekers.' Not even the members of the Public Welfare
Society were admitted.

The aged Mme Eynard-Lullin, 'la belle Eynard' of
the Congress of Vienna, placed a *salon* of the *Athénée*
at the disposal of the delegates, a pretty little build-

ing which had just been erected for the *Société des Arts*. After some labours, the program of social arrangements was worked out. Mme Eynard, Dunant and Moynier would give receptions at their homes, and each member of the committee undertook to entertain daily a number of the guests whose arrival was awaited with trepidation and suspense.

The representation at the congress exceeded all expectations. Sixty-two delegates appeared from sixteen nations, in addition to five delegates from the Swiss Welfare Societies of Neuenburg and Waadt and a delegate from the Prussian Knights Hospitallers, Prince Henry XIII of Reuss.

The aging General Dufour, attired in his black coat and wearing the rosette of the Legion of Honour, opened the conference. No one was better qualified than he. Born in 1787 in Constance of an old Geneva family, he became a student at the *École Polytechnique* in Paris. At twenty-five he was a captain in Metz, a talented military engineer in charge of construction work at Grenoble, Lyons and Corfu. In the Eastern Mediterranean, a French gunboat on which he was travelling was trapped one day in 1813 by the English and set on fire. Dufour leaped into the sea. Severely wounded and half dead, he was fished out by the English and made prisoner for a short time. Napoleon decorated him for his bravery with the cross of the Legion of Honour. As a second-lieutenant, he returned to Switzerland in 1817 and worked as a civil engineer before he reorganized the Confederated Army as Chief of General Staff. In 1831 he created the Swiss flag, the red field with the white cross. In the brief internal war that followed, Dufour was commander of the government troops. Napoleon III, whose instructor Dufour had been at the military school in Thun, on several occasions requested Dufour's confidential assistance. In 1857 he retired from service, performing his first peaceful labour, a topographical map of Switzerland which will always remain a masterpiece of cartography.

This general, Switzerland's good spirit, who in contrast to most of his fellow-professionals, had felt the sufferings of war in his own body, issued to his troops in 1847 before the outbreak of the war with the Sonderbund, a proclamation which deserves to be preserved in the memory of mankind forever as a humane document.

Be always moderate in the struggle, do not lower yourselves to excesses which can only embitter a population that we are seeking to win through mildness . . . Prevent at all costs the destruction of the churches . . . When the enemy is beaten, care for his wounded as if they were ours: show them all the consideration that is owing to misfortune. Disarm the prisoners, but do no harm to them and do not curse them . . . Let them return to their homes if they promise to discard their uniforms and not to take up arms again. When the enemy is guilty of atrocities, take care that we can be reproached with nothing of that kind. Under no circumstances, reprisals—they can only damage our cause. After a battle, quiet the fury of the soldiers, spare the vanquished. There is no greater honour for victorious troops . . . No matter how strong we feel, we must fear the desperation of our enemies . . . The leaders must inculcate these principles in their subordinates, and these in turn must make every soldier familiar with them so that they become law for the whole Confederated Army. It must exert itself to show the world that we are not a horde of barbarians . . . Under your protection I place the women, the children, the old people and the priests. Whoever lays his hand on a harmless person is dishonourable and has soiled his country's flag. The prisoners, and above all, the wounded, deserve your greatest care.

These Ten Commandments of General Dufour deserve to be engraved on each of the countless war memorials and mass cemeteries. We shudder as we contrast these rules of warfare (not yet a hundred years old) and the spirit that brought them forth, with the horrors of 1938 that take place day by day under our scarcely troubled eyes, and in whose shadow youth grows up and knows nothing of the humanity of a forgotten century and does not want to know.

On 26 October 1863 Dufour opened the session:

You know, gentlemen, that for the unfortunate wounded who remain on the field of battle the military hospitals in their present state afford only very imperfect aid . . . This inadequacy has struck everyone, but it has been described quite particularly, and with appalling truth in a work that is well known to you, and which was published after the Battle of Solferino by one of our countrymen, Monsieur Dunant. We have gathered here, gentlemen, to see if some possible way cannot be found to realize some of the humanitarian ideas expressed in that book . . . One cannot begin to imagine

the situation of a man who comes to the battlefield and
there, after he has fought for his flag, finds that suffering
is the wages of courage and sacrifice, a suffering that is
almost torture since every alleviation is lacking, and
which is often redoubled by the dreadful feeling that he
is abandoned.

Despite all the humanitarian efforts of the peace congresses, there will continue to be wars upon this earth.
Instead of pursuing the phantom of their abolition, one
should strive to mitigate the frightfulness of their consequences as much as possible, by supporting those whose
task it is to help suffering. We must create the means for
them which they now lack . . . This is the task we hope
to accomplish.

Does the very idea of accomplishing it, put us, gentlemen, in the land of dreams? Is the goal that we should
like to reach so lofty, and does it exceed our strength so
far, that a union of all our efforts will not suffice to reach
it? If that be the case, we can only bow to it. But the
merit will always be ours of having made the attempt
. . . We should not permit ourselves to lose courage in
advance because of a momentary failure . . . If it is
not permitted us to reach our goal, at least . . . we shall
have done what is fitting for men who love their fellows!

Dufour then gave over the chair to Moynier, who
in a long address acquainted the delegates with the
program of work and the contents of the projected
statutes. Then Dunant, the Secretary, arose and read
a great number of endorsements and proposals from
letters.

After this introduction began the discussions which
were to continue in an unexpected way for four days.
The scepticism which Dufour's greeting had plainly

enough expressed was not justified. The officers and officials who were sitting together there, the delegates of the all-powerful Second Empire and the representatives of the Prussian Army, the whole motley map of Europe over which the clouds of almost inevitable conflicts lowered, all submitted to the spell of sacred earnestness in which the plain men of Geneva had summoned them to discuss. They listened without sensitiveness or bitterness to the complaints that were levelled against the services to which they belonged—and this in itself was an immense achievement.

The hidden political and personal tensions were not glossed. Prussians and Frenchmen led the discussions. Dr. Boudier, an old military doctor with thirty-four years of service behind him, who attended as representative of the unwilling Minister of War, Marshal Randon, especially questioned the possibility that volunteer helpers could stand the test of the battlefield. 'From what social category will these helpers be recruited, how would they be able to accommodate themselves to military discipline?' Boudier met vigorous opposition, especially from the Prussians whose Knights Hospitallers, to whom the highest nobility belonged, had long assumed the obligation of giving volunteer aid in time of war.

The thirty-seven-year-old Moynier guided the discussions with great skill. He exhibited a happy mixture of youthful activity and legalistic pedantry. But he did not let slip the opportunity to punish Dunant for his impetuousness. He declared that the three points of the Berlin circular were not a subject of discussion, and over the passionate protest of Dr.Basting he had his way. But he could not prevent the idea of neutralization from arising again and again in the discussions, or from being adopted at last in the form of a 'desire.'

Especially impressive was the argument of the Spanish delegate, Dr.Landa:

. . . if something like the threat of war were not in the air, if all hearts did not entertain the dread of a convulsion which may make itself felt in every corner of Europe, if so many disastrous questions were not posed, the invitation from Geneva would not have found so warm a reception . . . The true ground of the inadequacy is the disproportion between the development of the means of protection and the means of destruction: the extraordinary progress in ballistics, for example, and the conical bullet, the effects of which are far more frightful than those of the spherical bullet. When I had to remove the conical bullets of our sharp-shooters from the Moorish wounded, I experienced a feeling of revulsion that I should gladly make every high-placed military person feel.

When in a single-combat the simplest rules of honour forbid taking advantage of any superiority of weapons, why should the same feeling not prevail in mass fighting . . . Why any refinement of the murderous weapons which are already so close to the exquisite cruelties of savages? . . . The soldier is really not begging for alms when he asks for a handful of lint, but for the payment of a debt of honour—and fortunately, I know of no government, no nation, that is willing to contest this . . . In every union of men there must be a common bond, and if their object is to do good works and not to make

business, they must look for this bond in the moral
sphere . . .

Are these mere phrases? No, to-day they would be
phrases. At that time there was no Red Cross. Since
then, seventy-five years have passed. This should
be an occasion for celebration. The organization is
great and powerful. In Geneva, the Palace of the
League of Nations overshadows the little hall of the
Athenaeum. Not only Europe, the whole world comes
together in Geneva. But whoever should get up and
make such a speech to-day would pass for an insane
visionary. The Red Cross has brought blessings. It
has not abandoned its principles and is outwardly
still intact. The powerful nations have not yet deserted it as they deserted the League of Nations. But
tongues in Geneva are tied because they feel shame
at the discrepancy between word and deed. For every
actual outbreak of hatred and rapacity shakes with
acts of barbarous and unheard-of cruelty the 'sacred
principle' of humanity of which Dunant dreamed and
which in 1863 was not yet a phantom. To-day it is
less than a phantom.

The conference at Geneva broke up on 29 October.
With a few small changes they reached a complete
understanding on all the points under discussion. On
Dr. Appia's motion a uniform emblem was proposed
for all members of the future relief societies, in the
form of a red cross on a white ground. A crowd of
officials, critical, incredulous and the slaves of regula-
tions, had become a band of active and enthusiastic
fellow-combatants in a common cause.

At the close of the final session, Dr. Basting took the floor:

> In view of the extraordinary significance of the noble pioneer work of Monsieur Dunant and the Geneva Public Welfare Organization, and in appreciation of the mighty echo which the measures drafted by this Conference must find in all countries and in all classes, I propose that the Conference at the close of its labours declare that Monsieur Henri Dunant, because by his persistent efforts he has called forth an international study of the means required for assisting the wounded on the field of battle; and the Geneva Public Welfare Society, because it so forcefully seconded the noble ideas of Monsieur Dunant, have deserved well of humanity and earned the incontestible right to universal thanks.

The whole assembly rose in sign of acquiescence. But Dunant, who had stood so much at the spiritual centre of this organization, whose name was mentioned again and again, and without whose activity the conference would unquestionably never have taken place, had taken absolutely no part in the discussions.

An extraordinary timidity kept him from hearing himself speak before so many people. He possessed a finished talent for convincing any man whom he could look in the eye. He was an apostle within four walls. But the multiplicity of any mass gathering terrified him. He was overcome and oppressed by the fact that his idea, which he had written down to free himself from a profound and instant anxiety, had come to have such a life of its own, had so grown and so changed. When he saw before him the crowd of important men who must bring his idea to fulfilment, each from his own motives and in his own circles, he felt how alien they all were to him. He was no leader. He had cried out, and the cry had been taken up through no effort of his. It ended in articles and resolutions, in committees and official documents. There was no other way, he knew that. But it was no longer a problem of his own life's need. It was a beginning. The misery and suffering of men were too great. It was a contest with God that he was waging. Wrong could not be solved by conferences. The agony lay on other planes of which these people knew nothing. He had so many companions now, but they left him solitary. That night he went home sadly.

X

The Forerunners of the Red Cross

INSTEAD of one advocate there were now many. Moynier, who for forty-seven years was to keep the leadership of the central organization in his firm hand, was taking over more and more definitely. Dunant was becoming more and more a functionary of Moynier's. With extreme prudence Moynier went about the difficult tasks that arose. The success of the conference did not deceive him as to the opposition he was to meet. Again and again he emphasized the provisional character of the Geneva office and the necessity that the individual national groups must be completely autonomous and independent, but guided by the same aim. The name 'international' which the committee had long since sovereignly conferred upon itself disappeared for the present. Not until the Brussels Conference in 1882 was it officially recognized. Now they must wait for the reaction of public opinion—and above all, the reaction of the governments—to the Geneva resolutions.

It turned out that those who were thinking about war were most receptive to the message of the Red

Cross. Prussia was the first country to found a national committee, preparations for which Dunant had made in Berlin. The smaller German states, with Baden in the lead, followed. In Italy it was the medical societies especially that took up the plan. In Milan Dr.Cesar Castiglioni founded an 'Italian Society for Aiding the Wounded and Sick in Wartime,' despite the fact that the Countess Pallavicini wrote to Geneva on 12 February 1864: 'The military is in general opposed to this kind of hybrid organization. They find it more important to busy themselves with improving their ambulances than to let others share in their plans.'

In Spain the enthusiastic Dr.Landa accomplished extraordinary things for the Cause in a short time. In Belgium, too, by February 1864 there was a committee ready to work. Russia, Sweden and Denmark contented themselves for the time being with goodwill. In England, since the Crimean War, hygienic conditions in the army had been thoroughly reformed. The Secretary for War was entirely opposed to the use of volunteer helpers and an article in *The Times* of 13 February 1864 was the first step in improving the attitude toward the Geneva project.

As before, the greatest difficulties were in France, and without the participation of France any practical success for the conference was unthinkable. France was still the greatest military power and the hostile attitude of the army removed all hope.

No one knew this better than Dunant. Immediately after the close of the conference he went to Paris. Once more he set to work with the obstinacy of a troublesome salesman who will make himself heard in the end. In a little Carmelite monastery near Passy, he sought out Father Hyacinthe whose sermons in Notre Dame were a rendezvous of distinguished society, and persuaded him to make an appeal from his pulpit. Through the former minister Guizot, a Jew, he won the support of his co-religionists. He did not shrink even from the radical Élisée Reclus. Meanwhile he sought out the Ambassadors from Mexico, Brazil and Japan. Mirza Hassan Ali Khan, the Persian Ambassador, told him, 'I believe that my master, the Shah, would much prefer to be asked to sign a treaty in which the princes of Europe pledged themselves not to make any further wars.'

Dunant had two things in particular at heart—the founding of a French committee and the preparations of a diplomatic step on the part of the powers which was now inevitable. For this, unity in Geneva was necessary. They must move the European governments to consent to a binding covenant. The accomplishing of this diplomatic innovation would surpass all the difficulties so far overcome. To summon a real diplomatic conference was essential, with plenipotentiaries who were empowered to make the necessary international legal commitments.

Even at the first session on 9 November 1863 a questionnaire to the governments was drafted and dispatched immediately. Among other things it asked:

Would the government participate in an international Convention the object of which was
   a) The neutralizing in time of war of ambulances

and military hospitals, the personnel of the official sanitary service, the volunteer nurses enlisted by the Relief Committee, the inhabitants who come to the aid of the wounded, and wounded military persons?

b) The acceptance of a regular uniform or emblem for persons belonging to the sanitary service and a regular flag for the ambulances and hospitals?

Would there, in the event that the last suggestion was agreed to, be any objection to the adoption of a white arm-band with a red cross?

The replies were in general favourable. In several war ministries there was evident hesitation. The final success must depend on whether the right form for the conference could be found, in order to create sufficient authority for the originators of this first attempt in history at a supra-national court.

At this moment Dunant intervened with a solution that once more was possible only for him. On 5 December he presented Napoleon III with a 'petition'—'a request to support the Relief Committee that is trying to organize in Paris.' The appeal was accompanied by a letter of recommendation from General Dufour, to whom, as his teacher, the Emperor showed a lifelong gratitude. Five days later, Dunant received this reply through Colonel Fave, the Emperor's adjutant:

His Majesty is in fullest agreement with the object of the Conference and the proposals for its realization. He desires to participate in your work by hailing the formation of a Relief Committee such as you are at present trying to form in Paris. He authorizes you to make full use of his sympathy for this undertaking. He promises to

request Marshal Randon to authorize a few high officers
of the army to take part in the Committee.

This was a triumph for Dunant, but in the hierarchy of the Second Empire there were countless
walls erected even around the highest will. It required
all the adroitness of diplomatic intrigue not to fall into
a trap. The delegates who had appeared in Geneva
with so much secret opposition revised their ideas to
conform to the Emperor's attitude, at least outwardly. On 29 December Marshal Randon sent a
questionnaire to Dunant: 'What will the object of
this Committee be? What persons will belong to it?
Who will preside? Where will it meet?' etc.

What a difference there was between the unified
attitude of Prussian militarism and the clumsiness
and divided energy of Napoleon's regime, which had
now become a dictatorship whose insecurity was
shared by the pettiest bureaucrat! On this fact alone
a political prognosis for the future could have been
based.

On 26 January 1864 Dunant replied to the War
Minister's questions. His letter was a masterpiece of
Dunantesque diplomacy. With the utmost circum-
spection he plays upon the Franco-Prussian rivalry:

> The governments have informed the Geneva Com-
> mittee of 1863 that they are in agreement with its resolu-
> tions. Especially the King of Prussia has taken a noble
> initiative in the matter of neutralization (which I wish
> France might have taken), and His Excellency Herr von
> Roon informs me that by royal command this chivalrous
> and important humanitarian question will be handled

by Prussia in a diplomatic way. I earnestly beg Your Excellency to evince the same initiative. For France has always taken the lead in noble and generous ideas and never yielded precedence to any. The reputation in questions of this kind has always been on the side of France, as Your Excellency knows so well, and as the material shows, which I have enclosed for Your Excellency.

This material was indeed convincing. Even during the Geneva Conference, the military physician, Dr.Loeffler, had referred to a treaty of Frederick the Great with France, signed on 7 September 1759 by General von Buddenbrock, and by Marshal de Rougé for Louis XV, in which an extensive exchange of wounded prisoners, mutual assistance and the protection of doctors was provided. Stimulated by the Geneva program, more and more such humane separate treaties were being wrested from historical oblivion. Dunant first collated them on March 1864 in his book *Relief Work on the Battlefield.* Later, the Swiss Dr.Brière and especially the German Dr.Gurlt took over this important work of exhumation. By 1873, 291 treaties for the exchange of prisoners from 1581 to 1864 were known, containing humanitarian provisions for military chaplains, women and children.

This pre-history of the Red Cross is encouraging and discouraging. It testifies to the eternal existence of human sympathy and the eternal nullity of human agreements. The reality of war was different from the history of its humanitarian contracts. Where they meant anything at all, they meant it almost exclusively for the officers. The common man was a cipher.

In 1762 de Chammousset, Commissary-General of the French hospitals, cries out: 'How is it possible that the civilized nations have not yet agreed to regard hospitals as sanctuaries of humanity, to be respected and protected by the victor!'

But much as these ancient yellowed documents, these feeble, unsuitable, even hypocritical attempts to reconcile the crime of killing with the Christian commandments were doomed to ineffectiveness, their rediscovery set the efforts of the Red Cross in an honourable historical context to which ultimately even the antipathies of a Marshal of France must bow.

'Your Excellency must agree that the resolutions of the International Conference are entirely in the sense of those magnanimous ideas which were born in reality of the French spirit,' wrote Dunant in conclusion.

Randon failed to reply; the Emperor, however, presented with Dunant's letter, answered:

Sir, I have had the honour to present to His Majesty the documents which were conveyed to me, reporting the progress of your work for the relief of wounded soldiers. As soon as you are in Paris, the Emperor will have you introduced to the Minister for Foreign Affairs so that he may examine your proposal for the neutralization of ambulances, hospitals, the wounded, and the sanitary corps.

Dunant wanted to manage matters so that the French government would officially support the calling of the congress. In Geneva there had at first been much hesitation lest an appearance of dependence on

France be the result. Finally, however, they let themselves be converted by Dunant. France's endorsement of the undertaking would provide a desired guarantee in the eyes of the Swiss government also.

On 23 April 1864 Dunant was received by the Minister for Foreign Affairs, Drouyn de Lhuys. The introduction was made by the Swiss Ambassador, Dr. Kern.

'The Minister assured me that if the Swiss Confederation, with the object of making the idea of neutralization an international law, would issue an invitation to delegates for a congress to be held in some Swiss city, France, as a military power, was willing to support it in its efforts and to urge the invited states to accept the invitation.'

There were differences of opinion. The Minister insisted on Berne for the conference city. Dunant insisted on Geneva. Meanwhile he managed to secure the invitation of the smaller German states while acceding to the Minister's desire not to invite the South American countries.

Immediately upon receipt of Dunant's letter with its happy message, the committee met in Geneva and decided to convene the conference for the coming August. Moynier went to Berne to conduct the negotiations with the Swiss authorities, who were to issue the official invitations. On 28 May he wrote to Dunant, 'This morning Drouyn de Lhuys' letter was officially read to the Diet. The gentlemen assure me that the affair will occasion no difficulties. Especially the President, Herr Dubs, seems ready to do whatever we wish.'

Once more Dunant had performed a decisive service for his Cause. On 6 June 1864 the Diet issued invitations to all the contemplated states to a diplomatic congress, which would meet on 8 August in Geneva. The circular letter of the French government recommending acceptance of this invitation followed a few days later.

The founding of a French committee, for which Dunant had striven so long, was now about to be realized. A little group of reliable friends was assembled, among them the great Genevese banker Theodore Vernes, the philanthropist Auguste Cochin, and a few courageous generals who were not afraid of their Minister of War. On 25 May 1864 'a small preparatory meeting' was held in the Rue de Londres, in the reception hall of the administrative board of the Orleans Railroad. The committee was to be formed. It was a monstrosity of names and offices honorary presidents, a dozen vice-presidents, a half dozen secretaries, charter members and sub-committees. What a wonderful opportunity to satisfy and injure vanities!

'Organizations are difficult things in France,' said *comte* Rohan-Chabot a month later when they were still not much farther advanced in the appointment of officers. *Baron* Darricau excused himself politely when offered the leadership. Finally, General de Fezensac became chairman, and Marshal Randon approved for himself the title of Honorary President of the French Relief Society for Wounded Military Persons.

A delegation appeared with the Duke in the Minister's office. Randon was not very polite. 'I hope that you don't have anything to do with those people in Geneva who meddle with matters that are none of their business!'

I attended this audience with the War Minister, standing silently with the other members of the Committee, and was not at all surprised at the Marshal's attack since he knew nothing of my presence, or at least pretended not to. He further vented his bad humour by abusing a 'certain Monsieur Dunant, a Swiss who takes it upon himself to criticize the French Service . . . ' It was like a cold shower. Nobody answered. The delegation returned little edified and deeply shocked from the audience.

It is small wonder that the French committee, although it was solemnly received a half year later by Napoleon III in the Tuileries, had only an illustrious but very passive sham-existence.

Now almost everything had been done which Dunant had set out to do. Napoleon had been won over. The French had a committee of the most resplendent names in the country. Neutralization stood in the foreground of the coming congress, and unless everything proved delusive, his dream of the 'sacred principle' must become law. The breathless intoxication in which Dunant had existed for months began to clear. The flight through the palaces, the life with their kings had left behind much emptiness and sadness. Everywhere Dunant had been listened to, but nowhere had his sorrow found surcease. He remained as ever the stranger with the invisible woe which none might share. His business affairs, which meant so much to him, lay somewhere far away in the dusk of those nights he passed alone. He had paid out 50,000 francs to bring together a catalogue of titles. The travelling apostle of humanity had sown the unrest of his tormented heart across the soil of Europe, and a barren convention would be the harvest. There was no more room for prophets. His friends in Geneva were not lacking in harsh and distrustful remarks. Since the incident of Berlin, they no longer trusted his temperament. Moynier, the new master, lived in perpetual fear of unexpected and overhasty steps. 'Too much talking does harm,' he wrote admonishingly to Secretary Dunant in Paris.

On the morning of 29 May Dunant was listening in the church of the Sorbonne to a sermon of the celebrated Abbé Perreyre. It was an enthusiastic appeal for Dunant's work. There sat the great gentlemen of Paris, Cousin, de Broglie, *comte* Duchâtel. And yonder he sat, wretched little Monsieur Dunant from Geneva. The voice of the priest uttered his name like one of the saints. He was terrified by the weight which this name had come to have.

What had become of him? Did he not feel within himself a nostalgia for the peace of ordinary life, an urge to omissions and commissions? He had wandered from the path. Fear seized him. He wanted to struggle. Hurrying home, he wrote to Moynier:

I believe I have by now done everything within my power to make our work a success and set it in motion. Now I wish completely to step aside. No longer count on me for active co-operation. I shall return among the shadows. The work is begun. I was only an instrument in the hand of God. Now others, better qualified than I, must push it forward and complete it.

In Geneva they were extremely bewildered at this sudden decision. Dunant's personality had become a European legend. In the interests of the Cause it would have been highly inconvenient to lose him now, just before the organization was stabilized. On 1 June Moynier replied, 'We are your colleagues, but no substitute. To leave us now would be the surest means of jeopardizing the work.'

Dunant remained. There was no way out for him. The ghosts of Solferino had him in thrall.

XI

The Danish War of 1864

MEANWHILE there was more lint to be shredded by
the ladies of Geneva. Bismarck's Prussian policies
had finished the preparatory phase and passed over
to aggression. On 1 February 1864 Prussia and Austria, on the pretext of protecting the people of Schleswig from oppression, declared war on Denmark. A
decade of struggle over the duchies of Schleswig and
Holstein preceded the outbreak of hostilities.

The causes of this war are an inextricable welter of
genealogical and legal complications. Since 1460 the
King of Denmark had been overlord of both duchies.
The inhabitants of Schleswig were overwhelmingly
Danish, those of Holstein largely German. In 1848
there had already been fighting. A claimant to the
duchies, the Duke of Augustenburg, had appeared
who annexed the territories for Germany. A conference in London in 1853 had regulated the controversy.
The claimant had sold out his rights for cash and
Schleswig-Holstein once more belonged to Denmark.
Later the Danish King sought a reasonable solution
by annexing Schleswig to the Danish Crown and

making Holstein autonomous. The German Diet was in arms against this.

The English were entirely on the side of Denmark, for the Prince of Wales had just married the Danish Princess Alexandra. In the House of Commons, Palmerston defended 'the independence, the inviolability and the rights of Denmark. If any forcible attempt whatsoever should be made to set aside those rights or jeopardize that independence, the author of the attempt must bear in mind that it is not Denmark alone with whom he will have to reckon.'

These were strong words from the powerful statesman and fortified the resistance of the little country. Once more the European family united in noble indignation over the rights of the weak. And once more it all meant nothing when might meant business. France remained neutral because Napoleon could not forgive the English for their refusal to help in the Polish insurrection. Russia was Prussia's friend. Austria did not wish to leave German initiative entirely in the hands of Prussia and so joined in for reasons of prestige. At the most critical moment, the Danish King died. The son of the claimant to the duchies again appeared on the scene and renewed his pretensions. But Bismarck was not interested in creating a new petty state. Kiel was an important harbour on the Baltic Sea and could become the base for a future Prussian fleet. Denmark stood alone with its 40,000 soldiers.

The Prussian army corps under Wrangel advanced against the Danish frontier, the guard against Kiel. The Austrians crossed the Elbe near Hamburg. It

was no very glorious war that followed. The allies
moved forward and before their overwhelming force
the Danes retreated. Before Dueppel there was a
pause and an eight weeks' siege. Then Dueppel fell
and the way to Copenhagen was open. The chorus of
European protest swelled, but no one lifted a hand.
There was a conference in London. Napoleon proposed a plebiscite. The professional diplomats shook
their heads at the incurably romantic methods of the
Emperor. The Danes' last stand was broken at Alsen.
Moltke and the Crown Prince had the final word. An
armistice followed. Toward the end of the year, Denmark ceded the duchies to Austria and Prussia in
Vienna.

Hardly had the *soirées de charpie* begun in the
salon of Mme Eynard when Dunant announced in the
Gazette de Lausanne that he was going to Denmark.
But his labours in Paris were too pressing and kept
him from his plan. It was obvious that the young
Geneva organization could not remain inactive in the
face of this new war. The news from Missunde, where
the Kiel students, at the risk of their lives, brought
off the wounded under fire, shook the world.

'General Dufour insisted on our obligation at once
to send two delegates, one to Germany and the other
to Denmark in order to safeguard our principle of non-
partisanship and internationalism.' (13 March 1864.)

They turned to a friend of Dr. Basting's, the Dutch
officer, C. W. M. van de Velde, who happened to be in
Geneva lecturing on Palestine. Van de Velde agreed
to take over the Danish mission while Dr. Appia went
on the Prussian side.

For the first time official representatives of the Red Cross appeared in the theatre of war. They were to have very diverse experiences. The reactions of populations, living under an enemy-psychosis, toward a 'neutral' foreign delegate who—and this was thoroughly novel—pretended to speak in the name of humanity, was difficult to predict.

Much distrust had to be overcome. When Van de Velde arrived in Copenhagen at the beginning of April, it was still bitter winter. The Danes were sitting in a fortress of ice, spiritually and materially deserted by the world around them. Two newspapers, *Folkets-avis* and *Dags-Telegraphen* immediately began violent attacks against 'the delegate of a partisan association whose indifference to the Danish cause is such that they have at the same time appointed a representative to the Prussian army.'

The idea of a neutral court of justice in the midst of war's hatreds was still too new. Even the representatives of the Red Cross found their role difficult. Van de Velde tried to identify himself with the Danes 'in a moral, but not a political sense.' He was told: 'The Geneva idea is beautiful and noble. But we Danes are too much occupied with our own cares and troubles at this moment to give much thought to other things.' They forbade him to go into the Prussian camp with a member of parliament to gather information concerning wounded Danish officers.

The attitude of the Red Cross can be compared only with the position of a doctor who is obliged to care for the needs of a patient without inquiring as to his moral worth. He may have ideas about the value or lack of value of any given life, but his profession enjoins undiscriminating aid. To the physician, as perhaps to other individuals, life in itself, its pure animal force, is sacred in every form, whether it be in a criminal condemned to die or in a genius. His unique enemy is anything which threatens the life with which he is entrusted. When he gives up this elementary principle of his professional existence—as happens very often to-day—he has given up himself.

Totalitarian states require the physician to subordinate his profession to national needs: he must appraise the value of a patient according to his value to the community. Thus he is compelled to choose between the hubris of a godlike function or the shame of lowering himself to the level of a politician. Between doctor and patient there can never be any other court of appeal. Nor can a non-partisan organization, whose purpose is to aid the wounded on the field of battle, conceive its mission in any other way.

The first representatives of the Red Cross in the Danish War were in many respects dilettante. Since 1863 there had been a kind of union, but as yet no firm moral dogmas by which they could feel themselves bound. Neutrality should not and does not imply moral passivity, as many believe. This danger, which the Red Cross faces in a heightened degree even to-day, existed then too in full force. The Red Cross has the right and the obligation to condemn open injury to human civilization which in the very nature of war reaches its lowest point then. In this war there were inhuman acts, like the senseless bombardment of Sonderburg, which public opinion of Europe would not tolerate. In Madrid and Paris they could not understand the silence in Geneva. Again it was Dunant whose uncompromising zeal showed a sure sense of the ideal tasks of the Red Cross. In a letter to Moynier (26 April 1864) he indicates that 'the duty of the International Committee, whose opinion has so much significance and influence, is to know and then to utter the whole truth, to publish this truth in all its good or evil, to set the facts straight or to stigmatize every kind of hateful occurrence.'

In this war Dr. Appia lost all critical judgment. He was a passionate militarist and fell under the spell of the wonderfully efficient Prussian war machine. In the beginning, he too had difficulties. A critical article of Dunant's in the *Journal de Genève* was received very badly in Berlin. But he managed to improve the feeling. The idea of the Red Cross found fertile and well-prepared soil in Germany. There were already the orders of the Knights Hospitallers, the Knights of Malta, the Deaconesses of Kayserwerth and Bethania, the brothers of the *Rauhes Haus* in Hamburg, who would rescue the wounded even under fire, and the students of the *Philanthropeum* in Duisburg.

'No, gentlemen, we were not dreaming when we expressed the hope that persons who did not belong to the army, without uniform and with only a simple arm-band, could busy themselves with saving and giving first aid to the wounded on the battlefield without endangering military discipline.'

Appia was given a recommendation from Roon and a Colonel was permanently assigned to assist him.

With the Red Cross on arm for the first time in history, he carried on an indefatigable activity. In
Rendsburg he was received by the eighty-year-old
Marshal Wrangel who impressed him profoundly.
'With his own hand he filled his officers' glasses.' He
admired the warlike spirit and bearing of the Prussian
soldier, 'martial figures, powerful bodies, medium
height, robust constitutions, expression of cheerful
bravery, nothing exaggerated, nothing overbearing,
especially nothing frivolous, a genuine and truly soldierly appearance.' Although he spoke in other places
of war as a 'collective wrong,' deep in his heart he respected it. ' War, like all the great trials of life, works
for man's perfection.' In another part of his report he
says again, 'I cannot conceal the fact that at the sight
of this evil I was so shocked that I nearly burst into
tears to see the numbers of victims, many of whom
no doubt were innocent.'

Appia was extremely active in the hospitals. In several instances he held regular conferences on the Red
Cross for the officers and doctors. 'I was always taken
seriously . . . Everywhere, both in the Prussian and
the Austrian armies, I found almost without excep-
tion, a cordial, sincere and convinced understanding,
and often when I least suspected it, a Christian humanity. Wars are made with the desire that they
shall be what unfortunately wars must be, but with a
desire too that mercy, moderate and mild, shall prevail.' So torn this way and that was Dr. Appia, so fascinated was his Prussian heart, which by a twist of
fate had strayed into the Genevese Republic, by the
charm of the perilous adventure. The gulf between

'Christian humanity' and the battlefield was not a
problem for him as for Dunant. Nor was he tormented
by thoughts of the super-power and the calculations
of politicians whose command sent innocent men to
their death. A year later, he, the official representative of a humanitarian and neutral organization could
send the Crown Prince his felicitations on the anni-
versary of the storming of Dueppel.

And yet his attitude is pardonable when one considers the relative decency of this war. Appia describes a scene, a touching soldier's story, that sounds
as if it were taken from our school-readers. He was
sitting in a wagon which was conveying to Sonderburg the coffin of a Danish officer who had died
among the Germans:

> We moved ahead slowly. Six soldiers who were carry-
> ing the coffin followed the wagon. Arrived at the bridge
> to Sonderburg, the middle of which had been destroyed,
> we saw a boat putting out from the other bank. It was a
> Danish officer: he had understood the signal. The Prus-
> sian officer advanced to meet him. They saluted and ex-
> changed a few words. 'How sad,' said the Prussian, 'he
> was undoubtedly an officer of whom great things could
> be expected.' At a given signal the six soldiers who bore
> the coffin advanced with slow funeral step to the bridge
> in order to give it over to the Danes. A last military
> salute was given the dead officer, then the Danish boat
> pushed off. The weird scene was ended. We climbed
> into our wagon again while the Danish batteries were
> silent.

It is a cheerless description, but it shows a respect
for death and a kind of chivalry for which one will

search in vain in the reports from Abyssinia, Spain or China. The taming of the individual by civilization intensified mass inhumanity. In the bloody shambles of an air-raid, piety would be senseless and decency out of place.

XII

The Geneva Convention of 1864

On 8 August 1864 the conference which was to frame the Geneva Convention began with all the preliminaries of a great political event. Of the twenty-five states invited by the Swiss government, sixteen responded to the call with twenty-four delegates: Baden, Belgium, Denmark, Spain, France, Hesse, Italy, Holland, Portugal, Prussia, the United States, England, Sweden, Norway, Saxony and Württemberg.

Who was not there? Austria declined because it considered its sanitary officials 'adequate for all requirements' and was not in agreement with 'several points of the program.' Bavaria and the Papal States emphatically declined. It appeared that they were afraid of encountering the ghost of Calvin in 'the Protestant Rome.' Brazil, Mexico, Greece and Turkey did not attend but sent messages of endorsement. The Confederation of German States permitted its individual members to send delegations, but declined a joint representation. The Russian delegation arrived after the Congress was over.

But it soon became clear that the ideas of the delegations as to what was to be done were widely diver-
gent. Fortunately, however, this first league of nations session in Geneva was, as regards its dissensions,
confusions and intrigues, only a feeble forerunner of
its mighty relative of the year 1919.

Moynier supervised the preparations with the most
meticulous pedantry, from the shape of the confer-
ence-table to the preliminary draft of the agreement
which he had composed jointly with General Dufour
and which satisfied, as far as could be foreseen, all
juridical and political requirements.

One of his greatest cares was to eliminate the Geneva authorities wherever possible and to ensure the
exclusive character of the gathering. The hatred between 'the people' and the 'patricians' in Geneva
was too deep. The Revolution of 1846 had not been
forgotten: 'It must not be treated as if it were a national holiday on which you cram people with entertainment from morning till night.' An illuminated
promenade on the lake was permitted, but 'it should
not be requested from the City Council who will invite all their "acolytes" and the celebration will
begin to smell a little of "*democrapule*," of the
democratic slum-pack.' (25 June.)

'Doormen and perhaps a fine functionary for the
sessions,' that was all that they wanted to see of the
Geneva government. Such fine gentlemen were we!
That year, in the same city, Johann Philipp Becker
founded the first section of the International Workingmen's Association, whose statutes Karl Marx
wrote. That year in France the right of the workers to

strike became law. Two great tendencies had begun to divide mankind. And no one sensed the danger.

Moynier assigned the functions. The Diet had turned over the whole business of organization to the Geneva office. Dufour would, as a matter of course, preside. Dr.Lehmann, the Surgeon-General of the Swiss Army, and Moynier, were the delegates from the Diet. The historian Dr.Brière was secretary. For Dunant there was no place in this plan. On this occasion, which was to crown his life's work and which could never have happened without him, Moynier assigned him to the tragi-comic role of head of the Entertainments Committee. Basting was kept officially in Holland. The rebels were eliminated.

Until the last moment, Dunant took part in the preparations. His two secretaries had worked day and night. Through a letter to President Lincoln he had substantially furthered America's participation. His name was the banner of this convention. But he himself was busy arranging for the refreshments and fireworks like a kind of illustrious Cinderella.

The Council placed two halls at the disposal of the congress, the same in which eight years later the 'Alabama claims' between England and America would be negotiated.

Many of the participants knew one another already from the year before. Boudier was back again, and Dr.Loeffler, his Prussian opponent. But this time, after the Emperor had so definitely expressed his interest in the work at Geneva, the French took over the leadership and the Prussians remained taciturn and somewhat irritated listeners.

Side by side with the main meeting, which continued until 22 August, a meeting of the relief societies was held, making it possible for the many friends and observers of the movement to follow the course of events without disturbing them.

Dufour had reduced the agenda to the simplest possible formula: ' We want one thing only—the neutralization of the ambulances and sanitary personnel by the belligerents.'

But what a bold and stupendous task it was to bring sixteen nations to agree to that sentence!

In none of the descriptions of the congress have its inner struggles and crises appeared clearly enough. A document from the archives of the United States government, never before published, gives an uncommonly vivid picture of the events in Geneva and the persons who played a role in them. It is the report of Charles S.P.Bowles, who had come to Geneva as the representative of the American Sanitary Commission. This classic example of diplomatic reporting deserves to be better known. Not only because the long-range viewpoint of the American observer enabled him to judge the political situation much more clearly and objectively than all other eye-witnesses; but especially for the light it throws on America's important part in the realization of the Geneva Convention and the reason why the United States was almost the last of the civilized countries to agree to the convention.

On 23 May 1864 Bowles received from Dunant a semi-official invitation to the Conference: ' From its inception, our European branch has been in active correspondence with Mr.Dunant and the Geneva

Committee. We have been able to give a practical support to this cause in Europe through our documents and other material, which has perhaps been essential to its successful progress.'

On 24 May, Bowles returned to America, where he was appointed 'Foreign Agent in Europe of the United States Sanitary Commission.' He went directly to Washington to discuss the business of the Geneva congress with Secretary of State William H.Seward.

Washington stood firm in the spirit of John Quincy Adams' Monroe Doctrine of 1823, which had since determined American foreign policy. Grant's final victories came in 1864, and then there could be little question what the outcome of the Civil War would be. Napoleon's troops were still in Mexico as a very unwelcome reminder of European interference. Something must be done soon to terminate this occupation. Lincoln expressed his sympathy for the Geneva idea and his wish to 'co-operate as far as lay within his power.' But Seward's official declaration read:

Our Government, while always ready to forward all humanitarian action, has a well-understood policy of holding itself aloof from all European congresses or compacts of a political nature; that it had sent delegates to the Postal Congress at Paris, the Statistical Congress at Berlin, and to those relating to Agriculture, in other parts of Europe; but that the Congress now proposed to be held at Geneva, being for the modification of International laws of war, and the signing of a treaty binding upon our Government, while in the midst of war with a relentless and barbarous foe, was one of greater significance, and the sending of a delegate or delegates, officially empowered to represent and act for the United States, was, from the very difficulties apparent, nearly or quite impossible. That, nevertheless, the United States Government stands ready to treat with any one, or with all other Powers individually, for the accomplishment of the grand objects of the Geneva Congress, or even to adopt later the treaty stipulations which shall wisely emanate and result from that Congress. The Government wishes to act as a free agent, with option in these premises, and in its own good time.

After long discussion it was finally decided to send Bowles, in his capacity as Agent of the Sanitary Commission, to act as semi-official observer at the conference. He hastily returned, appearing in Geneva on 4 August.

'Upon presenting myself I was cordially welcomed by Mr. Dunant and the International Committee.' On his arrival, Bowles received the agreeable news that George G. Fogg, the American minister in Berne, had received instructions from Washington to attend the congress as an informal representative.

On the evening of August 7th, I was present at the first informal meeting of the delegates at the Athenaeum, by the invitation of the authorities. As this meeting was a very important one, I propose to give an exact account of it. The delegates of fifteen or sixteen Governments were present. And here let me previse by stating that the Swiss Government had called this Congress for the framing and signing of an International Treaty or Convention upon the basis of Resolutions already, in their opinion, amply discussed and considered in the proceedings of the previous October. Any discussion therefore, except such as was necessary for the legal embodiment of the principles contained in those resolutions, was not only not the object of this Congress, but it was precisely what it wished to avoid, in the fear that it would be endless, and probably result in the dissolution of the Congress without the accomplishment of its aim. I have not seen the official invitation given out by the Swiss Government, but must suppose that it did not sufficiently convey this meaning, as a very large part of the delegates, on their arrival at Geneva, certainly had but a general and indistinct idea of what they had come to do.

Thus Russia at first declined to send a delegate, and only consented after being urged to do so with explanations by the French government. The Russian delegation, although appointed and sent, did not arrive at Geneva in time to take part in the negotiations. And Austria not only showed, by her reply, that she did not understand, but that she misunderstood, and in consequence refused to send a delegate at all. Other Powers had sent delegates, but at the meeting above referred to, at the end of the first half-hour, we discovered that, among those present, only the representatives of Switzerland and France were furnished with full powers permitting them to act, and to sign the Treaty consequent! Two or three others had what they called full powers, but their papers were, in fact, either informal or defective. Animated and unsatisfactory discussion followed this discovery between those who were plenipotentiaries, those who thought they were, and those who knew they were not. Question arose as to the practicability or even possibility of carrying out these advanced ideas; as to the working and practical nature of Sanitary Commissions, and their relations to Government. These were the very questions which I had come prepared to answer. I was there as the real and palpable representative of an institution of which they had all heard (by means of the numerous pamphlets and other documents distributed by our Branch), but which, nevertheless, they were still half disposed to consider a myth, or at least as the unreal creation of an, to them, incomprehensible people. But I was able to prove to them that this same 'mythical' institution—the United States Sanitary Commission—had long since met with and overcome the very difficulties which they were now predicting and recoiling before; had long since solved, and practically too, the very problems which they were now delving over. Moreover, I had just arrived from the scene of these labours in the United States, and with the battle-field, hospital, and burial ground freshly pictured upon my mind, could speak to them but too earnestly of war, the disease of nations, and its known or proposed remedies. It was in this always present consciousness, and as the representative of a nation now suffering fearfully from this very disease, that I endeavoured to impress upon them the importance of the present Congress, of its high and philanthropic aim, and that through all discussion and action, our guiding thought should be Humanity first, Policy afterward. The meeting broke up without arriving at any harmonious or definite result, and we all looked forward with uneasiness to the first meeting of the Congress at one o'clock the next day.

The members of the French delegation were much perplexed, and the principal, M. Jagerschmidt, a diplomat of capacity, finally declared to me that the whole affair was a failure, since that he and his colleagues, vested with full powers from their sovereign, could not treat with those not so qualified, even admitting that they were bona fide delegates from their respective Governments. I said what I could to impress upon him the necessity for action of some kind; the disgrace and ridicule of breaking up the Congress without it. I suggested, finally, that the plenipotentiaries having the requisite powers should say nothing about them, and enter the Congress on a par with the rest for the framing of the Treaty, in the hope that, when this should be ready for signing, a sufficient number of delegates, after explaining their position to their Governments, would receive these powers, authorizing them to sign. He made no definite reply, but said he would go as far as was in his power to save us from a failure. Although anxious for the result, I could not but feel hopeful, and I had also the satisfactory conviction that my coming to Geneva had already been more than justified; that if the Congress should succeed, it and the world in general would be largely indebted to our own Sanitary Commission, whose unparalleled achievements furnish a lever, so powerful for its representatives to work with.

The next morning several delegates met at my rooms, and although the subject of qualification was avoided, I saw with satisfaction that the plenipotentiaries had unbent, and showed a changed and more fraternal manner toward the rest of us.

I had taken rooms at the Hotel des Bergues, and no less than thirteen out of the twenty-five official delegates to the Congress had come to this hotel, where they remained throughout the session. From their central situation, and balcony windows fronting upon the Lake, these rooms at once became the favourite resort of the delegates resident in the house, and finally served as a sort of head-quarters or rendezvous for the Congress out of session. This was just what I sought to make them. The reflection and greater part of the work of a Congress of this kind is done outside. To stimulate this reflection, and influence the minds of the delegates by conversation, and by the material proofs which were there laid before them, would bring about gradually and clearly that full understanding of the subject which was so necessary to harmonious action in the session. The importance of this will be more fully realized when it is remembered that the subject of unofficial or volunteer Relief Committees was either entirely new, or at least problematical to nearly all the delegates to this Congress.

I had brought with me from the United States the latest reports and most valuable publications—medical, statistical, and other—of the Commission; some large engraved diagrams, showing its working organization; a number of large coloured lithographs of the Philadelphia Fair buildings, and five or six dozen of the beautiful bronze medals which were struck off in commemoration of that Fair. I had also photographs of the principal depots and buildings of the Sanitary Commission, with hospital plans and improvements of various kinds—developments of our war; photographs from life of the Field Relief Corps, with its men, waggons, horses, tents, and their arrangement and action. These life pictures, books and practical proofs, produced an effect as great as it was valuable. It was to many of them—earnest men, seeking for light with their whole hearts in the interest of a long suffering humanity,—like the sight of the promised land. They had been working in the dark, and this was the opening of a window, letting in a flood of light, and putting an end to all darkness and doubt. . . .

All these books and matters were freely circulated by Mr. Dunant and myself, previous to the organization of the Congress. . . .

Of these resolutions,[1] the last two—lettered B and C—relating to Governmental sanction or protection of Volunteer Aid Committees, was objected to, on the grounds that it was a matter proper enough, doubtless, for the consideration of a Conference, but quite outside of the legitimate bounds of International Law, and therefore beyond the scope of the powers of the present Congress. Not to discuss the matter here, I will say that whatever I may have thought, I did not push the proposition, knowing full well that the power of Sanitary Commissions comes from the people, and not from their governments. Even had it been wise or necessary to urge such action, I should have been forced to combat, nearly alone, both unbelief and official jealousy. The latter sentiment showed itself plainly, in men, too, who were otherwise liberal-minded and really Philanthropic. The point in question was, therefore, withdrawn by the Swiss Government.

The choice of General Dufour as President was an extremely happy one—a man loved and respected by all who know him, and whose energies and mental abilities, the cares of more than seventy years have only tempered, but in no whit impaired. He was the first military teacher of Napoleon, and has enjoyed his respect and favour ever since. His opening address to the Congress, delivered with all the sincerity and earnestness of a truehearted, conscientious old man, is not to be forgotten by those who heard it. As General-in-Chief of the Swiss Republic, his position, as well as his high personal character, gave dignity to the Congress itself, over which he presided to the end most ably.

The Congress Hall was plainly but tastefully arranged with desks to the number of about forty, placed

1 The resolution of the International Committee.

in horse-shoe form, facing the elevated desks of the officers. In alphabetical order, in French, our seats were between those of the Spanish and French delegates.

This was very important. For as the Americans were only unofficial participants, they could take no part in the debates, even when they did not share the opinions presented. However:

This was particularly trying in the debate which took place upon Volunteer aids, which was not as thorough and clear as it should have been. The ideas of the French Government expressed in this discussion are undoubtedly those of all the military powers of Europe at present. Still it is not a little strange to find the representatives of France taking such a course, when the Emperor himself is well known to be the supporter of this movement, and of the present Congress. At one moment these representatives refuse to acknowledge Sanitary Commissions, refuse to Florence Nightingale and those of her type the privilege of neutrality; and at another, pen and put forward Article Fifth of the Convention, which gives to people who care for the wounded in their own houses that very neutrality, and further advantages, which it denies to those who go beyond them in noble efforts and good works. The same apparent inconsistency was shown throughout the session, and the explanation of this seeming paradox is, I am told, that as the Emperor wills it, the Minister of War submits; but, with all the narrow-mindedness of a French official, does what he can in a small way to retard the movement. The very idea of associations independent, even in a humanitarian way, of the Government, is presumptious, and too democratic for the limited comprehensions of such persons. It is an idea wholly foreign to everything in their own education, and one which the traditions of their forefathers utterly ignore. It is, however, only just to say that this unfavourable influence was in a measure counteracted by the liberal spirit of the delegates themselves, who, though obliged to follow the line of their instructions, nevertheless stretched it as far as they could when the spirit of harmony and the good of the Congress seemed to demand it. In fact this spirit of harmony became in itself so powerful an element of unison, that although the discussions, both inside and outside the Congress, were often high, and opinions differed widely at times, yet the charm was never once broken by an unkind word or feeling between any two of the members. At times it was threatened, as when it was proposed to nullify in effect our whole work, by the insertion of the clause or article giving to generals-in-chief the right of making their own exceptions, and at such times as they might judge proper! And again, when the French delegation resisted the neutralization of the sick, declaring that the object of this Congress was to secure that privilege to the wounded *only*, and that they had instructions not to include the sick therein. But both of these difficulties, although at one time serious, and which, had they been maintained, would have probably led to disputes and partial failure, gave way before the pressure of the large majority, and of the general good will and understanding which existed.

Trivialities, hair-splittings, or verbosities were all indifferent, so long as the main principles for the establishment of which they had come should be left unharmed, so long as the iron framework of a new and practical humanity should emerge from the forge intact, and without other than the surface-flaws caused by insufficient or misdirected blows.

The result of the Congress is a Treaty which, although less than perfect, is far more than was really to have been expected when the difficulties and contending interests are properly appreciated. Its grand test, future practicability, remains to be applied. To reconcile humanity with the exigencies of war, or inhumanity under another name, is a task of almost unsurmountable difficulty.

And even if the treaty should be evaded or violated, it is still there upon record—its influence will be felt, and the justice of its principles acknowledged, and those who violate it will at least be morally accountable.

It will be marked by the future historian as a forward step in the civilization of the nineteenth century.

We were encouraged in these hopes, and somewhat repaid for our labour of difficulty, when, two days after the completion of the treaty, M. Jagerschmidt announced that the French Government had expressed itself entirely satisfied with the results, and had congratulated its delegates and itself thereon. It had at the same time assured them of its belief in the value of the treaty, and of an unqualified ratification of it in due time.

At this stage of the proceedings, when nothing remained to be done but to sign the treaty, the delegates not especially empowered to sign found themselves in a false position. We were, and had been, upon a footing of entire equality, but at this moment the delegates of the United States, England, Sweden and Saxony, were found to be without the requisite powers to sign.

They had fought, and helped to win the fight, and they had now to see other nations share its honours on record for the future to the exclusion of their own. They submitted to the necessity as such, consoled by the thoughts of the good that had been wrought to the world as a whole, and contenting themselves individually with hopes of the appreciation of their fellow-countrymen, and sympathisers with the cause.

On Monday, the 22nd day of August, the Treaty was duly signed by the plenipotentiaries of twelve Governments.

The Congress of Geneva then closed with a few heartfelt words of thanks through the medium of M. Fenger, of Denmark, to its well-beloved President.

During our stay at Geneva, nothing could have surpassed the hospitality which we received from its citizens, from the International Committee, and from the City and Federal Government.

The wealthy citizens of Geneva, warmly espousing the good cause, seemed to vie with each other in magnificent entertainments in honour of the Congress and for the diversion of its members. Fetes, regattas, illuminations, and excursions on the Lake which is the most beautiful in the world—followed in daily and nightly succession.

These entertainments were followed by complimentary dinners, given to the Congress by the Federal Government and the City of Geneva.

At the one last named, given at the Hotel de l'Écu, on Wednesday, August 17th, an event took place, worthy of special record by us. Most particular attentions were paid to the U.S. delegates, as being the representatives of a sister Republic. They were placed in the first seats at the table, next to or opposite the President, a mark of preference which is held in great esteem by Continental peoples. In the centre of the table was a large piece of confection, representing a fortress, with its garrison, and sanitary workers, distinguished by the red-crossed brassard, pursuing their vocations. The tower was surmounted by small silk flags of the Swiss Republic and

Canton of Geneva, around a central flag with a red cross on a white field, the emblem of our neutrality, just adopted by the Congress. After the first toast, this flag was taken from its place by the President, who turning to me as the representative of the U.S. Sanitary Commission, presented it as a token of appreciation of its labours for the good of all humanity. To this kind and unexpected compliment to our Commission, and to the accompanying speech of the President, I replied as well as I could, but the act, the sentiment, the acclamations of surrounding friends, and withal, the proud consciousness of a deserving cause, almost overwhelmed me. The full outburst of a chorus from ' William Tell,' given by the Genevan Musical Society, in the hall outside, though it covered my retreat, did not add to my equanimity; for from the windows of the dining-hall we could almost see the spot on which the republican here shot Gessler. These associations, and the music of Rossini, sung by Swiss compatriots upon that historic ground, made an inexpressibly powerful impression upon me. Those of us who, amid darkness, doubt, and the exultant sneers and insults of aristocratic despotism, have been forced to watch from abroad the second great struggle for the maintenance of our country's liberties, will best understand the force of pent-up feeling which events like these at Geneva could not have failed to let loose.

I have simply endeavoured in this report to give everything which might interest you, or, by pointing the value of our work in Europe, serve the cause and stimulate us to new action. To show that for the spreading of intelligence, and of trustworthy knowledge and proper appreciation of our country's affairs, for the development of international good feeling, and for the rendering thus of efficient aid to our country and its cause of liberty, there is no channel so direct, no agency so powerful, as that of the Sanitary Commission.

Its power is beyond that of any policy; for the reason that, while it may embrace policy, it can touch the heart, while policy affects the mind alone.

In closing, I wish to call attention to, and acknowledge here, the obligations which we are under to the International Committee of Geneva for their sincere and unceasing kindness during our stay. And most particularly to Mr. J. Henry Dunant do we, both individually and in common with all mankind, owe a debt of appreciation and gratitude. With all his resources, mental, influential, and pecuniary, and with his courage and great energy, he has been at once the pioneer, prop, and successful promoter of this work in Europe. He is at work still, and bravely the work is progressing.

We must continue to do our part, and maintain thus the lead which our nation has taken in this as in other progressive movements of the civilization of our day.

I remain, Mr. Chairman and Gentlemen,

Most respectfully yours,

CHARLES S. P. BOWLES

The report of this American, who with his sound common sense and his republican enthusiasm sat unembarrassed and alien in the councils of these Europeans, ossified by tradition, gives a wonderful picture of European 'harmony' and the extraordinary mixture of sentimental pathos and mutual distrust in the year 1864. From the confection and the choir to the diplomatic ponderousness and intrigue, everything is there which characterized this first truly international assembly of the nations.

As to the ten articles of the 'Convention for the

Amelioration of the Fate of Wounded Soldiers of
Armies in the Field,' there were unfortunately definite defects. It was especially regrettable that the
neutralization of the wounded was not specified
clearly enough in the convention, but could only be
construed indirectly. As to naval warfare there had
been no agreement; that was reserved for a later
time. The red cross on the white ground was now
officially recognized as the emblem of the neutral
helpers. Its similarity to the flag of the Swiss Confederacy, whose colours it simply reverses, was an in-
tentional act of esteem for the little land that had
supported the Cause in so exemplary and disinter-
ested a way.

How much Dunant contributed to the success of
this congress is clear from Bowles' objective report,
much clearer than from the official reports of the
organization. He was excluded from the leadership,
but he worked invisibly behind the scenes in his
tenacious and suggestive way, which brought spirits
together when discourses merely riled them.

In connection with the entertainments that Bowles
was to praise so much, the figure of poor Dunant
played a melancholy-festive role. Everything possible
was done to adjust the standards of Geneva to the
regal splendour of the ambassadors. The Genevan
patricians were secretly a little ashamed of their republican state in the heart of monarchist Europe, and
it gave them a deep satisfaction to display their ful-
some hospitality before the hated 'people' who had
ruled the city since 1846. It was a very local resentment which concerned the great world but little, yet

it had an unfortunate influence on the development
of the Red Cross. The regime of the anti-democratic
Geneva democrats was very useful as a result of their
authority with the governments and the generals,
but it created an atmosphere of feudal distance which
impaired the confidence of the masses. And because
of this the Red Cross forfeited the radicalism of its
spiritual position and was unable to fulfil the ultimate logic of its existence in the present social order,
namely, the struggle against war.

The festivities of the congress were more typical
of this attitude than the sessions. Between war and
peace, between the recognition of war and the glorification of peace, they created a dangerous and suspicious precedent for the future spirit of the League
of Nations which, with the key to happiness in its
hands, has conjured up so much unhappiness.

First there was a gathering at the beautiful estate
of Moynier's mother-in-law, at Séchéron near Geneva, where the gold-braided uniforms of the foreign
diplomats were much admired. On 11 August there
followed a promenade along the lake to Versoix.
Here the wealthy banker Theodore Vernes, who had
hurried back from Paris, received the delegates. A
military band accompanied the guests and Vernes
presented the musicians with a silver goblet 'in
memory of the work which has just been accomplished in Geneva.' Toward evening, the steamer
Helvétie brought the congress home and the day
ended at *la Grange*, the splendid palace of Colonel
Favre, who was the doyen of the Genevese aristocracy. Dunant had prepared these festivities with

much loving care. Now he wandered a little forlorn, an almost ghostly and legendary symbol of himself and his work, through the hubbub of the halls, among the crowd of glittering names, on which his heart hung so very much.

The next day the delegates gathered in the Greek hall of columns at the home of Francis Bartholomy on the harbour. Down on the lake the sail-boats were waiting for the signal for the regatta. Two steamers floated past. From one came the blare of trumpets, from the other, men's voices singing a cantata composed for the occasion. Darkness fell, the terrace of the villa was illuminated, and thunderous and resplendent fireworks mounted into the night.

On Saturday an official banquet was held at the Hotel Metropole, for which President Dubs had made a special trip from Berne. The choruses and blare of trumpets left nothing to be desired.

Finally, there was the banquet given by the Geneva Council.

It was the banquet at the *Hotel de l'Écu* about which Bowles wrote such an impressive account. Councillor Vautier could not be restrained from making a long speech in praise of peace, and there was much concern lest the tender feelings of the assembled warriors might be wounded. But the incident passed.

During the latter days, the sky was overcast as if too much good had already been done. The cheerful lake lost its peaceful aspect and a savage storm lashed the shores.

On the afternoon of 22 August the conference assembled in a festive final session. Suddenly, firing was heard from the far side of the Rhône. Like forked lightning it struck into the peaceful act of signing.

Dissension in Geneva had come to a dangerous outbreak. In the election the 'independent' Conservatives had defeated the Radical candidate, James Fazy, by a majority of votes. The election bureau declared the elections invalid. The 'independents' got up a protest demonstration and marched through the streets with drums. In the working-men's quarter, St. Gervais, there were shots and several demonstrators lay in their blood on the sidewalk.

The aroused mob stormed the *Rathaus* to settle accounts with the Radical members of the Council. But there was no Council there, only a gathering of foreign dignitaries who were about to reform the rules of warfare for the world. The shouting and uproar of the infuriated citizens who filled the courtyard became so loud that Dunant sprang up to bar the doors of the main hall and lock the windows, for people had begun to climb up in hopes of assaulting the Council members. The greatest effort was required to convince the mob that the persons they were looking for were not present. At last they went away.

In spite of the dull sounds that reached their ears, the plenipotentiaries did not permit themselves to become discomposed. But after the respected representatives of the philanthropic princes who had sent them here to accomplish a humanitarian work had appended their signatures, they disappeared as quickly as possible to observe the beauties of a governmental system which differed so greatly from that to which they were accustomed at home.

It is understandable that Dunant should have been annoyed and ashamed. For this parting climax was not on the program of the Entertainment Committee. But was not that blood on the pavements a warning cry from heaven, in whose inspirations he devoutly believed? Was it not a sign that something was false in the idea of the Geneva Convention, that if hatred was to be chained up, some stronger means was required than a charitable agreement by the haters while they were still in a sane state of mind? Dark and heavy were the clouds over Lake Geneva: cries of rebellion and indignation echoed through its streets. Dark and heavy were the clouds over Europe too. The blood of slain men, that for thousands of years had drenched this earthly paradise, was seething and channelling underground. Like a boil, the crater of the coming war must swell and burst, and the crash of bombs, the bellowing of the wounded, the stench of corpses, would wipe out everything in their deluge—confectionary and conventions. But Dunant still believed in fireworks and male choruses. Never did any mind, to which in an extraordinary hour the voice of humanity had spoken, cling more tenaciously or stubbornly to the hallucinations of a sham-world whose right was might. The trials he had suffered were still not enough.

'General Dufour and I remained at the *Rathaus* till the last. I had a carriage brought and took home the distinguished chairman of the Congress, who was very troubled and unhappy. Then I came back to make some last arrangements and to take away the papers pertaining to the Congress.' Meanwhile Moynier had placed a part of the documents in safety:

When I was leaving the *Rathaus* shortly after, I received word that my brother, Dr.Dunant, had been wounded while treating the victims of the outbreak. I immediately hurried to the lower city to look for him. When I reached the shore-drive, which is usually very lively at that hour, it was perfectly empty. The same solitude, the same stillness, prevailed on the *Pont des Bergues*, except for the whistling of a few stray bullets . . .

The festivities were ended, with their martial and well-bred mirth, their touching over-sumptuousness and nineteenth century luxury. The rain streamed down on Dunant. The restless monotone of the waves filled his ears. Like a dark fortress rose the black walls of the cathedral to a blacker sky. Still the voices of Solferino were not silent. The work that he had willed had been completed. But the air about him was heavy, sultry and hard to breathe.

The diplomats dispersed in all directions to their fatherlands. In their dispatch-cases lay a document—the Geneva Convention.

XIII

Restless Europe

THE ratification of the Geneva Convention took some time, for diplomatic mills grind slowly. By the end of 1866 twenty states had adhered to the Convention. Russia followed in 1867. In 1868 the Papal State finally decided to sign.

The year 1865 began and political apprehension grew while the subterranean activity of the couriers, who with their secret papers spin the web of war in every corner of Europe, also grew from month to month. The riddle of Prussia became more and more fascinating.

In Paris the first volume of *Julius Caesar* appeared and its author Napoleon III read with satisfaction the favourable reviews of the German university professors. The mild dictatorship of the Second Empire went on, more and more riddled with democratic concessions which the Emperor's slackening strength accepted stoically. Offenbach's *Belle Hélène* made persiflage an institution of the regime. Ibsen was sitting in Christiana, grumbling and embittered at the display of force that he had seen in Denmark.

A deep unrest which might be characterized as the reorganization of force had broken out in Europe. Once more the theories of demonic might were seeking to invalidate the moral and biological basis of humanity, the immutable ten commandments of mankind.

With the beginning of the nineteenth century, warfare was to undergo a fundamental change. The armies of Napoleon I were the first mass armies, the *levée en masse* of revolutionized France was the first totalitarian war. Henceforth the 'masses,' which sprouted like sinister weeds from the soil of Europe, became a technical instrument of warfare whose utilization at the hands of the field-marshals and statesmen proceeded ever more systematically, like the utilization of all other technical 'achievements.' The existence of the masses and their new reactions gave a sinister stimulus to their exploitation and destruction. That the masses could be experimented on, thrown into states of psychic intoxication, driven to prescribed reactions, mentally stultified to the point of self-annihilation—this was a new discovery of the century of natural science: the application of religious ecstasy to an amoral, all too rational, worldly political field.

The wars of the eighteenth century were differences between dynasties. They caused suffering to the people, of course, but jeopardized non-combatants relatively little. The armies of Frederick the Great consisted more than half of non-Prussians. War was still a special trade. The wars of the nineteenth century more and more became wars of annihilation between nations. They drew their moral justification from the idea of nationality, and Napoleon III, one of its first and most zealous champions, was to go down in the earthquake which he himself had caused.

At the beginning of the century things were still different. In 1805 Pitt and Alexander I concluded an Anglo-Russian treaty in which 'all the great powers of Europe should participate and through which their rights and their possessions, as they existed at that time, should be fixed and recognized. They should mutually engage to protect and support one another against every attack or injury. A universal and inclusive system of public law should be restored throughout Europe to prevent future attempts to disturb the general security.'

The same spirit was at the bottom of the 'Holy Alliance' drafted by Alexander after Napoleon's overthrow, and of which Goethe said, 'Nothing greater or more useful to mankind has ever been created than the Holy Alliance.' It was Alexander's idea that all governments and men should openly declare their intention of following the principles of Christianity:

> They are permeated with the extreme conviction that the many-sided and changeable relations of the powers must rest upon the pure truths of the holy religion of our Redeemer. They regard themselves, in relation to their subjects and their armies, as the fathers of a family, who desire to guide them to the safe-keeping of religion, peace and righteousness. They regard themselves as the members of a single nation, which in reality has no other Ruler save Him to Whom alone all power belongs.

This document was sent to be signed by all the princes. They could not laugh openly at the Tsar: he possessed too much worldly power. But Castlereagh thought the document the 'height of mysticism and nonsense.' He and the Duke of Wellington 'could with difficulty remain serious' during their perusal of it. And Metternich 'examined every practical possibility for suppressing it.' This Holy Alliance, this Christian League of Nations, the lack of respect for which could according to Goethe 'be blamed on an inability to recognize greatness,' in reality envisaged a politically purposive community which reactionaries, with their self-seeking, anti-liberal methods, destroyed.

The phantom of Christian national harmony was displaced by the phantom of nationalism. Said Mazzini: ' A nation is not a territory that grows stronger by expanding its surface, nor an aggregation of people speaking the same language, and guided by a leader, but an organic whole, unified by its objectives and its strengths, living in the strength of its own faith and its own traditions.'

Once more there appeared the promise of a better future which became a reality by ending a half century of peace in Europe with a series of wars, and demonstrated that the liberated nations almost always combined their new feeling of freedom and strength with a desire to attack and oppress the weak. The subsequent peace treaties contained only very feeble attempts, or none at all, to link the new rights, which the victor had forced from the vanquished, with the moral idea of peace. The idea of the League of Nations was first resumed at the point where the Holy Alliance failed.

Religion once, and now nationalism gave war that sanctity that it enjoys to-day and which endows its crimes with the spiritual semblance of heroic deeds, though its only real heroes are the innocent victims of its crimes. European nationalism, which on paper is so simple and happy a formula, forces not only its armies, but entire nations to the love of war and the psychosis of hate. Napoleon I began conscription, though in a very imperfect way. But the Prussian General Scharnhorst, in order to get around the limitation of the army by treaty, created the system of universal military service which in a brief course of training turns the entire male population of the state between the ages of eighteen and forty-five years into soldiers. Almost every European state except England quickly adopted this system. Thus peace became a prelude to war. Never for one moment could the idea of war disappear from the citizen's mind.

It will surprise no one that this ideology found its philosopher, and naturally he was a Prussian, General von Clausewitz, whose book *On War* laid the basis for the doctrine of force. This military Machiavelli led an almost unknown life. After his death in 1832 his widow published his writings posthumously, and his inexorable theories received scant attention until they took shape in the hands of Prussian militarists, and to-day dictate the mechanics and the spirit of modern war.

'War is politics continued by other means. The moral effect of its vigorous preparation is of inestimable value. Everyone feels certain of success: that is the best way in which to strengthen the spirit of a nation.' From the science of war as taught by General von Clausewitz it becomes apparent that Napoleon I was a strategist of genius who was destroyed because of his civilizing ideas. Ideas have only a propaganda value and are not to be taken seriously. War must be short, cruel and decisive. Whoever begins a war must retain the initiative. War must not be waged against an army but against a nation. The civil population must be made to feel the harshness of war in order to desire its end. The more harshly the conqueror treats the country, the quicker the war will end. The army must take advantage of the best and earliest opportunity to begin a war. Secret preparations, sudden invasions ensure success. The adversary's weak moment must be exploited. Preventive war is the most successful war. A spirit of aggression must inspire the whole population even before the outbreak of war. 'The passions which war brings out must already be latent in the nation.' War is independent of morality. 'There is no moral concept outside of the state and law.' International law consists of self-imposed limitations which are hardly deserving of mention. 'The method of disarming and conquering an enemy without a great blood-bath . . . is an error which must be rooted out.' Force must be used without stint and without regard for the shedding of blood. 'In such dangerous business as wars, the mistakes that proceed from kindness are the worst.'

While the Prussian General Staff was working in the spirit of these principles, which were in appalling contrast to the spirit of Geneva, Napoleon III, the spiritual author of high nationalism, who was not un-influenced by the ideas of Louis Blanc and Auguste Comte and Cobden's system of free trade, beheld only a league of European nations united in peace. Not that he was himself in any way disinclined to use force.

To Bismarck, Europe was simply an appendage of Prussia. He hated the idea of mediation as much as Hitler. His sword was raised and made the green table superfluous. He was a master of bilateral agreements. He preferred to yield of his own free will rather than be persuaded by others, and he never took more than he had willed to in advance.

The Habsburgs must finally surrender the leader-ship of Germany to Prussia. The plan was quickly drafted and the drama of preparations for the war was improvised with the sure touch of a skilful dramatic poet.

Bismarck created a Rome-Berlin axis, and the sit-uation rather resembled that of 1937. In September 1864 Italy and France reached an understanding ac-cording to which Florence was to be the capital, Rome was to remain unmolested, but the French garrison, which was still protecting the Papal State against the Italian nationalists, was finally to be evacuated. Napoleon the Liberator disappeared from Italy and left behind a deep resentment at his half-hearted and indecisive policies. Bismarck the Liberator appeared and promised what Napoleon had thrown away— Venice. A treaty was concluded whereby in case of a war with Austria, Prussia and Italy would come to each other's assistance with all their forces, while Prussia would make no peace without the cession of Venice to Italy.

In October 1865 Bismarck went to Biaritz to see Napoleon III. There must surely have been much talk about the rights of nations: France was not displeased at the prospect of a long war between the German brothers. The Emperor was more than satisfied: 'France and Prussia are the two European nations whose interests fully coincide to the greatest extent.' A grotesque historical bull.

Meanwhile the relations between the two conquerors of Schleswig-Holstein were becoming more and more critical. Duke Christian von Augustenburg, the mysterious claimant to the duchies, was again active, and to Prussia's annoyance was protected by Austria. By the end of the year war was imminent, but the differences were provisionally settled by the Treaty of Gastein. Prussia was not yet ready. For it was not merely a question of Schleswig-Holstein: the problem was to detach Germany.

In June 1866 Prussia proposed a reform of the Constitution to the German Diet which led a pale and impotent existence in Frankfurt. The present Diet should be dissolved and a new national constitution framed, excluding Austria. Austria, with the support of a few South German states, accused Prussia of violating the Constitution. It was the prelude to war.

By all contemporary reckonings, Napoleon's among them, it should have been a long, indecisive, murderous struggle which would waste the German countries like the Thirty Years War. It lasted seven weeks.

Moltke wrote: 'It was a war long foreseen, superbly prepared for, and sanctioned by the Cabinet, not as a struggle for territorial aggrandizement, but to secure the establishment of Prussian hegemony in Germany.' Clausewitz' seed was bearing fruit.

Prussia acted with a decisiveness such as until then Europe had never seen. One remembers the slow development of the campaign of 1859. In fifteen days the South German armies were paralyzed by the defeat of the Hanoverians at Langensalza. Three weeks after the outbreak of war, on 3 July a decisive battle was fought near Sadowa or Königgrätz in Bohemia, at which a young Prussian Lieutenant named Hindenburg was present. Great masses of Austrian troops were pinned in the south by the Italians, whose defeats at Custozza and the naval battle of Lissa could not affect the outcome. King William and Moltke were for a continuation of the war and a march on Vienna, but Bismarck opposed them with the utmost energy. He wanted to avoid anything that could lead to a European intervention. On 23 August 1866 the Peace of Prague was signed. Italy received Venice, the Prussians Schleswig-Holstein. Austria withdrew from the German Confederacy. A North German League, having close relations with the South German states was founded; these, however, retained their 'international independence.'

The defeat of the Austrians at Sadowa was one of the most terrible defeats France ever suffered. 'France was beaten at Sadowa,' said Randon. 'What has happened is the greatest misfortune to France in four hundred years,' said Thiers. The Prussian mili-

tary system of the national army had conquered the
states which, like France, still clung to professional
armies. The new German needle-gun had conquered
the French *chassepot* rifle. German offensive tactics
had conquered the French tactic of the slow advance
and siege. As a result, Napoleon committed one diplomatic blunder after another. He strove desperately
to manage some territorial gain in order to restore
the 'disturbed balance of power in Europe.' An expansion on the Rhine? No! The annexation of Belgium? No! The purchase of Luxembourg from the
impecunious Dutch King? No!

Everywhere Bismarck's iron 'No!' barred the way.
It was no longer a Prussian 'No,' it was a German
'No.' A great power had awakened beside France and
taken the fate of Europe in its hands. The power of
the Second Empire, the health and power of resistance of its dictator was shattered.

'When the War of 1866 broke out,' wrote Moynier,
'it found the Red Cross in real chaos. No one had
expected that the Geneva Convention must receive
its baptism of fire so soon. Above all, there was the
difficulty that one of the belligerents, Austria, as well
as several of the lesser German states, were not sig-
natories and in part had been definitely hostile in
their refusal to adhere. What would be the consequences of this situation, which had not been practically foreseen? Our fears were soon laid. Prussia declared at once that she would employ the provisions
of the Geneva Convention without restriction against
all her opponents. On 23 June 1866 King William issued an order to the High Command in Bohemia,

which was to be transmitted to the Austrian commanders, that the Prussian troops would expect
mutual agreement in applying the provisions of the
Geneva Convention protecting the Austrian sanitary
officials and premises.' By this exemplary act Prussia
created a kind of legal precedent whereby other similar situations have almost always been regulated.

Here again Dunant played a decisive role as an intermediary. He requested the chairman of the French
Committee, the *duc* de Fezensac, to take steps through
the French Ambassador in Vienna, the *duc* de Gramont, with a view to bringing Austria at last to sign
the convention. At the same time he wrote to Queen
Olga of Württemberg, whose country in this conflict
was on the Austrian side. The voice of France, which
had just announced its neutrality, meant much in
Vienna. Shortly after the outbreak of the war, that is
to say, shortly after Königgrätz, Austria adhered to
the convention. The South German armies, too, on
9 July 1866 followed an order of the day of their
Commander-in-Chief, Prince Alexander of Hesse, who
commanded them to observe the Geneva Convention.

In this way the War of 1866 became the first in
which the Red Cross could unfold its full organizational strength. Its practical efficacy was demonstrated during this campaign. Thus some young Bres-
lau students, who were acting as volunteer nurses,
would co-operate with the Knights Hospitallers and
doctors of the Berlin Committee to save from certain
death 383 Austrians wounded in a clearing in the dark
forest of Horwitz, after they had lain for two days
without doctors or nourishment.

Dunant had spent almost all his time in France where he devoted himself to building the French Committee which little by little was overcoming the original opposition. MacMahon became its head. The Emperor, the Empress and the young Prince permitted their names to appear on the lists of subscribers. The propaganda was making headway in the provinces, thanks especially to the help of the Lyons advocate, Léonce de Cazenove, whose book *War and Humanitarianism in the Nineteenth Century*, which appeared in 1869, was one of the source-books of the movement.

Dunant's relations with Geneva were becoming constantly cooler. His work there was finished. What remained was in firm hands which were not at all friendly to him. The world of the Second Empire was familiar ground to him. The atmosphere of speculators and visionaries, the conservative and cosmopolitan bourgeoisie around the sick and aging Napoleon III, lured him again and again like magic. In May 1865 he was back in Algiers. He describes an invitation to the former summer residence of the Dey, which was now occupied by MacMahon as Governor-General. It was a party in honour of the Emperor who was paying his African capital a visit.

At nightfall thousands of Bengal fires illuminated the Moorish sculptures, the white marble arcades, the avenues of orange-trees, the mosaic fountains at which tame gazelles went to drink. Below in the roadstead lay English, Italian and French warships which had appeared in honour of this high visit. It was the Arabian Nights, the mirage of the 'best of all possible worlds,' the ironic-tragic looking-glass world of Voltaire.

Dunant sat among a group of English and French ladies whom the wife of the Marshal had gathered about her. In the background stood the mighty Arabian chieftains in their picturesque robes. 'I am one of your disciples, Monsieur Dunant,' said the powerful and enchanting woman, and Dunant's heart thrilled with joy.

The Emperor conversed with him at length and in detail about the progress of the Red Cross. 'He wanted to do good. Under a taciturn and unfeeling exterior he concealed a noble side, and he possessed in a high degree a sense of his responsibility. It is very sad that he was not better understood. Perhaps he might have realized a few of the reforms and peaceful social utopias of which his mind was full.'

On 23 June 1866 the Emperor issued a decree recognizing the French Committee as a publicly beneficial organization. 'It is France's misfortune that it is almost exclusively the *haut monde* that understands this great movement. The people pay no attention to it.' The people, Monsieur Dunant, who were so deliberately left out, had other worries! He would soon have a personal understanding of that.

But his prophetic glance did not yet see into the distance not even as far as the misery that was waiting just around the corner. Dunant had a new idea. In March 1866 he divulged his plan for a 'Universal and International Society for the Revival of the Orient.' Did he see so clearly in advance the evil that was brewing in aged and fanatic Europe and which would degenerate at last into an inconceivable race hatred? Once more it was a touching mixture of the apostolic spirit, the humanitarianism of the century and a sense for business speculation that made him the legitimate forerunner of Theodor Herzl and Zionism and finally led his plan astray. In the *Bibliothèque Nationale* is a single copy of his extraordinary eight-page memorandum on this project. Palestine was to be neutralized in the interests of a great colonial society. And in the following year the International Palestine Company was actually founded, with Dunant as President; it proceeded to make contracts with Jewish societies until the enterprise broke up.

Nevertheless, the Palestine project had flourished so far that by 1867 Dunant could discuss it with the Empress Eugénie in the presence of the French Ambassador to Constantinople, Monsieur Bourée. The Empress, whose beautiful face had begun to harden under her troubles, received him in the Tuilleries. The conversation was memorable because in the course of it Eugénie expressed the wish that the benefits of neutrality should be extended to wounded sailors, shipwrecked marines and the ships and persons that brought them help, through a broadening of the Geneva Convention.

The Empress was still under the impression of a dreadful episode from the war of 1866, which the Austrian Admiral Tegetthof had described to her a few days before. During the naval battle at Lissa, in the Adriatic Sea, the Italian warship *Rè d'Italia* was sunk with nearly a thousand men, without the possibility of giving them the slightest help. The Empress repeated in a horrified voice the facts that the Admiral had described to her—knots of men beside themselves with terror and despair, clinging to and smothering one another, climbing on each other's shoulders while the ship went down. Afterwards the unfortunate men swam around helplessly while the battle continued, until one after another they sank without friend or foe being able to raise a hand to save them. 'And yet they could have been saved if a rescue-ship protected with your international banner had been there!'

Dunant replied that he believed his task was ended—it was the first time he mentioned his resignation—but that the French government was in the fortunate position of being able to take the necessary steps. 'No! *You* must do it!' said the Empress, pointing to him. And Dunant declared himself ready, through the *comte* de Serurier, who was the leader of French society at that time, to make the efforts which this time, too, finally brought success.

Dunant was still considered, although his inner estrangement from his colleagues was definite, as the obvious exponent of the Geneva idea. In September 1866 he received an invitation to Berlin from Queen Augusta of Prussia, to participate in the festivities in honour of the returning troops. The streets were bedecked with fir branches. At almost all the windows and on the roofs the international flag of the wounded waved beside the Prussian flag. Even on the triumphal arches and on the public squares it was not forgotten. Prince Otto von Stolberg-Wernigerode, the chairman of the German Committee, accompanied Dunant officially. He was honoured like a king.

During the march of the troops on the *Schlossplatz*, the palace and the royal tent were decorated with the Red Cross. Dunant stood on a tribune with the Knights Hospitallers who also wore the Geneva armband.

In the evening, a huge banquet was held in the basement of the Palace. Long tables ran straight across the enormous hall, and Dunant took a place at the extreme end until he was discovered and brought to the King's table. After the banquet there was a reception in the main hall. Thick rows of generals, high government officials and nobles stood in a circle about a free space in which the royal family moved and drew first one and then another into conversation.

'I noticed at one corner of the hall, motionless and silent, the pale face of the great Minister Count Bismarck, who was wearing the uniform and helmet of the White Cuirassiers. His characteristic head and athletic form, rose above everything around him and towered over all the guests who were standing near. He did not talk to anyone.'

The King spoke to Dunant.

When you came to Berlin in 1863, I was the first prince in Europe to appreciate and encourage your work. At that time I did not think that we should need it so soon! But our enemies compelled us to start shooting. Now all the countries have agreed to the Convention. Austria was the last to join. On July 20 we made peace and on the twenty-first she signed the Covenant! That was a little late! The Austrians left us their wounded. We did everything that we could for them. They were better cared for than our own men.

Dunant was deeply touched by this noble-minded sarcasm. Everyone crowded about him, everyone wanted to see him and press his hand. It was as if the adepts at Clausewitzian inhumanity were asking absolution from the saint of Geneva humanity, as if the war against Austria had been a benefit got up in honour of the convention. The Queen, the Crown Prince, later the Emperor Frederick, the Grand-Duke of Saxony Weimar, the Duchess of Mecklenburg-Schwerin, who was the King's favourite sister, all these proud majesties and highnesses of irreproachable extraction, spoke a few friendly and honouring words to Herr Dunant.

My glances turned once more to the giant figure in the sparkling uniform who was still standing silent and motionless at the end of the hall where I had seen him when I entered. The great man considered me firmly and critically. Our glances met. Was the famous statesman seeking to guess the identity of this modest stranger who alone in this hall filled with the elect and this welter of dazzling uniforms, was dressed like a bourgeois in a simple black coat, and who was given such a reception by the mighty Hohenzollerns?

Undoubtedly the silent Bismarck at his corner of the hall knew the identity of the little Swiss civilian whom they were courting at this victory celebration as if he had won the laurels of Königgrätz. Prussia stood half way. A good army needs a good Red Cross. But he did not shake Dunant's hand.

Two days later Dunant was invited to a little repast at the palace: 'The steward in attendance struck the marble floor twice with his halberd and cried solemnly, "The King! The Queen!" Their Majesties entered. The Queen came straight up to me and showed me the arm-band with the red cross that she wore on her left arm. "See, I'm wearing your arm-band! I did not put it aside all during the war. To-day I wore it in your honour!"'

After dinner the Queen drew Dunant aside and had a long conversation with him.

> One day I found on my work-table your book, *Recollections of Solferino*. Who had loft it there I do not know, but it was probably Pourtales! I understood you at once. I was so moved that I gave it to the King to read. He returned it to me with the words, 'We must do something to make this work effective!' Afterwards, when you came to Berlin in 1863, both of us, the King and I, followed all your efforts with the liveliest interest . . . At the beginning of the war I had to supervise everything myself. The King left me behind in Berlin with the cholera. All the world was with the army. There was so much partisanship and lack of unity! I was so unhappy! But your work drew us all together. The spontaneous volunteering was wonderful. It surpassed all our expectations. I thoroughly approve of your idea that the Committee should be permanent. In peace time it should be well organized and always in readiness . . . '

The Queen told him how, at the time of the Geneva Congress, she had visited her old teacher, Soret,

there, and told him proudly how much she had admired the work from the beginning. She was an
ardent disciple of Herr Dunant. She continued, 'The
King is very international. He issued express orders
that all captured and wounded Austrians should be
well treated . . . If a war were to break out with
France, the French wounded would receive the same
treatment. You may be sure of that . . .'

The Queen rang and a splendid alabaster statue
representing the Archangel Michael was brought in.
She had had the cross, which was carved in relief on
his breast, painted red.

When Dunant returned to his hotel, the statue was
already standing on his table.

Dunant paid a visit to the dowager Queen, the wife
of Frederick William IV, at Sans Souci, and examined
Frederick the Great's famous mill. The old Queen
was an aunt of the Emperor Francis Joseph, and the
dissensions in the family had caused her much grief.
During the war she had herself taken to the station
at Potsdam in a wheel-chair in order to comfort the
wounded. Beside her easy-chair was a huge flower-
bowl with a chiselled cross, the arms of which were
filled with roses.

As we see, there was a real Dunant cult in Berlin.
At the cradle of modern war, of the national war, in
which everyone from the Queen to the poorest
mother had her part, the bloody handiwork took on
an almost patriarchic appearance. In fact, this war
was relatively mild and civilized, to a degree never
known before or after. Quick, bloody, and aggres-
sively short: that was General von Clausewitz'

recipe—and it seemed to hold good. The Archangel Michael with the red cross on his breast—it was a symbol of Prussia and its martial piety before which Europe had begun to tremble. The kind-hearted Queen was simply doing her duty when she visited the victims of the battlefield on their beds of pain.

But was that the vision which had come to Dunant from the shrieks of Solferino? Was he not thinking at that time of saving mankind from the filth and corruption of battle? Was he not thinking of some unarmed, unarmoured goodness whose very existence and sacrifice would suffice to strike the instruments of murder from the hand of the war-fury? When he saw that sentimental royal trash, the alabaster statue, standing before him, was he not seized with dread for his work which was so falsely understood? Was he helping along this frightful false doctrine that peace must be a continuation of war? Did not war in this way become the continuation of a deceitful and vicious sham-peace, and was not the result a distorted, horrible, brutalized condition, an anti-humanity of momentous dimensions?

In short, is a Red Cross thinkable that does not solemnly and publicly denounce war?

The Geneva agreement was concluded. Dunant let the victors shake his hand. Enchanted and bashful, he walked across the parquets of kings—half a miracle worker and half a recipient of favours. But his destiny was not yet ended.

XIV

A Beggar in Paris

DUNANT was forty years old. He was the 'man whom kings invited.' His reputation was world-wide. He was too old and too famous to begin again. His work was finished. Yet he was too young to live, like a coupon-clipper, on his reputation.

The year 1867 passed in an atmosphere of misfortune and operettas, of frivolity and tragic suspense. The pressure of the masses was more tangible and serious. With their consciousness of being an active element in the political struggle grew also the need to participate at least nominally in responsible political leadership. The first volume of Karl Marx' *Capital* appeared that year. In England an embittered struggle between the industrialists and the authorities over recognition of the trade unions was ruffling the Victorian calm. In Prussia universal, equal, direct and secret suffrage was introduced, and Bismarck gazed with growing concern at his new opponent—the people. In America appeared the National Labor-Union. In Lausanne the second Congress of the International Workingmen's Association was held: in Geneva a 'Peace Congress' assembled. It included an extraordinary mixture of bourgeois idealists, like the German Fanny Lewald, anarcho-socialists like the Russian aristocrat Michael Bakunin, whom an adventurous life and Siberian imprisonment had driven around the world, and the very bellicose revolutionary, Garibaldi, who would shortly afterwards attempt the forcible 'liberation' of Rome despite the French guarantee of the Papacy. In the *Journal des Débats* appeared sarcastic and indignant accounts of the unpeaceable peace meeting in Geneva.

Napoleon, sick, was drinking the waters of Vichy. The Second Empire which had begun so youthfully and violently was becoming a prematurely aged and increasingly unpopular prefectural bureaucracy. In Brussels appeared a pamphlet which in pretended conversations between Machiavelli and Montesquieu ridiculed Bonapartism: the impudent plagiarism of it in the *Protocols of the Elders of Zion* would achieve much tragic notoriety through the race insanity of the twentieth century.

Napoleon saw the necessity of undertaking something 'decisive and liberal.' 'Only it must not look as if I were begging pardon for my defeats in Mexico and Germany.' In the Tuileries, the radical Ollivier was seen mysteriously to come and go. A ministerial post was offered him. When the Emperor's solemn proclamation to Premier Rouher appeared, it was a feeble concession to freedom of the press and parliamentary formality, of which nothing now remained but a growing bitterness. In foreign affairs there was a state of latent panic. The unexpected and crushing victory of Prussia left a Gordian knot of problems. What had been decided by the sword they sought to offset with money. The House of Rothschild wanted to finance the sale of Luxembourg. But the German national soul was boiling furiously, and the South German states were one by one making alliances with North Germany. The process of German merging could not be prevented. Austria was beginning to reorganize, settling the difficult Hungarian question, seeking a halfway conciliatory solution for the awakened urge to independence of its motley populations. In Francis Joseph's dual monarchy the long last act of tragic dissolution was beginning. Italy's friendship had been definitely lost. Napoleon had no allies left.

The army had to learn from the Prussian lessons of Sadowa. A new Minister of War came in, Marshal Niel. The exemptions from military service were restricted. On the model of the Prussian *landwehr*, which the professional soldiers had regarded so scornfully, the *garde mobile* was formed. The people were unsure, and public opinion was asking critical questions of the army.

But Paris did not let the visible signs on the horizon disturb its customary gaiety. Once more on the *Champs de Mars* a world exposition displayed the thousand wonders of progress. The transatlantic cable was shortly to link the two hemispheres. The goods and gifts of the earth were taking wings. In Egypt the machines of bold Monsieur de Lesseps were shoveling away the sands of the desert at Suez. Among the cranes and the ploughs people were admiring the new, brightly-polished cannon of Frederick Krupp of Essen: they received the *Grand Prix*. The Geneva committee convened the first International Congress of First Aid Societies in Paris and these gatherings became a permanent institution.

The parade of the kings began. Napoleon sat erect on his horse between the Tsar and the King of Prussia, and held a review at Longchamps.

But the real conductor of cosmopolis was Jacques Offenbach of Cologne. The melodies of *Orpheus in Hades* and *The Duchess of Gerolstein* rose like tuneful smoke above the chimney-pots. Hortense Schneider's staccato enchanted the city, and Bismarck, the menacing, monosyllabic giant in the boxes, seemed heartily amused. Gounod's new opera *Romeo and Juliet* brought the melting warmth of the Provençal sun while under the gas candelabra of the *Alcazar*, and in the discreet houses of the side-streets, chanteuses sang with the impudent grace that thrives only in Paris.

No one noticed the unfortunate Empress Carlotta of Mexico, who went from the station to her hotel in a miserable hack. With the end of the Civil War, the United States had declared itself openly on the side of the Republicans. Washington sent an official representative to Juarez. The recognition of Maximilian was refused. France had to reckon at any moment on a European war: In 1866 Napoleon withdrew his last troops from Mexico, and thereby sealed Maximilian's fate. Carlotta returned to Europe. In St.Cloud she fainted in the Emperor's arms. In Rome she swooned at the Pope's feet. In Vienna she learned that they did not desire Maximilian's return. Her spirit grew dark before their stony stares. One day the shots of the court martial sounded in Queretaro where the lost Archduke had fled with a few loyal followers. Morny, the writer-minister, was dead. Jecker, the writer-banker, was shot a few years later during the Commune. One of the greatest of historical infamies ended without the world's taking much notice of it.

Only the preter-sensitive noses of the speculators sniffed the scent of downfall and of change in the air and they watched the fever curve of the stock exchange with a physician's care. Much money was lost there and squandered. Much money was used there for cannon and uniforms, for railroads and fortifications. A dictator on his way out is useful only to the munitions business. Grist mills in the desert were not bid.

One day, in May 1867, Dunant was bankrupt.

Toward the last, there is no denying that Dunant had fallen a victim to Sadowa, to the victory which he had helped so ardently to celebrate, a victim of the Prussian archangel with the painted red heart.

Bankruptcy belongs to the bourgeois disgraces of the first order, but like all such disgraces, it is easily pardoned if the game is played according to the rules. But for Dunant bankruptcy was the catastrophe of his life.

Dunant was no longer a banker, he was an idol of the bourgeoisie. He hardly lingered now among the living. His image stood crowned at the international exposition as a symbol of noble humanity. Who would believe that this idol of progress, whose work had just been awarded the gold medal of success, was actually running desperate about the boulevards without a franc to his name?

Dunant had possessed the confidence of so many. Had not his rise into exclusive spheres been tenderly fostered? Had not his virtues been rewarded with so much goodwill, honour and appreciation? Had they not made of his worthy bourgeois appearance an example of liberality and lack of prejudice? Had they not willingly let themselves be carried away by his pious enthusiasm? And now this man who seemed to be guaranteed as a well-situated apostle and yet could touch the heart with the manners of a gentleman—Dunant was a bankrupt, a man suspect to everyone, a man whom no self-respecting family could any longer ask to dinner.

They had never inquired into his income when he, the banker, who must know that even philanthropy has its price, gave months of his time and enormous sums of his fortune to the success of the Cause. He belonged to that proverbial circle of the Genevese Protestant plutocracy whose generosity was as famous as their prudence, whose war contracts were as important as their piety was spotless.

But while ordinary mortals have the privilege of anonymous poverty and unseen demoralization, Dunant's failure was a headlong fall of terrific momentum.

It was, according to bourgeois legal concepts, a fraudulent bankruptcy. Many of his friends were undoubtedly drawn into his affairs and suffered severely,

and the reproach was easy to raise and hard to lay
again that by all the rules of business he had dealt
fast and loose with those concerned. But was not the
Napoleonic business world, which had upheld so
many of the traditions of the *juste milieu*, a mass of
adventurous speculations, of political ambitions,
national ambitions, caste spirit and the hunt for
profits? Unbridled opportunism in politics and unbridled opportunism in business were not so easily
separated and, as usual under a dictatorship, the
adventurous spirit of the dictator was the model for
the nation. His luck failed him—and with that the
luck of his loyalest followers failed them too.

Dunant's fate lay entirely within the magnetic-
field of this larger fate. The magic power of suggestion,
which he possessed in so high a degree in dealing with
humanity, waned with the waning star of the Second
Empire. As stubbornly as he believed in the right and
the victory of his Cause, he believed in the future of
the mills of Mons-Gemila, the phantom against which
this nineteenth century Don Quixote would tilt again
and again in vain. Raising grain in Algeria was surely
no more Utopian for a banker than humanizing the
rules of war in Europe.

The tension with Geneva, which had secretly existed for so long, broke sharply now that the good
name of the organization was involved. It would
cause plenty of trouble. What worse thing could
Dunant have imagined to do to them than this failure with all the earmarks of a public scandal? For
years they had been striving to keep the Red Cross
aloof from the masses, to give the impression that

only among Genevese patriciandom, which had nothing in common with Genevese *democrapule*, could so noble an idea flourish, without corruption, without the humanitarian mouthings of the demagogues, without concessions to the electoral majority. And now one of their own number, in fact the illustrious author of it all, had committed the incredible treason of losing his money in questionable ways. That a man whom they had already made into a monument should fall beneath the blows of common fate! A reconciliation was not to be dreamed of. In the city of Calvin there is no forgiveness. To believers in the predestination of good and evil, failure could only be taken as evidence of a lack of divine grace. But as Dunant's name could scarcely be rooted out of the Red Cross, and as they clung passionately to their work, they resolved to leave Dunant the symbol alive, but to forget Dunant the living man.

This inhuman partition succeeded perfectly. Dunant was buried alive. To men like Moynier, it was a question of the Cause to which they had obligations and whose interests they must protect. There could be no doubt that further work with Dunant would jeopardize the Cause. Dunant's path and that of the Red Cross must part. When, several years later, someone inquired in Geneva for Dunant's address, he was told that they knew nothing about Dunant, that he must be dead.

Yet in the first shock of misfortune Dunant did not stand completely alone. Efforts were made to straighten out his affairs. An Alsatian industrialist, Monsieur J. J. Bourcart, began an action, and the

Emperor declared himself ready to assume half of Dunant's debts. He was the only one who felt, from some dark foreboding of common destiny perhaps, responsible for Dunant's fate.

But Dunant perceived with terror that not one heart was on his side. Until that hour his whole life had been a struggle against the angel of misery. Now he realized that in the houses of his patrons, advisers and disciples he had always been only a guest whose memory disappears like bread crumbs when the table is cleared. On his soul's wild hunt there had been no tarrying. Who had ever embraced him at parting? Who had ever asked for, granted, been grateful for happiness? When he was sealed into the dark loneliness of sleep, the angel of suffering awoke beside him, the only voice he was familiar with, and which would now be beside him for the rest of his life.

No one could help this man, who was so poor in thought, so rich in vision, whose talent for life and whose possibilities of happiness were so few, and he was incapable of letting himself be helped. With that sure intuition which far surpassed his intellectual powers, he recognized that poverty was a destiny which he must take upon him, the only future which promised peace to his unrest, the only possibility of saving the meaning of his work from destructive reality.

He was a humble sinner full of penitence and self-reproach.

If one has never tasted misery, it is hard to have any real idea of it. In such circumstances there are a thousand indescribable agonies which would be unbearable if they lasted long, especially in a state of continual disillusionment, with bleeding heart and defeated spirit, with the consciousness that one is not rightly understood, and that mistakes which were the result of a whole unfortunate chain of circumstances, as well as my bad luck and personal imprudence, are judged too harshly by others.

The world in its great generosity credited me with abilities that I did not possess. It was believed that I was clever. The exact contrary was true. I was misled by a restless imagination, a too excitable nature, and a too trusting character. I was a victim of inappropriate confidence. I meddled with things of which a poor literary man like me understands little or nothing, and I was deceived. I have had to suffer cruelly as a consequence of my simplicity, my incompetence, my inexperience and easy credulity, the more so, as through my own misfortune other persons suffered losses, others to whom I had hoped to be useful, and for whom I would gladly shed my blood to keep them from harm.

For Dunant, the banker, the son of a Genevese patrician, his apprenticeship to poverty was a hard and astounding dream, and he described it with the same naïve relentless impressionism as he did the terrible adventure of Solferino. The humiliations of this period must have been inconceivable, the stages of his Passion, which brought him from amateur diplomat to Franciscan, from capitalist to beggar.

But this *via crucis* fulfilled in Dunant a deep metaphysical need. Previously he had known the world as it looks from above looking down. Now he knew how it is distorted and debased when one is prostrate on the ground. Previously he had known the signs of helplessness and misery in others, now he knew weakness and poverty in himself, knew, too, how outside help looks, how it is taken by the victim and endured by him, and how the bacterial world of poverty and filth breeds hate, cramps the body, petrifies the mind, and yet develops the inner freedom of a man through his stubborn resistance to his abject and sordid imprisonment. Dunant saw how possession, which makes one carefree, distorts the standards of distress: only that man is able and willing to give real help who is himself in danger. If the people knew nothing of the Red Cross it was because the trumpets of the Red Cross were directed upwards and did not carry to the depths. Dunant felt the bitter and pervading suspicion of the poor toward authority with its brutal power to reach into the alien vegetating world of misery. He had stepped across the threshold which divides the groaning board from the bare boards of hunger, a fabulous world of poverty yawned before him, a world of hells and wonders.

I was myself to learn about the misery of Parisian life, descriptions of which I had read in my youth, descriptions that I regarded at the time as fancy's brain-children. I too, when overtaken by misfortune, led the most wretched life and knew all manner of deprivation. I too have belonged to those who on the streets gnaw at a roll which they have hidden in their pocket, who darken their clothes with ink and whiten their collars with chalk, and fill out a shabby formless hat with papers. The water soaks through their shoes. In the soup-kitchens where they eat they get nothing more on credit. When they come home at night the key is refused them because they cannot pay the rent. They go to bed without light, their fire gives off more smoke than heat, their stomachs ache because they have not eaten enough or because what they ate was spoiled. Still, the cruelest thing of all probably is when a very poor, but sensitive man must watch his linen go to pieces and not be able to buy more. Night after night I have had to spend under the open sky because I could not pay the rent for my room in the humblest quarter of Paris, and so did not dare to go home. There was often nothing left for me when, overcome by fatigue, I must rest somewhere, but to go to the waiting-rooms of one of the great railway stations which because of the number of night-trains are open all night.

In such circumstances, I learned really to pity the poor.

Darkly and with scorn and sadness, Dunant recalled his youth. Guided by his kindly mother, he had spent his free time reading from travel-books to the inmates of the Geneva poor-house. That had been almost thirty years ago. Thirty crowded years of bourgeois life had not sufficed to open his eyes to the knowledge that the prestige of income and investment belongs to the least pacific and most provocative elements in human society, and that the social arrogance of the propertyless classes, which had begun to flower so rankly, had better arguments on its side.

A man in Dunant's position should have killed himself: then his mistakes would gladly have been forgiven him and the legend of his life could have been saved. But Dunant was too pious and too honest to connive at such deception. He could have tried, with his tenacity and ambition, once more to climb the social ladder from which he had been so pitilessly kicked off. But then he would have become and remained a wretched renegade to poverty, that poverty which for the first time had shown him a way to silence those cries that had pursued him since Solferino. Not through escape, not through palliation, not through conventions—but through attack, through real sympathy, through rebellion. Dunant might have become one of that anonymous army of wage-earners who carve their crust of bread from the stones with a pick-axe. But he was much less than an unskilled worker. He had no patience, no persistence, no muscles, no strength for the monotony of hard day labour. But Dunant did have the vision of a just and benevolent humanity. His childhood belief that power and goodness go hand in hand was now—finally—destroyed. Slowly he began to suspect that wars and industry and hierarchies and stock exchanges and philosophic cob-webs are all the same poisonous breed whose evil network covers the earth. The helpless wounded on the battlefield were not only the victims of the lack of organized first aid, they were the tragic victims of accumulated ignorance, greed, exploitation and hysteria.

Dunant's poverty was to strip many veils from his eyes. At the very point where the hopelessly disordered account of Dunant, the banker, ended his work, Dunant, the beggar, resumed it.

Dunant without money was poorer than he could ever have dreamed. He no longer had any family to

whose patrician origins he could proudly point. There
was no list of honorary committees to play upon his
vanity. At the great boulevard restaurants and the
iron-grills of elegant mansions the invisible sign of no
admittance was hung out for him as for all other beggars. His handsome whiskers were unkempt and were
growing long and stringy. His gold watch-chain was
long since at the pawn-shop. Bit by bit the degrada-
tion of bankruptcy robbed him of the marks of bourgeois opulence. He played the sad game of trying to
conceal the signs of progressive dilapidation. He
struggled against holes, thin places and spots. More
and more his appearance took on the broad unpressed
disorder of a Bohemian idealist. Soon the well-dressed
patrician resembled a shabby democrat—a little
more and he would look like a socialist *emigré*. The
radicalizing of his clothes preceded the radicalizing of
his spirit. From the provinces where he went to lecture, complaints were received about his 'careless appearance.' They had expected an impressive dignitary and saw only a poor itinerant preacher of the
most threadbare kind.

As Dunant was thrown more and more upon himself in his shabby shell, he was appalled by his own
vacuity which until his fall, decorations and diplomas and business had so well covered up. He had read
little, had had no chance to look about him, did not
know enough. He discovered with surprise and alarm
that the world had changed a great deal since the
abolition of slavery in Algiers, and poor and denuded
as he was, he willingly let himself be enriched by the
wealth of progress. He felt the intoxication of his

century for changes, improvements, accelerations, discoveries that promised mankind happiness, peace and unity. And as he made everything that he encountered his own, and as he could think best in appeals and projects of a hazy vastness and boundless optimism, in October 1867 he founded the *International World Library*, whose program he signed in the name of an imaginary founding committee.

Our epoch has seen the birth of a new world, which is becoming greater day by day, the world of international ideas. These ideas have already resulted in the international exposition, the dredging of the Suez Canal, the relief societies for wounded soldiers, the international congresses and the seats of international culture.

The development of international culture is thus called upon to be a powerful lever of moral and material progress . . .

Therefore, it is necessary to organize and publish a complete collection of the masterpieces of the human mind which shall include everything of importance that is to be found in the greatest public libraries. It will create the necessary basis for an individual education and be a fount of culture for every family . . .

We hope to organize an international exposition of the mind by bringing before it the progressive development of civilization, by uniting the scientific and literary masterpieces of all nations and times, and bringing them together according to their natural relationships. In this way we shall supply the means for making the highest human knowledge accessible in the easiest and surest form. Whenever we show the contribution of any nation to the common labour of civilization, we destroy many prejudices, increase the sympathies between nations, and in time, create a happier more permanent reign of peace and justice among men.

This is the task which the founders of the International World Library have set themselves . . .

The idea was not bad. There was a need for the wealth of culture in a comprehensive form. There was a dim feeling of anxiety at the new and unfamiliar haste and vastness of the world. A number of such universal libraries compiled in those years, especially in Germany, have kept their reputation even to this day. Dunant, who lacked all the prerequisites for such an undertaking, would have made a very good reader for his library—as its editor he was hardly qualified.

He had no political and no intellectual concept of his own. He could not even bring himself to accept a strange one. Previously he had lived in the mistaken notion that world history was determined by the genealogies of royal houses and a few great families who ruled Europe. Human progress depended on the intellectual freedom of the individual: this truth he had recognized, but how that freedom was to be determined, guaranteed and achieved, he did not know. Banished from the bourgeois traditions of his home, he was an orphan without intellectual heritage or intellectual standards. He tossed helplessly in the wild wide currents of those years which also did not know their own goal.

XV

The Franco-Prussian War

THE last act had begun for the Second Empire: it was also the last act of the Prussian trilogy. Inexorably, as they had been planned, the differences between France and Prussia were moving toward the end. Europe held its breath, and in the stillness Prussia shone 'like a mighty iron-clad from which came no sound but the tramp of men at drill and the crash of giant cannon on their axles.'

There were negotiations between Paris and Vienna. Napoleon and Eugénie went to Salzburg. The Austrian imperial couple made a return visit to Paris. But nothing resulted save a prudent friendship and several quieting reassurances from Napoleon. 'There are dark clouds on our horizon, but I foresee a new era of greatness and well-being for our fatherland.' In Italy Garibaldi's assault on Rome had not yet broken. In Spain the army rebelled and Queen Isabella fled from San Sebastian to Biarritz where Napoleon greeted her respectfully at the station. She left behind 14,000,000 pesetas in debts.

In the harbour of Brest, one armoured cruiser followed another. From the drill-grounds came the rattle of mitrailleuses. The Bakuninist Anarchists founded the International Alliance of Social Democracy, and at the third congress of the International came to an open break with Marx. In Germany a new industrial system was introduced. At a Congress in Eisenach in 1869, The Social Democratic Labour Party was founded. Twenty-eight-year-old August Bebel and Wilhelm Liebknecht laid the ground-work for the most powerful and disciplined proletarian movement of the century, which after a generation would be destroyed by command and without a struggle. In Vienna was held the first Workers' Industrial Exposition. The machine-seed sprouted from the torn-up earth, and a new kind of war was preparing in which the stock exchanges were the general staffs, and factories the battle-grounds, and no Red Cross could reconcile the hate

Step by step the Second Empire retreated before the mounting flood of discontent. The restored freedom of the press was used for immoderate attacks. Gambetta's brutal force and Henri Rochefort's corrosive sarcasm led the chorus. *La Lanterne*, Rochefort's magazine, was read in thousands of copies and the red wrappers were like a blight over Paris. When the censor forbade the magazine after a few issues, Rochefort went to Brussels: every railroad train smuggled untold numbers of the little magazines across the frontier while Paris was eagerly waiting for them. A martyr was dug up, Boudin, who had fallen on the barricades during the *coup d'état* of 1857, and the ghost of this neglected dead man, after lying in the earth for eighteen years, awakened to haunt the sick and weary dictator, to revive the shades of the past and cry pathetically for vengeance. The prosecution of a newspaper in this connection gave Gambetta an opportunity to reveal the backgrounds of the *coup d'état* as if it had happened yesterday. Napoleon was about to summon a liberal government. Overnight his opponents painted him as the usurper he had been in his youth, and distrust of the sphinx, whose secret was now known, grew resistlessly.

Eugénie went to the Orient to open the Suez Canal. Her yacht was the first to sail through the narrow desert strait whose building the English had opposed with so much suspicion. The miracle was wrought by ten years of labour. For the first time the magic tones of *Aida*, which Verdi had composed expressly for this festive occasion, mounted to eastern skies. France had a national hero, Ferdinand de Lesseps, the Dunant of technology, the visionary of the canals. Like the visionary of the Red Cross, he was to live through his Mons-Gemila almost twenty-five years later, in 1893, in the swamp of the Panama scandal.

The fateful year of 1870 arrived. A liberal ministry under Ollivier governed France. A new constitution was prepared and by a plebiscite on 6 May, adopted by an overwhelming majority. Rochefort, the trouble-maker, was in prison. A glorious climax of domestic and foreign peace seemed to be crowning the 'Liberal Empire' of the dreamer Napoleon III. Ollivier, the confirmed exponent of peaceful evolution, was taking steps in London with a view to

European disarmament. England was pleased to play the intermediary. Lord Clarendon made a statement in which he regretted a state of affairs 'which is neither peace nor war, but which disturbs confidence to the point where people almost long for war with all its terrors in order at least to have the certainty of peace at last, a state of affairs which keeps millions of hands away from productive industry, which taxes the people heavily to their own detriment and foments discontent with their rulers.'

The fate of this plan did not differ in the slightest from that of its countless successors. The conference, whose objectives were the exchange of guarantees and a proportional limitation of forces, never got beyond the stage of Bismarck's polite evasions.

Summer came. Lord Clarendon died and Palmerston succeeded him. Lord Granville declared that at the moment no clouds were troubling the European horizon. King William was taking the cure at Ems. Napoleon was resting at St. Cloud. Bismarck was on his estate at Varzin.

Then in the portentous heat of July, which has so often brought storms of war to Europe, the news from Spain broke.

With the expulsion of Isabella, Spain, after toying briefly with the idea of a republic, had decided to establish a constitutional monarchy. Not without Bismarck's interference, the choice had fallen on Prince Leopold of Hohenzollern-Sigmaringen, a member of the Catholic branch of the house of Hohenzollern, which had annexed the Romanian throne a short time previously in the person of Prince Charles.

It must have been clear in advance that France would not tolerate a Prussian on the Spanish throne. Gramont, who had become the Foreign Minister, issued a sharp statement which Ollivier underscored: 'The government desires peace. It passionately desires peace. But it must be a peace with honour.'

Excited negotiations went on. The French Ambassador Benedetti went to the *Hôtel de Bruxelles* at Ems to negotiate with King William. On 12 July Prince Leopold withdrew his candidacy. France was elated by this diplomatic triumph. 'Sadowa is avenged,' cried Thiers. Napoleon assembled his henchmen at St. Cloud. Ollivier, the Premier, was not present. In the exuberance of triumph they decided to demand a written acknowledgment of the renunciation from King William. Benedetti delivered the demand. William politely declined to discuss the matter further. He sent his famous dispatch to Bismarck who was highly dissatisfied with the King's conciliatory attitude and threatened to resign. Bismarck edited the telegram. An admonishment to reason became an abrupt and challenging rupture of relations. That was on 13 July. Bismarck gave the new version of the telegram to the press immediately. On 14 July Paris learned the alarming news. On the evening of 15 July the Chamber decided to mobilize the *Garde*. In Berlin and Paris crowds filled the streets demanding reprisals and revenge. The war they had been talking about so long had come: a war, painstakingly prepared, light-mindedly invoked, and before it could be decided already the prelude to new wars.

The art of beginning a war in the nineteenth century was *théâtre intime* compared with the heroic opera music of our times. Unpaid debts, contested inheritances, wounded family honour formed a patriarchal backdrop of primordial feuding to the bloody scene. The shrill clash of conflicting ideologies was not yet heard. But always, in the past as in the present, the sinister drama of war psychosis is repeated, the sudden mass outbreaks of hate and desire for destruction, to which all the voices of reason blindly succumb. If nothing else were assumed or proved, this periodic intoxication of blood lust and death lust, which overtakes an otherwise kindly humanity, would confirm the pathologic origin of the mental disturbance called war. For even if it is understandable that the feeble-mindedness or self-interest of the irresponsible scoundrels, to whom humanity so blithely entrusts power, sets the nations to fighting each other, it has never been discovered by what poisonous process the harmless sheep are suddenly turned into raging hyenas. There remains nothing but the metaphysical consolation that the misused human soul, deceived in its happiness of life, seems to release its stored up despair in acts of anarchy, and that some day it will mature enough to discharge its anger against its real enemies. But we have certainly not got that far yet.

The war of 1870 may be compared with the action of a machine that with superhuman precision and care crushes mouldering stone into a thousand pieces. France's plan was based on Napoleonic wishful thinking: South German neutrality, help from Aus-

trians, Italians, Danes. When the wishful thoughts
evaporated, there was nothing left but a confused
muddle. Emotional with age, with chronic pain, with
concern for his son, the Emperor began his wanderings behind the front. Only with difficulty and great
agony was he able to keep on his horse, next he took
to a carriage, then to the miserable filth of a farm-
wagon. A staff of generals, whose names were asso-
ciated with the proud victories of the Empire, tried
to dissuade him. But he continued to follow the dic-
tatorial orders of Eugénie who was trembling in Paris
for the fate of the dynasty and the mood of the
crowds in the streets.

On 6 August MacMahon was decisively defeated in
Alsace, near Woerth, and Bazaine near Spichern, in
Lorraine. The country lay open to invasion. Paris,
which wanted news of victories and not defeats, over-
threw the cabinet of Ollivier. A seventy-five-year-old
general whose participation in the campaign in China
had earned him the curious name of Pelikao took his
place. Shadows began a shadow government of
twenty-four days. The Emperor was at Metz. With
difficulty he escaped the encirclement of the city
which cut off Bazaine's army of 200,000 men. Napoleon resigned the supreme command to MacMahon.
He was waiting at Châlons to hear if the plan of the
expert strategists to retire on Paris would be approved.
But Eugénie had decided otherwise: ' Without a victory, it is impossible! It is a dishonour!' MacMahon
followed her orders. He tried in vain to make contact
with Bazaine. The Emperor's carriage rolled along
behind. 'It is true, it looks as if I had abdicated.'

On 30 August, they were in Sedan which was held tighter and tighter in Moltke's iron grip. The next morning the battle began. By ill-luck, MacMahon was one of the first to be wounded. Napoleon mounted his horse for the last time. Planless, with rumpled white hair and bristling moustaches, and groaning with pain, he rode among the batteries. All about him the soldiers were falling across the gun-carriages. For him there was no bullet. He dragged his invulnerability around with him. The accumulated horrors took away the remnant of his strength. When two Prussian officers appeared and demanded the surrender of the town, he wrote by the last glimmer of daylight to King William: 'As it was not granted me to die at the head of my troops, there remains nothing for me but to lay my sword in Your Majesty's hands.' The Emperor of France was one of 104,000 prisoners.

Napoleon saw Bismarck in Donchéry. He saw the King of Prussia. He saw the Crown Prince. Tears ran down his sunken face which at the end of all his struggles took on the appearance of a weather-worn buffalo. Bowed by fate, humbly, honestly, blaming himself, he wrote to Eugénie:

MY DEAR EUGÉNIE,

It is impossible for me to tell you what I have suffered and what I am suffering. We marched against all principles and common sense. The catastrophe had to come. It is complete. I should rather have died than have been witness to so frightful a capitulation, but under the circumstances it was all that could prevent the slaughter of 60,000 men.

If only my torments were concentrated here at least! But I am thinking of you, of our son, of our unhappy country. May God protect it! What will happen in Paris?

I have just seen the King. He had tears in his eyes when he spoke of the grief that I must feel. He has placed one of his castles near Hesse-Cassel at my disposal. But what do I care where I go! I am desperate! Adieu, I embrace you tenderly.

NAPOLEON

Napoleon was on his way to Wilhelmshöhe when on 3 September the improbable news petrified Paris. Then the rebellion broke out for which so many fists were waiting. Still the moderate republicans had the upper hand. In the *Hôtel de Ville* a government of national defence was formed with Trochu, Jules Favre and Gambetta. While they were tearing the eagles of the Second Empire from the houses, Eugénie spent the night at the home of an American dentist who guided her safely to the coast the next day where she could board a ship for England.

Everyone had hoped and expected that, as after Königgrätz, Bismarck would take advantage of the decisive victory to end the war. But when he met Favre near Paris, on 18 September it was learned that France must sacrifice Alsace-Lorraine. Favre declared that they would not give up one foot of French soil and the lost war continued. Paris was besieged from 30 September to 28 January 1871. Gambetta escaped to the provinces in a balloon and organized an army of 600,000 men. Suddenly, capable leaders appeared, Freycinet, Faidherbe, Chanzy. But the heroic peasants and citizens of France could do nothing against a nation of trained and disciplined soldiers. There was enthusiasm, perseverance, contempt for death, but also insubordination and political disunity. Bazaine, the incurable Bonapartist, betrayed the Republic and capitulated at Metz. After the war he was tried, condemned to death, but escaped and died in Spain. Bourbaki and the aged Garibaldi's volunteers fought around Belfort, but their army of 80,000 men was forced back and half frozen laid down its arms in Switzerland. Paris began to feel the pinch of hunger. All sorties were bloodily beaten back.

On 18 January 1871 William of Prussia was crowned as German Emperor in the Hall of Mirrors at Versailles. There was a violent and truly German struggle behind the scenes as to whether William should be called the Emperor of Germany or the German Emperor. But Bismarck saw his work completed: his 'Second Reich' was founded. On 28 January there was an armistice. France elected a new Parliament which was to receive the sentence of the German peace terms in Bordeaux.

It was a barbarous peace. Alsace and Lorraine were annexed. The representatives of both provinces declared that this was done 'in disregard of all justice and by an atrocious abuse of force.' Two million pounds sterling had to be paid as war indemnity. An army of 30,000 Germans would hold a triumphal march through Paris. Victor Hugo, who left the Parliament in protest against the vote, declared: 'Henceforth two nations will inspire dread in Europe—one because it has conquered, the other because it has been conquered.'

On 1 March the treaty was signed. The Prussian parade rumbled down the *Champs Elysées* and the tormented population of Paris faced the terrors of the Commune.

The quite different effectiveness of the two armies was paralleled by the preparation and readiness for action of the two Red Cross organizations. Two figures clarify the situation: in Germany the Red Cross collected more than seventy million francs, in France only seven million were raised, and that despite the fact that the enemy was in the country. In Germany in the few years of its existence the idea of the Red Cross had taken firm hold. Its meaning was understood and widely recognized by the people. In France it was a club for outworn aristocrats; neither the army nor the people knew what to do about it. The ambivalent character of the Red Cross was clearly expressed in this decisive conflict between the old and the new militarisms. 'In 1870, the relief organizations could better than ever before oppose their weapons of mercy to the weapons of force, and wage their hard war against war.' (Moynier.) The Prussian soldiers gladly permitted this enemy in their ranks. There was too much talk about humanity at this time. No one could or even wanted to root out the pious Samaritans who went so well with the sword. The feeling of a schooled and disciplined first aid organization raised the fighting spirit. The compromise between humanity and bestiality was easily arranged, and immoral as it was, seemed suited to the barbarous-civilized transition state of the century. The face of the hero still bore a trace of noble emotion. International humanitarianism had not yet been outlawed as a defeatist, suspiciously Christian movement, an enemy of the state, as the new religions proclaim it to be to-day.

The war of 1870 wrenched Dunant out of that aching numbness of poverty and apathy which had lain on him for years. It must have hurt him to think that the French relief society which he had built up stone by stone with endless effort and devotion, should fail completely. It seemed as if they had never even heard the name of a Geneva convention. There was neither money nor materials: no arm-bands with the Red Cross were to be seen. An interpellation of Breniers in the Senate was drowned completely in the uproar of the session.

Dunant wrote to General Trochu, begging him earnestly to have the articles of the Geneva convention published in the *Moniteur Universel*, the official organ of the government. On 20 August 1870 he received a reply that there was no time at present in which to test such questions.

Dunant refused to be satisfied. On the same day, he inquired of the Empress: 'Does not Your Majesty deem it a fundamental necessity to propose to the Prussians that they neutralize a certain number of cities to which the wounded could be sent? In that way the men would be preserved from the hazards of the battle-fields while the population that received them, would share in the protection which is assured in such cases by the diplomatic Convention . . .'

It was a great and new idea which is still waiting to be realized. The Empress who from her *salon* in the Tuilleries was dictating the most important and unfortunate decisions on the front, at Metz and Châlons, replied that she did not feel competent in the question, and referred him to the Minister of the Interior whom this proposal certainly did not concern. It was never discussed. It probably did not even come to the knowledge of the Red Cross at that time. But it deserves even to-day to be put on the agenda of the next international conference. For in the wars of the year 1938, with their bestial bombing of harmless, non-combatant populations, where a Red Cross on the roof is simply a welcome target, the neutralizing of cities for the wounded would at least create a few havens of refuge the disregard of which no diplomatic pretext could excuse.

But Dunant's voice was not to be silenced. Like the fanatical Voice of One Calling in the Wilderness, he showed his true greatness in the hour of need. Everyone else had retired in anger. But a few days later, Dunant sent a second note to the Empress Regent:

Does not the French government consider that in the impending circumstances the various points which were resolved in the convention ratified by all the European powers on 22 August 1864, shall be strictly observed? The most important points are:

1. An order of the day shall be issued to the entire army (active army, National Guard, *Garde mobile*, Volunteer corps) covering the substance of the Convention so that every man under arms understands it.

2. The entire official personnel of the hospitals and ambulances of the army shall be supplied with the armbands of the Red Cross, which are recognized diplomatically (in conformity with Article 2 of the Convention).

3. Explanation to the population of France, and especially the inhabitants of Paris, of the meaning of Article 5 of the Convention which reads: 'The inhabitants of a country who administer aid to the wounded shall be free and unmolested.'

4. Since the War has necessitated the formation of new Volunteer Corps, and the hasty equipment of a part of the *Garde mobile*, whose uniforms must be either incomplete or heterogeneous, it should immediately be stated in the press and through diplomatic channels that these corps are under the Ministry of War, are official parts of the army, and are not to be considered by belligerent powers as illegally armed inhabitants.

In conclusion he repeated his demand for the neutralization of concentration points for the wounded.

The Empress did not reply and nothing happened. The disaster of Sedan came. The collapse of the Empire made even the most hardened bureaucrat tremble: at last Dunant was heard. On 11 September he was received by Jules Favre, Minister for Foreign Affairs in the Government of National Defence, who published Article 5 of the convention on the following day in the *Journal Officiel* of the Republic. A day later, Dunant was named an honorary member of the medical committee of the new government. But the honour was superfluous. Aroused from the long torpor of despair, he wanted to act and to bring order into the panic and disorganization of those evil days.

On 21 September 1870, together with *baron* Dutilh de la Tuque, he organized the 'General Association to Provide for all Citizens Under Arms.' The tasks of this organization, which were soon extended, were at first limited to a sort of information service for the men who had been called out, to supplying them with warm clothing and the most necessary materials for first aid and bandaging.

It is significant how completely Dunant's 'unofficial' work for the Red Cross was differentiated from the official efforts of the Geneva Committee. The latter developed a vast and fruitful activity. Huge sums flowed into Switzerland from all the neutral countries and were apportioned strictly on the basis of neutrality. Presently an International Agency was organized in Basel which undertook to trace and supply information concerning the wounded. Two thousand five hundred French incurables were repatriated in the course of the war. Bourbaki's 80,000 men, who were in desolate plight, were received in the most generous way in Switzerland. An International Institute in Basel provided artificial limbs and sanatoria. Lists of French and German wounded were published.

The English distinguished themselves by their prompt and generous help: they collected 7,500,000 francs, more than all France. When a call came from Pont-à-Mousson for two hundred and fifty beds, they were there in forty-eight hours. Lord Vantage himself went to the scene of operations. On 15 October he delivered half a million to beleaguered Paris, and the next day gave another half million to the King of Prussia at Versailles. The King bowed. ' You are very impartial, indeed,' he said in English. Lord Vantage wrote in his report:

> The fact that I was conducted through the lines of advanced posts by a Prussian officer, on my way to bring

help to their sick and wounded enemies in the besieged
city, could only have occurred under the protection and
in the spirit of the Geneva Convention. That I could
make a journey from Le Havre to Paris, in the course of
which I had to pass through the advance posts of both
armies, is for men like me whose experience of war ante-
dates the new order created by the Geneva Convention,
a truly amazing thing. Never did I have to wait as much
as two minutes, and the white flag with the Red Cross
was honoured by soldiers and peasants alike . . . The
leaders on both sides acknowledge that the organizations
for the sick and wounded in this war, which has already
taken at least 100,000 lives on each side, have performed
inestimable services.

In fact it was the Franco-Prussian War, if rather
preponderantly on the German side, that showed
what the Red Cross was really capable of doing. It
was one of the great surprises of this war. Dunant
mentions the testimony of a Frenchman, Hector
Malot, who writes in his *Recollections of a Wounded
Soldier*:

I personally experienced the superiority of the German
medical organization at Pont-à-Mousson. Volunteer
helpers, Knights Hospitallers, Deaconnesses and Sisters
of Charity were busy among the French and Bavarian
wounded. While on our side, thousands of obstacles were
put in the way of private activity, one being ridiculed,
another discouraged, and all given the answer that the
military authorities needed no help and were quite capable of caring for the wounded themselves, the Germans
urgently requested the organization of volunteer ambulances which followed the army and assisted the military

ambulances . . . Our military surgeons, who either did not know the Geneva Convention or disregarded it, were taken prisoner at Froeschweiler because they were not wearing the Red Cross, and the few ambulances which the French Relief Society had got together could not remove the countless victims of Gravelotte, St.Privat and Sedan.

Napoleon, who in Wilhelmshöhe was writing his pamphlet on *The Causes of the Capitulation at Sedan*, did not mention these abuses, the fruit of old Randon's refractoriness, by their right name. Dunant and his futile calls for help were fearfully justified. But even here he was disappointed and misunderstood. The Red Cross had made itself a nest in the charnel-house of war and created one place at which the heart need not stand still. But how different were its principles already from the will of its founder!

Moynier in his account of the Franco-Prussian War writes:

The Geneva Committee and its experienced agents in Basel, positively refused to render assistance to unwounded men. They abided strictly by the rule to aid only the sick and wounded. The Red Cross is the sign of the Sanitary service and may not be employed as a protective emblem by associations, which are not devoted exclusively to this branch of the administration. When the International Committee was approached with a view to its superintending the fate of the prisoners of war and the French soldiers interned in Switzerland, it declined this mission.

During his entire term of office, Moynier maintained this inexorable division between the wounded and the unwounded. No doubt he won the favour of the war ministers by so doing, but his role became that of a policeman who interferes only after the murder has occurred. By this position, the Red Cross has avoided possible conflicts, but it has sacrificed moral strength. The Red Cross, according to Moynier's interpretation, became a technical organization for cleaning up battlefields, a sort of volunteer street-cleaning department for removing the wounded. This was not in Dunant's mind when he uttered the cry of Solferino: that was a cry against war, not an appeal for the better organization of war. It is inhuman to make aid to a threatened life contingent on the random path of a bullet. Dunant meant to deal war a blow when he founded the Red Cross. War to him was a natural catastrophe, like an earthquake or a famine, and his demand for the extension of relief to mass misfortunes of that kind was consistent. The future has justified him: the campaigns, especially of the American Red Cross, against the outbreaks of natural forces are among the glorious acts of the organization. But social epidemics demand before all a social prophylaxis—the changing or removal of the conditions under which they occur. This can hardly be expected from those who call forth and defend those conditions.

In general the sanitary services of the armies now function splendidly, but this is a secondary service of the Red Cross. The volunteer international relief organization which desires to safeguard its meaning and its justification on the battlefield, must not merely remove the debris of mass murder, it must in the name of humanity prevent misfortune and wrong before they have occurred. Further, it must seek to lessen the sufferings of war in war's victims, whether it be a bullet in the belly or a case of cholera, for the distinction between military and civil will be very slight in the totalitarian wars of the future. It must be inspired by the spirit of the work as Dunant conceived it. Dunant's futile proposals were intended to confine the explosion once it had occurred, and to prevent catastrophes which could be foreseen. He thought socially and therapeutically. Geneva thought technically with a dash of piety. That success was on the side of the others was one of the evil consequences of Dunant's tragic situation. His life went to pieces completely in the great storm which swept France after the defeat.

The Third Republic began as a typical post-war republic. The Parliament at Bordeaux consisted of an overwhelming majority of monarchists. Its president, Thiers, the old Orléanist, was a republican by virtue of necessity and shrewd politics. Everyone with any money fled Paris. The German garrison had robbed the city of the remnant of its nerves. It remembered its revolutionary tradition.

Trouble began on 18 March with the removal of cannon that had been placed by the people on Montmartre during the siege. The people used force to stop Thiers' soldiers. Thiers felt himself weak. He had not more than 20,000 men at Versailles. He withdrew his troops, pending the return of 100,000 prisoners who were embarking from Hamburg. Bismarck needed a strong and capable government in France. On 26

March the Paris Commune was constituted. The city was in the hands of insurrectionists. But the Commune had a faulty and unclear political program. 'Centralization' was declared to be the arch enemy. 'Centralism is despotism.' A voluntary union of completely autonomous communes was to unite France. The Communards were virtually without a leader. One replaced the other. There was a Pole, an Italian, the American Cluseret. Delescluze was the leader of the 'Committee for Public Security.' Their hopes with respect to the provinces were not realized. Paris, the old citadel of the Fourierists and the St. Simonists, stood alone.

MacMahon, his wound healed, took command of the government troops. The attack began on 29 April. There followed a frightful fratricidal war which ended only on 28 May with the storming of the last barricade. Ten thousand had been slaughtered on both sides with the greatest bitterness and cruelty. The *Hôtel de Ville* and the Tuileries went up in flames.

On 24 May the Archbishop and a number of other prisoners of the revolution were executed in reprisal for the crimes of the government at Versailles. The only tangible result of the atrocious blood-shed was the wild determination with which Paris supported the continuance of a Republic.

Dunant was nervously active during those days of hatred and ruin. Tirelessly he sought in both camps for voices of reason that might save the city from the inevitable bloodbath which must take place in full view of the German troops.

The *Daily Telegraph* reported from Paris on 8 May 1871:

Henri Dunant, the author of the Geneva Convention and the First Aid Societies is here to try to save the women and children of Paris from the horrors of a threatened conflagration in this vast city, a conflagration which is certain to follow either bombardment by the government or the actions of the Commune, which for its defence is blowing up whole road-trains at several points.

As a Swiss subject, and in view of his universally known humanitarian work, Monsieur Dunant is in the fortunate position of being able to negotiate with all parties without causing distrust.

A personal friend of the Prince of Saxony, whose noble and humane character is well known, Dunant was able to ensure the compliance of the German authorities in Compiègne in carrying out his humane purpose. The government at Versailles assured him of its warmest co-operation and assistance in case the possibilities, which are feared, should transpire. On the other hand, he has received similar assurances from several of the influential members of the Commune. Thus prepared, Monsieur Dunant has founded a committee in Paris under the chairmanship of Firmin Marbeau, the founder of the Paris crèches, to which several foreigners of distinction also belong.

An article in the *Moniteur Universel* strikes an even more desperate note.

Unfortunately, the work of the last few weeks in Paris is a prelude to dreadful street-warfare from behind the barricades which are all too strong. Paris today is filled with picric acid, dynamite, bombs and mines. One fire must start others. The disorganized fire-fighting forces will certainly break down at the critical moment, and may God grant that no wind rises in these disastrous days. Where would the women and children flee? Paris, surrounded by the troops of Versailles and bombarded on all sides, will afford no refuges. Where can these women, these children, these innocent victims, who may be dying of hunger, where can they go? Who will take them in? Who will give them bread? Monsieur Dunant's plan must be earnestly considered!

But never yet has a well-prepared madness allowed itself to be prevented. Soon Dunant had no more time to worry about the feeding of children. He sat in the ante-rooms of the Communards, he stood in the court-yards of the prisons, trying to rescue his friends from death. Dutilhe de la Tuque, the co-leader of his relief organization, was already condemned, but Dunant was able to snatch him from the court martial. For the Archbishop, Monseigneur Darboy, for his old friend, Abbé Deguerry, the priest of the Madeleine, he could do nothing though he begged all the powerful persons in the Commune, one after another for their lives—Vermorel, old Delescluze, the painter Courbet, who was described to him as approachable.

At last one night they stood the Abbé against a wall: two salvoes rang out. He sank down wounded, but still alive. More shots were fired. One bullet shattered his left wrist, others pierced his breast and his skull. The same night about three o'clock (it was the night of the twenty-fourth or the morning of the twenty-fifth of May) the murderers of this noble martyr carried his body to the cemetery of Père Lachaise and threw it into an open grave filled with liquid mud.

While he was waiting at the *Hôtel de Ville* for Vermorel, a writer who had earlier supported the Red
Cross and was now a member of the Commune, and
who fell a few days later fighting bravely on the barricades, Dunant witnessed the disorder which so regu-
larly brings the scum to the top in the opening phase
of every revolution, until the old chairs are moved
back into place again with the new masters in them.

> There was a mob of petitioners of every kind, National
> Guards, women with little children, crazy people and all
> kinds of hungry sufferers, all mingling in a motley crowd,
> though without making very much noise, in that vast
> hall under the gilded panelling, or sprawling in the bro-
> caded easy-chairs; eating, smoking, snoring, or just sit-
> ting quietly, playing cards and swearing in low voices,
> cursing, scolding, and even drinking. But how much real
> misery there was, and how much grief! . . .
>
> But all my efforts were in vain. I even ran the risk of
> being arrested by a tipsy and over-zealous Guard. As I
> was observed under these circumstances in the *Hôtel de
> Ville* by the plain-clothes detectives of the opposing
> party, spies of the lowest kind who knew neither my
> name, my position, nor the humanitarian motives for my
> being there, these agents later denounced me without my
> knowledge as an anarchist, nihilist and a communist,
> 'one of the leaders of the *International*!'

It was crazy enough to have happened yesterday!
At the beginning of the war, when the Red Cross first
emerged publicly from its distinguished seclusion, the
populace used to call it 'the international.' This fateful similarity of names caused the peaceful Red Cross
to be confused with the revolutionary association of

Karl Marx and Bakunin. With the defeat of the
Commune the historic moment arrived when the
word 'international' was first used as an epithet,
something akin to high treason. Membership in the
International was declared to be a crime against the
state by Thiers, and the criminal was under police
surveillance for life. And as reaction is always even
more stupid and blind than revolution, Dunant was
considered a traitor, and narrowly missed the fate of
the many martyrs who in such periods of infamous
bloodlust are commonly shot 'by mistake.'

> For years I have had to suffer all too much from such
> fateful confusions and errors which became the source
> of injustice, false condemnation and secret annoyance,
> when I was sadly roaming about abroad, in misery and
> trouble, no longer able to speak of the happy days of a
> time long past, melancholy and lonely, reflecting in the
> midst of my restless and thankless labour, on the words
> of Dante: '*Nessun maggior dolore che ricordasi del tempo
> felice nella miseria.*'

The adventure of 1870 and 1871 was the turning-
point in Dunant's life. As a banker and patrician, he
had fared forth to do business in millions, and returned with the unbearable burden of Solferino. As
the merchant of humanity with growing credits, but
also growing debits, he had been crowned and honoured, hated and suspected, bankrupt and impover-
ished. Unbowed and unterrified he laboured on. His
reward had been the threat of death and total de-
classment. At last, Dunant began to be ashamed of
his suffering and to develop that timidity in the
presence of people, which had always been uncon-

sciously latent in him, and which now threw up a great wall between him and the world.

He was certainly anything but an exponent of the theory of class struggle. Now that peace was restored, his whole effort was directed to make the individual work of the Red Cross part of a great and comprehensive political and social movement for peace. His horizon was broader but not clearer. He misunderstood, or he overlooked and did not understand at all, the deep and elementary changes which underlay the mounting social conflicts. In his indescribable credulity, he did not know that in the struggle for economic power, in the struggle over wages, foes far more morose and brutal confronted each other than in the struggle for political power. The savage aggressiveness of the class struggle, which as an idea was so close, but in practice so far from him, appalled him. He still believed, and he would never give up this belief, that human affairs can be regulated by understanding and goodwill. His own experiences proved the contrary. But his optimism appeared to be incurable. Again and again, he was drawn to those cultured bourgeois circles whom reform and progress delighted and who believed—or pretended to—that man is a civilized creature. The pause from exhaustion after such a dreadful bloodletting as war is favourable to such opinions, and the watchword, 'Never again!' was willingly believed. So he swam for a few years longer in the broad shoreless stream of plans for human happiness, which in every system of paranoiac delusion seem flawless and perfect up to the point of the unknown X. For Dunant this unknown X was still—mankind.

XVI

Flight into Oblivion

THE war was over. Surprisingly enough, it left behind no wreckage. For victor and vanquished, the wars of the nineteenth century had an almost constructive character. They led to the building of railroads, to technical organization and to 'reconstruction' on broader and better bases. Faults in planning and production were diagnosed. Inner political cleansings were effected, political powers concentrated, social conflicts better recognized and understood. But all this, in the last analysis, was subservient to the main object—to be better prepared for the next war. It was a vicious circle that began with destruction, and with the tools of progress forged new weapons for further destruction.

In France, Thiers was guiding a republican regime that was monarchist and clerical at heart. Merciless toward the left, and unyielding toward the conservatives, he performed the miracle of reconsolidating France in a surprisingly short time. The enormous war indemnity to Germany was paid apparently without difficulties. The German garrisons had to leave the country.

But the reactionary chamber was waiting impatiently for the return to a monarchy, and as there was no sign of this, Thiers was overthrown, and Mac-Mahon, the conqueror of the Commune, became President. It is one of the rare instances in which a nation has turned over the power to the commander who lost the war.

But MacMahon was no conqueror this time. He came to restore the monarchy and he founded the Republic. There were too many candidates for the throne of France. Napoleon was again busying himself with day-dreams of a *coup d'état*, until his physician declared an operation necessary, from which he died on January 1873 in his English exile at Chislehurst. The Prince Imperial met his adventurous death in 1879 as an English officer in the war against the Zulus. The *comte* de Paris was the candidate of the Orléanists. But the *comte* de Chambord, who was living in quiet seclusion near Vienna, was the legitimate successor of the Bourbons, but he refused to recognize the tricolor which had waved beside the guillotine of Louis XVI. The embarrassment was great. The bye-elections for Parliament strengthened the republican minority and, on 30 January 1875, by a majority of one, a law governing the election of presidents was passed which put the Republic on a firm foundation.

Thus as a result of this chance vote—Wallon was the name of the man who proposed the law—the strongest and securest democracy of the Old World arose.

In other countries, too, the war had its consequences: Italy finally captured Rome, and Russia took advantage of the disturbance in Europe once more to open up the Black Sea which had been sealed since the Crimean War.

But naturally the greatest developments were in Germany. Its militarized citizens and officials with intense industry and great ability, with the French millions and a specific kind of delusion of grandeur, were creating a world power that the British Empire, which through the long Victorian peace had been almost invincible, was soon to feel.

The motor of the new German Reich, that ate up the oil of indemnity so ravenously, was the Berlin Bourse, which was more and more becoming the central point of the European credit system. Capital, which had fled abroad during war times came penitently home. The German states quickly repaid their war loans and 800 million homeless marks threw themselves into stocks. The Reich, seeking safe investments for its surplus, took part in the race. As the good paper was soon sold out, new had to be whistled up: the 'founding fever' began. The capital became the centre for a kind of California gold craze that attracted packs of dark and criminal financial jackals, and severely taxed the consciences of 'honest' business men. In the 'founding' period between 1871 and 1873, 985 German stock companies were founded with a capital of 3,600,000,000 marks. The compulsory licensing of stock companies was set aside. Compulsory filing of prospectus with fixed liabilities was not introduced until 1896. Utopian companies sprouted up whose prospects were inflated fantastically by a paid press. A board of directors of excellencies and privy councillors could always be got together. When the price of stocks had been driven up to dizzying heights, the founders sold and the air-castle collapsed.

The spectacle of this new wealth on the solid Berlin pavement was hardly edifying. Speculation and Prussianism are an almost incredible mixture, but nobility, industry, and middle class yielded to the allurements of the boom with Prussian precision. Only a section of the intelligentsia, who as officials, teachers and officers, were traditionally the inviolable source of Prussia's strength, held aloof from the new trend with loathing and contempt. Treitschke wrote that it seemed as if the bounds of human stupidity had been immeasurably widened.

The big-scale profiteer established himself in Germany, and this fungus was never again uprooted. For the first time, he gathered all the fateful breed of horizontal and vertical trusts into the hands of a single selfish speculator, that tragic forerunner of state capitalism, whose genius was an unconscionable greed for profits. At first people were proud of such types, then they cursed them, from Strousberg, who precipitated the great depression of the eighteen eighties, to Stinnes who ruined the Weimar Republic.

Strousberg's real name was Straussberg and he came from the East. In London he got himself baptized and made his first fortune as a journalist. The *London Magazine* belonged to him. In 1855 he went to Germany and began to build railroads, first for English firms and then independently. The state gave private initiative a free hand. Strousberg's rails ran right across Germany. Presently he bought the largest German locomotive works, near Hanover, acquired coal mines and iron foundries, had an enormous estate in Bohemia. Dukes and counts were happy to sell their names to him. He paid his contractors in the shares of his railroads. As the contractors needed money, the market was flooded with Strousberg shares. In 1875, Strousberg failed in Germany, Austria and Poland. In Moscow he was arrested and spent a few years of exile in Siberia. In 1885 he died, poor and outlawed, in Berlin.

The effect of Strousberg's collapse was terrific: it was a kind of German Sedan. A world of illusions went to pieces. People recognized the irrational and fabulous power of capital, against which they felt more defenceless than against French cannon. Strousberg was the 'Devil, the Jew.' A wave of excessive anti-Semitism swept the country.

The economic depression which followed and which dragged along far into the eighteen eighties struck other countries as well. Even if other reasons played their part abroad, the psychological consistency is the same. In the United States there were serious financial disasters, the failure of the Ohio Life Insurance Company and of the powerful banking house of Jay Cooke and Company. In England, the failure of the City of Glasgow bank in 1878 brought on a long crisis. It was a universal early panic of high capitalism, a blight which it overcame and continued its dazzling development more resistlessly than ever.

While money was still flowing, the arts of humani-

tarianism flowered. It is one of the tragic peculiarities
of private philanthropy that it can be most magnanimous when it is least needed: the socialization of welfare and social insurance belong among the great
ideas of the twentieth century.

In the hectic post-war convalescence, the great
optimist Dunant was once more to do good. He was
active in several directions. The Welfare Society of
the war period transformed itself with peace, but did
not give up its activity.

If, according to the new militarist doctrines, the
war spirit must be prepared in times of peace, the
spirit of peace must also arm against the coming of
war. This was already a very dangerous, almost pacifist idea. Dunant's plan of social pedagogy proposed

> to raise the moral and intellectual level of the citizen in
> military service, to develop in him the desire for educa-
> tion, for useful occupations and even for the arts; to cre-
> ate the means for his further training in his earlier call-
> ing or his primitive manual dexterity; to form libraries
> and temperance societies; to organize welfare work in the
> jails and military prisons where none exists; to instruct
> the young citizen who is called to the colours, to moralize
> and humanize him; to awaken and develop in him ev-
> erything that can favourably influence his character—
> that is the goal we hope to attain. It is a new form of
> protest against national hatreds, a greater and nobler
> patriotism, whose function it is to develop the whole na-
> tion for those great efforts which kill egoism, ignorance
> and prejudice.

A great and touching plan, this Utopia of a democratic national army, this training of the storm troops

of decency and peace. A plan for future centuries—
but Dunant in his rashness did not shrink from ven-
turing its immediate realization. A 'Universal Alliance for Order and Civilization' foregathered and on
3 June 1872 began its deliberations. The old guard of
humanitarianism were together again: Frédéric
Passy, Firmin Marbeau, Ferdinand de Lesseps, the
Archbishop Dupanloup, and old General de Beaufort,
upon whose advice Dunant had once made a trip to
Solferino.

They wished 'to advance by every possible means
the regular progress of civilization, and to exert themselves for the maintenance of political and social peace.'
It was one of the few bourgeois attempts to create a
front of social responsibility outside the socialist
movement. On 8 April 1872 *The Times* reported:

> One of the most interesting societies on the European
> Continent is the *Alliance universelle de l'Ordre et de la
> Civilisation*. According to their program, they represent
> the legitimate interests of the family, of labour, of pri-
> vate property and of the progress of civilization. It is
> their object to prevent all violent social disturbances by
> a decorous and moral solution of the social questions.
> One of the topics of their first congress is a historical
> investigation of courts of arbitration for disputes be-
> tween nations.

The fate of prisoners of war and the problem of
arbitration, these were the two tasks which they
placed in the foreground.

On 16 April 1871 Marbeau discussed the plan, which
Dunant had suggested, in the *Moniteur Universel*:

The most important improvement we are studying is the introduction of a great international court to which could be referred all disputes that are serious enough to involve the threat of war. It is to the interest of all nations, great or small, to prevent these dreadful slaughters at all costs. It is within their power: they have only to wish it. Such a court, in which all nations would be represented by delegates according to their population, would in no wise limit national independence, it would in fact for the first time fully guarantee it. No disadvantages are conceivable, only powerful advantages would result for the well-being and strength of every state in this league, while the brotherhood of nations would become a fact, to the good fortune of all. Every nation would be secure in working for itself and would thereby increase the general well-being of the great human family.

To-day the Peace Palace stands in The Hague, and stands, for the most part, empty. The Court of Arbitration, gathered from among the most distinguished jurists in the world, ponders insignificant questions. To-day the League of Nations Palace stands in Geneva, and the prevention of war is one of its duties. It is unfit to perform that duty.

Toward the end of 1872, Dunant was in England. On 6 August he spoke before the National Association for the Promotion of Social Science, and before the Social Science Congress in Plymouth, on the court of arbitration and the proposed convention in the interest of prisoners of war.

Dunant's ideas could not be simpler or clearer:

A plan will be worked out for a diplomatic convention which should be as short as possible. As a basis, a convention will be used that was signed between England and France during the Crimean War with respect to Russian prisoners. This plan would obligate all the civilized nations to treat captive officers and soldiers according to agreed rules. It would place them under the high protection of the diplomatic corps in every belligerent country.

To-day the Red Cross has been in existence for seventy-five years, and in the cities of Spain, and before the gates of Nanking, thousands of defenceless prisoners are slaughtered.

Dunant had a complete success in England. The press wrote enthusiastic accounts of him and of his work: *The Times* on 18 June; the *Morning Post* on 19 September; the *Army and Navy Gazette* on 10 August. Florence Nightingale wrote him on 4 September: ' Allow me to congratulate you on the success of your noble work, a work that has truly been done in the spirit of God and of God's civilization.' A Permanent Committee was formed with *comte* d'Houdelot as chairman, and under the patronage of the Tsar there was a conference, without results, in Brussels in 1874. The delegates pored over a document of 148 articles and could not agree.

In the summer of 1875 Dunant's voice was again heard. He composed a 'memorandum on the present state of treatment of the Negro,' the old theme of his youth, which in March came before the International Committee against Slavery. On the occasion of severe floods in the French Midi which brought forth a movement of solidarity from all over Europe, he broached his long cherished plan for a Red Cross of

Peace, which could be invoked in every emergency to protect mankind against the seven plagues.

The famous English physicist Tyndall mentioned his name once again in the same year at a meeting of the British Association, where he delivered a lecture on 'Heat'—'Henri Dunant—a name dear to all the friends of humanity.'

Then for fifteen years there is a gap on the chart of his life. At forty-seven, when most men expect to reap the fruits of life, Dunant disappeared in a dark and mysterious errancy through the primeval jungles of misery and solitude. When he was found again, he was an old man of sixty-two.

All the great, the simple and righteous plans which no reasonable man, had the decision been left to him, would have rejected, trailed off into nothingness or less than nothingness—into a false and apathetic reality.

1875 was the year when life went out of profiteering and speculation for a while. Not many of Dunant's friends could bear to be poor and not worry about themselves. Only aristocrats make proud beggars. The bourgeois pities himself.

When the money went, so did goodwill. Dunant was now utterly forsaken. The progress of the century did not halt, but a harder tone crowded out the mild enthusiasm of such appeals as Dunant's, whose confidence and ingenuousness have an almost painful sound to our ears to-day.

A scepticism arose that thought everything was possible. The mania for physical explanations darkened the soul. Figures were the new gods and the old God was a myth.

When Dunant returned to this world from a word-less, deedless darkness that must have been worse than death, he had a long white beard and was sitting in the bare room of a poor-house, mild and wrathful as the legendary God the Father.

XVII

America Joins

A PEACE ensued in Europe which, if we disregard the events in the Balkans, was to last for forty-three years. It was a peculiar kind of prior 'peace of the nations' which, at least in retrospect, reveals every sign of instability. But it was more than an armistice. The European balance of power seemed to function, though it was the balance of a break-neck acrobat whose fall we momentarily expect with beating hearts. The ease and quickness of communications led of necessity to a new fullness of international relations which were not exclusively dedicated to mutual hate. Capitalism sought and found its markets without undue tenderness for national sensitivities. The working conditions of the people were everywhere much the same, for machines will work for any master in any environment at the same speed. The international organization of the workers made irresistible progress. The partition of Africa and the general plunder of colonies created a certain solidarity of European interests, while the preoccupation abroad deflected attention from inner-European conflicts.

But this flourishing of the olive branch could serve to reassure only the peace societies, which had also begun to open their petals again. Actually what was going on was the envenomed friendship of rivals with the same goal, each of whom dreams of outstripping the other and taking the goal for himself. Hence the talk was all about disarmament and courts of arbitration—and there was a lot of talk about them—and a complete agreement as to their uses, but also a complete refusal to use them. The doctrine of national honour precluded any possibility of employing the international moral concepts that were pumped into every school-boy. The army budgets were consistently bullish, while the munitions industry created the Iron International, the only one that has never broken down. The world was endowed with splendid new methods of murder accompanied by insane 'instructions-before-using' known as 'an armed peace is the safest peace.'

Then bloody clashes in the East led to differences between Russia and Turkey, to the creation of a Europeanized Balkans, and finally to the great systems of alliances—France and Russia, on one hand, and on the other, the Triple Alliance, Germany, Austria and Italy. The World War of 1914 was brewed in that dangerous corner of Europe.

Russia freed herself in 1871, as we have said, from the chains of the lost Crimean War. Since the Pan-Slavic Convention in St.Petersburg in 1867, Russia was more and more frankly playing the role of guardian over the allied Slavic peoples of the Balkan Peninsula, which she wished to unite under her

leadership. A further step was the setting up of a
Bulgarian Exarch, as the Slavic head of the Church,
independent of the Greek Patriarch in Constantinople. This led to violent strife between them, but
Slavic nationalism was awakened. There were uprisings against the Turks which were suppressed with a
cruelty that left Europe aghast. In the summer of
1876 war broke out between Serbia and Montenegro
on one side, and Turkey. Romania and Russia joined
in. The campaign ended with the taking of Adrian-
ople in January 1878. All Armenia was in the hands of
the Russians. Abdul Hamid, who only a few months
before had taken over a sultanate that was to be filled
with deeds of blood and blows of fate, had to sue for
peace. On 3 March 1878 it was concluded in San
Stefano.

The Russian victory was a severe blow to the Eastern policies of Turkophile Disraeli which had em-
broiled him with Gladstone. The Peace of San Stefano, by means of which Alexander had created a
Greater Bulgaria stretching from the coasts of Greece
to present-day Serbian Macedonia, seemed intolerable to England. A secret agreement against Russia
was concluded between Lord Salisbury and Abdul
Hamid. Bismarck fished in these troubled waters and
demanded a congress in Berlin, which met in July.

The congress became a brilliant diplomatic duel
between Disraeli and Bismarck. The map of the Balkans was cut up like a jig-saw puzzle, and before
Russia knew what was happening, she had been
stripped of every political advantage of her victory.
Bosnia and Hercegovina fell to Austria. Serbia came

into the sphere of influence of the Dual Monarchy. This was according to Bismarck's plans. Greater Bulgaria shrunk to a third of its extent. Russia made a slight territorial gain in Bessarabia at Romania's expense. Turkey retained its Asiatic possessions upon promise of humane treatment for its Christians, which was followed by decades of martyrdom and the brutal uprooting of the Armenian people.

The congress was a masterpiece of the political black arts. Disraeli was made a lord and Bismarck was satisfied. But the whole plan bore the stamp of that political astuteness which is pure and simple stupidity because the earth is peopled with human beings and not chess-men. The oppression of Macedonia was the prelude to a long period of suffering, terror and force. Austria's gains proved a fatal snare. The injury to Serbia left an open wound. Bulgaria had no intention of becoming a Russian province. A brief regime under the Tsar's nephew, Alexander of Battenburg, ended in 1886 with his forced abdication, and he was succeeded by Prince Ferdinand of Saxe-Coburg, who pursued a definitely anti-Russian policy. The friendship between Germany and Russia on which Bismarck had built the greatest successes of his life was hopelessly broken. The Balkans struggled in a web of dissension and conspiracy until the shot at Sarajevo, thirty-five years later, set the whole world in flames.

For the Red Cross this Balkan War, which was waged with Asiatic savagery, brought an abundance of difficulty. The situation resembled the years 1870 and 1871. While the Russians made an effort to fulfil the obligations of the Geneva convention, in Turkey at the outbreak of the war they were no more than an abstract idea. The Turkish Army refused on religious grounds to bear the symbol of the Cross, and finally an agreement was reached legalizing the Red Crescent as the sign of the Geneva organization. As a result there were constant confusions with the almost identical national flag.

It was almost a rule that a country had first to feel the bloody pressure of events before it took the Red Cross seriously. This was the case with Austria in 1866, with France in 1870, with Turkey and Serbia in 1876. When from 1879 to 1881, war broke out between Bolivia, Chile and Peru with an exotic violence, these states and the Argentine also joined the convention. San Salvador had been the first Latin American country to sign the agreement—in 1874.

The list of countries which adhered to the Geneva Convention was now more than thirty, but the United States was still missing. It would require a hard fight to overcome the opposition and indifference of people who were far more interested in the battles which young Rockefeller was waging for the Standard Oil Company than in the victims of future and imaginary wars.

But here too there was to be an individual who struggled for the forlorn and hopeless cause—Clara Barton. She embodied a peculiar type of American Victorianism. She was hard, aggressive and ready for battle, but more humorous, quicker at repartee, more emancipated and also more sentimental than her English sisters. With her big strong mouth, her prominent pointed nose, her frank and enthusiastic eyes, her abundant hair drawn tightly back from her high forehead, she combined the qualities of a lady and a pioneer woman.

After the hardships of the Civil War she suffered from nervous disorders and speech-impediments. In an effort to restore her health she went to Europe in 1869 and fate took her to Geneva. For the first time she heard of the existence of the Red Cross. She was unable to answer the question why the American government was so passive with respect to this humanitarian work. Dr. H. W. Bellows, the leader of the Sanitary Commission, who had just returned from attending the second International Conference in Paris, tried in vain to interest Washington in the Geneva Convention.

When the Franco-Prussian war broke out, Clara Barton was lying ill in Berne. There she received a visit from the Grand-Duchess of Baden, the only daughter of King William of Prussia, and one of the most zealous supporters of international relief work. A sincere friendship developed between the two women, and presently Miss Barton threw off her covers to hasten where she was needed.

At Sedan she cared for the wounded; she entered Strasbourg with the German troops, and organized sewing circles of unemployed women who for fixed wages produced 1,500 garments a week. It was one of the first examples of productive relief for the unemployed and it succeeded beyond all expectations: for eight months the needy helped the needy. During the terrible days of the Commune she was in Paris, toward the end of 1871, back in northern France.

When I saw the work of the Red Cross in the field, when I saw how, through systematic organization, it accomplished in four months what without its help we were unable to accomplish in four years—no mistakes, no needless suffering, no waste, no confusion, but order, abundance, cleanliness and comfort wherever the little flag made its way—a whole Continent organizing itself under the Red Cross—when I saw all this, took part in it, cooperated with it, I said to myself: 'If ever I return to my country alive, I shall strive to make my people understand the Red Cross and this Convention.'

Clara Barton kept her promise. After a long winter of severe illness, which she spent in London, she sailed in 1873 for America. For almost four years she lived, unable to work, at a sanatorium in Dansville, New York. When the Balkan War broke out, she again took up the fight, which Dr. Bellows, after struggling in vain with two administrations had given up as 'hopeless.' With a letter from Moynier to President Hayes she made a trip to Washington. She spoke to influential members of Congress and of the War Department. She was received by the President and the Secretary of State, Hamilton Fish. But again and again they insisted on the danger of entangling alliances. Nothing happened.

President Garfield took office. Clara Barton sat with Moynier's letter in his ante-room. This time she had better luck. The Secretary of State said that 'the Monroe Doctrine was not promulgated for protection against humanity.' But in 1881 Garfield was assassinated.

Clara Barton decided that the fate of the Red Cross

could no longer be made dependent on changes of government. Shortly before Garfield's death, she founded, in Washington, The American Association of the Red Cross, and in August 1881, at her sanatorium at Dansville, the first Red Cross Society in the United States. Soon after, tremendous forest fires broke out in Michigan. The little community of Dansville went to work actively with money and relief, giving the first practical demonstration of the need for a relief society.

Arthur was now President and again Clara Barton was sitting in his ante-room. She had an appeal to the President, the Congress and the people of the United States which closed with the words:

> It is my highest and greatest endeavour to wipe from the name of my country the stain of a disgraceful lack of human feeling, and to cleanse it from the reproach of barbarism. I have said that by 1869 twenty-two nations had adhered to the agreement. Now there are thirty-one. For since that time, Romania, Persia, San Salvador, Serbia, Bolivia, Chile, Argentina and Peru have come over. If the United States is fortunate and diligent enough, perhaps it will make the thirty-second on the list of humanity and civilization. If not, it will remain where it is, among the barbarians and heathen.

This was such language as no woman before had dared use in public. The ladies of the land were shocked. But Clara Barton did not worry about that. She wrote to Frances Willard:

> It is hard and difficult and bitter. The bullets of ill-will and slander are falling thick. But I have to stick by the helm and bring my ship into port. The Geneva Conven-

tion must be assured. I have only one way to carry it through. It is beset on both sides by cannons manned by the society ladies of the Capital and the nation. The Red Cross, a little, foreign ship from abroad, with the banner of peace and love and its message of world-embracing mercy, is seeking refuge and shelter in our broad havens and has chosen me as pilot. It runs upon the chains that have shut it out so long—special loopholes of the government, like 'non-intervention,' 'isolation,' safeguarding against 'entangling alliances,' 'Washington's Farewell Address,' 'Monroe Doctrine,' apathy, indolence, universal ignorance, national darkness, national distrust, the wish to maintain the barbarous old privileges of privateering and piracy, which we have defended as a precious good against every humane treaty since we began . . . Never has a message of mercy been received in a more unfriendly fashion, but the poor pilot has faith in his ship and in God, and the day is not distant when in spite of everything we shall sink our firm iron anchor in these coasts and hoist a little streamer to the mast-head: 'Agreement Signed.'

It speaks well for the nation that it not only tolerated this lady's furious activities, but even let itself be convinced by her. Clara Barton did much to assure for the American woman that conspicuous public influence, especially in cultural and political matters, which she enjoys to-day. From the Franco-Prussian battlefields she wrote home in 1870:

Woman ought to be able to raise her voice in matters of war, either for or against, and the fact that she is not allowed to is no justification for robbing her of other privileges. She cannot prevent war, and when war comes she cannot take part in any way. And because she cannot take part in war, she cannot have the ballot. And because she cannot vote, she has no representation in the government, she is not a citizen. And because she is not a citizen, she has no rights. Because she has no rights, she has to submit to injustice. And because she submits to injustice she is nothing.

Clara Barton rebelled. She was one of the first suffragettes. The blood of the Pioneers flowed in her veins. Her own civil war against the United States ended in victory for her. On 16 March 1882 Congress voted unanimously for ratification of the Geneva Convention, which President Arthur had signed on 1 March. America was the thirty-second country on the list at Geneva.

The American Red Cross became the most powerful, most influential and most active organization within the national relief associations. From the beginning, it rendered aid in every kind of catastrophe within its scope. It did not restrict itself to war. Thanks to its influence, the 'American amendment' was adopted, which realized Dunant's old plan for a 'Red Cross of Peace.'

For twenty-two years, from 1882 until 1904, Clara Barton acted as President of the American group. She was sixty-one years old when she undertook it, but her strength seemed inexhaustible.

In 1884 her relief boat, Joshua V. Troop, steamed under the Red Cross flag as an angel of salvation in the raging floods of the Ohio and Mississippi. In 1885 in the famine district of Texas she organized the same kind of self-help she had organized in the Franco-Prussian War. In 1888 she appeared with her helpers in Florida to fight against yellow fever. In 1889 she was at the Johnstown flood. In 1893 she was on the sea islands of South Carolina where a hurricane had done terrific damage. The grateful negroes named their girls 'Clara Barton' and their boys 'Red Cross.' In 1891 she sent a relief expedition during the famine in Russia. In 1895 she was in Turkey, bringing aid to the survivors of an appalling Armenian massacre. In April 1898 the Spanish-American War broke out, which would bring the United States control of the Philippines and Puerto Rico and a mandate over Cuba: she took care of the wounded after the blowing up of the Maine in Havana harbour. At the head of the American fleet, her relief boat with the Red Cross Flag at the mast was the first to enter the harbour of Santiago. Her prophecy was fulfilled: she was a good pilot of mercy. In 1900 she was on hand after the tornado at Galveston. Her name and her mission of mercy were bound up with every misfortune that swept the earth during those years. When in 1902, at the International Conference of the Red Cross, she stooped to give the prescribed kiss to the hand of Tsarist Majesty, he checked her: 'Not you, Miss Barton!' She was eighty years old.

She was, as her biographer, William E. Barton, wrote, 'normally susceptible to praise and abnormally sensitive to criticism.' Her dictatorship must often have been difficult for her co-workers. When she returned from Russia in 1902, and discovered that in her absence nothing had been done for the victims of Mont Pelée, she pressed for a further increase of her powers. There was a palace revolution. They charged her with the reckless and uncontrolled use of funds. The Congress instituted an investigation. The result was nothing but a boundless embitterment for the aged woman. They offered her the post of paid Honorary President. She refused. Since that time the President of the United States has been President of the Red Cross.

The dethronement of Clara Barton may have been a necessary step. If any organization needs the help of youth, it is the Red Cross. Whether it was necessary to make a second Dunant case of it, is another matter. During that century a career in philanthropy, like diplomatic careers, was open only to rather wealthy people. Clara Barton left this world poorer than she entered it. She did not forsake her work. From 1905 until 1912, she was President of the American National Society for First Aid. At the age of eighty-nine she learned to typewrite. But her last years were not happy: 'If only someone could show me a way to get out of America. Cannot you inquire of the Mexican authorities, if a woman who can no longer live in her own country can find a home or at least a resting place there!' She thought of emigrating to China.

When she died on 12 April 1912, at the age of ninety-one, shortly after Dunant's death and shortly before the vast death of 1914, her last words were: 'Let me go! Let me go!'

She belonged among the great veterans of humanity who were spared the holocaust of the World War. But her work stands. In 1918 the American Red Cross had a membership of nearly thirty millions.

XVIII

The Peace Movement

ONE can easily compare the long pause from 1875 to
1890, until we find Dunant again, with that acute
phase of heightened activity and euphoria which appears in the initial stage of paralysis, and which is
never free from symptoms of delusions of grandeur
and an over-estimation of strength. The insanity in
the European situation appears above all in the quest
for involved secret alliances and criss-cross treaties,
whereby one partner endeavoured to hoodwink and
deceive the other, and which by degrees became such
a bewildering maze that even the originators of this
system of lunacy did not understand it, and were
forced to take steps which no longer depended upon
their free will.

Clausewitz' theory that war is politics continued
with other means found its meaning here, for such
politics could lead only to war. War was in fact the
ultimate wisdom of the great statesmen of the nineteenth century. Napoleon I and Napoleon III, Bismarck, Cavour, Metternich—they knew how wars are
artfully prepared. The mania for alliances broke out

261

the moment Bismarck had to pursue a policy of peace.
It was exactly the case of the inspired bank director,
whom we have come to know and fear from our de-
pressions and crises, whose financial policy pyramids
up to an involved and intelligent structure of stupendous failure. The only European people who knew
how to connect the idea of politics with the idea of
reason, the English, were powerless before this development.

The masses of Europe were threatening to crash the
frontiers. The populations were starving for bread.
The machines were starving for raw materials. England was a century ahead of the European appetite
for colonies. By the middle of the century the conquest of India had been completed. Canada governed
itself, as did Australia and New Zealand. In the Cape
Colony disputes were going on between the English
and the Boers. In 1881 came the second Transvaal
War.

France had her colonies in North Africa and Indo-
China. By April 1881 she felt sufficiently strong to
annex Tunis. Clemenceau was the only deputy who
voted against this act 'because it will effectually alter
the European system and cool off precious friendships, which were cemented on the battlefield.' He
saw beyond 1914 to 1938 when Italy, struggling for
her position in the Mediterranean, would confront
France. The Suez Canal, which was built by the
French against the will of the English, passed by Disraeli's purchase of the majority of shares from the
khedive of Egypt into English hands. The overthrow
of Arabi pasha in 1882 ended the Anglo-French re-

gime. The English remained masters in Egypt, although presently to be faced with the long and difficult war in the Sudan against the Mahdi. Twenty-three years of serious tension lay behind the French and English, during which time the latter made several futile overtures to the Germans.

Russia made enormous conquests in Central Asia, Siberia and far into China. On the Indo-Afghan frontier there was almost war with England in 1885. But the road to China stood open and unguarded. Turkistan and Samarkand, the mythical lands of Genghis Khan and Tamerlane, were soon wrested from the Chinese. On the Pacific, the goal of all Russian yearning, a harbour grew up at Vladivostok. In 1892 the Trans-Siberian Railroad was built and every mile of track brought the Russo-Japanese War that much nearer. In 1902 the Anglo-Japanese Alliance was formed—against Russia.

In 1884 Bismarck suddenly emerged as a colonial competitor. In that one year, German Southwest Africa, Cameroon, Togoland, and German East Africa were taken over, more than a million square miles of German territory.

And finally, between 1878 and 1884, Leopold II of Belgium, after Stanley's wars of exploration, which he financed, developed the Congo Free State, the richest section of Africa, which was soon anything but free, but was a Belgian colony exploited according to all the rules.

The partition of Africa and a vast area of Asia was a series of 'peaceful' piracies. But there were too many pirates in business not to accumulate a store of jealousy and resentment, which must some day lead to a terrible explosion.

In Europe Bismarck began the fateful building up of his alliances. The estrangement from Russia was 'cordially' effected and consummated, in 1879, by a secret offensive alliance with Austria whose capable Foreign Minister Andrassy long resisted. The eighty-two-year-old Emperor William looked on helplessly. Almost immediately afterwards, in 1882 (the year in which Alexander II was assassinated and followed by Alexander III) a new and open alliance was formed—the League of the Three Emperors, between Russia, Austria and Germany. But the next year a new secret alliance was concluded between Germany, Austria and Italy—the Triple Alliance directed against France. Nor was this by any means all. In 1883 Austria concluded a secret treaty with Romania against Russia. When in 1887 the League of the Three Emperors came to an end, Bismarck demanded in the Reichstag an enormous military credit and raised the standing army to 468,000 men, and a new, so-called 'reinsuring treaty' was signed between Germany and Russia, which was aimed against Austria's Balkan policies.

The consequences of Bismarck's bilateralism soon showed themselves in the diplomatic conflicts that arose in the Balkans over the future of Bulgaria. Once more war was avoided. Bismarck threatened in the Reichstag and the memorable words were uttered: 'We Germans fear God and nothing else in this world.' Russia was completely isolated. The breach with Germany was complete, and in 1891 there resulted the *Entente Cordiale* with France, which, in 1893—again secretly—was extended to include a military alliance.

Meanwhile, in 1888 the Emperor William II had come to power. Soon there were differences of opinion between the twenty-eight-year-old Emperor and the seventy-five-year-old Chancellor, especially on questions of domestic policy. In 1890 Bismarck resigned. (A young scholar named Thomas Woodrow Wilson was at this time a professor at Princeton.) A new chapter of European history had begun. On the Continent there reigned the peace of a zoological garden where the beasts are glaring through the bars. People spoke of war as of something inevitable, yet in that Europe of genius and stupidity, humanity and power politics, hearts, hands and minds were resisting the imminent disaster. Only the methods, the views, the motives of the opponents of war were too diverse. The tragic situation was already clear enough, the advocates of force knew what they wanted: the enemies of force were wrangling.

There was the ever stronger international working-class movement, which had peace written on its banners, but the eight-hour day in its heart. In 1881 Samuel Gompers founded the American Federation of Labor. In the same year Germany began a unique and model state social policy with the introduction of workers' insurance. In 1883 followed the sick-benefits law; in 1884, accident insurance; in 1889 old-age and invalid insurance. All this took place under the iron pressure of the anti-socialist laws which Bismarck had passed, following attempts against the life of William I, in 1878. It was clear even then that social achievement and liberalism were to go separate ways in Germany. Social progress in Germany was an expression of the state principle of orderly and disciplined organization. Social misery was rust in the machine. But the numerical strength of the masses, which was to prove so brittle, grew irresistibly. Eighteen hundred and ninety was the first year in which the proletariat in all the civilized countries celebrated the first of May. It seemed as if peace would be served at least by that.

A 'peace movement' seemed to be forming. It was militant and had capital. Many millions flowed to it from munitions and explosives manufacturers suffering twinges of conscience. But it remained bourgeois, it never found a way to win the masses and was too infected with a pathetic faith in progress to be able to think realistically. There was never even any approach to religious pacifism.

The peace movement had its roots among the American Quakers around 1820. In 1828 the American Peace Society was founded. The first peace conference was organized by the blacksmith, Elihu Burrit, the son of a shoemaker from New Britain, Connecticut. A self-taught man, he studied languages in Worcester, in order to read the Bible in the original text. In 1846 he went to England where he founded the League of Universal Brotherhood 'to work by all legal means for the abolition of war throughout the world.' In 1867 the Society of the Friends of Peace was founded in Richmond, Indiana. In the same year Charles Lemonnier founded, in

Paris, the International League for Peace and Freedom. In 1880 there was an International Society for Arbitration and Peace. In 1889 Frédéric Passy and the Englishman, W.R.Cramer, founded the Interparliamentary Union. In 1889 the first World Peace Meeting was held in Paris. It was the year in which Bertha von Suttner published her memoirs under the title: 'Lay Down Your Arms!' The book was written in the romantic style of the eighteen nineties, and its sensational success did more for the cause of peace than all the peace societies together. Bertha von Suttner was the daughter of the Austrian Field-Marshal Kinsky. Through a remarkable coincidence, she became the secretary and confidante of the Swedish inventor of dynamite, Alfred Nobel, during the last years of his life. She converted the aging oil and explosives magnate to a friend of peace, and when he died in 1896 he left his enormous fortune built by the destructive force of dynamite, cordite and ballistite to the Nobel Foundation, whose Peace Prize is awarded so regally and solemnly for the 'greatest service to international brotherhood, for the limitation or abolition of standing armies, or for the organization and advancement of Peace Congresses.' In 1891 the International Peace Bureau was opened in Berne, and since 1919 has been in Geneva: Bertha von Suttner became chairman of the newly founded Vienna Union of the Friends of Peace. Peace Congresses followed in Berne, 1892; in Antwerp, 1894; in Hamburg, 1897. In 1892 the German Peace Society was founded by Alfred F.Fried. In 1894, Pope Leo XIII issued his bull on peace, *Praeclara gratulationis*, and each of the succeeding Popes, Benedict XV and Pius XI, has renewed the Christian appeal to mankind.

It is a long and tiresome list of dates. But what a sum of idealism, earnestness, care, effort and failure is bound up in it. Pacifism had its great day toward the end of the century. It seemed as if it had reached the ear of power. A more realistic tendency won leadership of the movement and sought to force moral norms on politics. But it all collapsed pitifully, and to-day pacifism throughout the greater part of the world is hated and outlawed like the plague. For other forces side by side with it proved more seductive and successful.

France experienced a physical reaction to its defeat in a wave of nationalist furore that may be regarded as a feeble forerunner of post-War German nationalism. In 1880 the poet Déroulède founded the League of Patriots. In 1886 it brought to power General Boulanger who as Minister of War stirred the army to *revanche*. Only the wise moderation of Bismarck prevented the outbreak of war. Boulanger was overthrown, he attempted a *coup d'état:* France came very close to a military dictatorship. Boulanger fled to Brussels with his wife, was sentenced *in contumacium* to deportation, and in 1891 killed himself at his wife's grave. The Dreyfus scandal, which broke in 1895, deserves credit for decisively shattering this movement. But it has never been laid to rest, and gleams to this day in the columns of *l'Action Française*, a lineal descendant of Boulangerism, though apparently no longer a political force.

In Italy, irredentism was active: the tune of *mare nostrum* was heard, piping the march via Federzoni and d'Annunzio, direct to Fascism.

Germany, under the leadership of William II, pursued its industrious and orderly course toward world power and chaos. Shrill rasped the peace trumpets of the young Emperor. But they were of Krupp steel and the mouth that uttered them resembled the long bore of a cannon.

XIX

Dunant Re-appears

ONE day, 'it was probably in the year 1889 or 1890,' Wilhelm Sonderegger, who taught school in the small Swiss health resort of Heiden, in the Canton of Appenzell, came home and noted, 'there must be a remarkable man staying in Heiden. In school the children told him that a gentleman, dressed in black with a little velvet cap on his head and a white beard falling to his knees, is going around the streets looking for little white pebbles which he puts in his pocket. He was extremely friendly with them, but doesn't understand German very well.' A short time afterwards the teacher met the stranger. 'It is the Genevese, J. H. Dunant, the man who brought about the work of the Red Cross. He lives in very modest circumstances at the Hotel Paradise with the Stahelin family . . . I shall never forget the impression which this splendid man made on us at first glance. His countenance radiates love, goodness and distinction.' So Frau Susanna Sonderegger reported.

Dunant had altered. But his beard did not fall

quite to his knees: the children had made of him an almost fabulous figure. He looked like a venerable Santa Claus, who put stones instead of presents in his bag. Dunant was Heiden's secret. The world still did not know where he was or how he had got there. It thought he was dead.

Dunant was a tender, fragile, sensitive old man with whom intercourse was difficult. The bitterness of his flight was uncontrollable. He suffered delusions of persecution. But was he not persecuted? It was a mania of loathing for the insanity of the 'normal' world which more robust men escape only through habit or resignation. But Dunant's whole greatness consists of the fact that he could never accustom himself to the world as it was. After his fall, he had gone the hard road of the 'unknown contemporary,' over whose grave no cenotaph will be raised. The road wound through hell. He had seen and suffered such accumulations of injustice, had experienced the sorrow of existence in the depths so fundamentally, that fear and horror joined in him for their final struggle.

The pious missionary of the *Alliance Évangélique*, the worshipper of kings, had become an enemy of the Church and State. About his exile almost nothing is known. For some time he lived with the Pastor Dr. Wagner, and with Dr. Rudolf Mueller, a professor at the gymnasium in Stuttgart. Usually he seems to have gone under another name. The avenging angels of Geneva pursued him constantly. In misfortune he cherished more than ever his great plans for human happiness: the visions of human well-being and peace nourished the hungry man. He was too proud to beg for help. But privation and the struggles of his conscience weakened his body which had never borne much. Pain sat in all his limbs. No one was there to say a word of courage. He was no longer able to earn the absolutely indispensable bite of bread. His family allowed him a paltry income of 100 francs. He found accommodations in Heiden for three francs a day. This left him ten francs a month for special expenses. At least, it was a state of regulated poverty.

But it required several years to accustom him to this new residence. He constantly feared that he was surrounded by enemies, constantly he scented treachery and disloyalty. He was right in thinking he had been betrayed. His thoughts, filled as before with humanitarian ideas, hovered more and more about the idea of peace betrayed by mankind. Between peace and anarchy he saw no way out. The Red Cross of war was only a beginning.

The voice of the prophet waxed strong in him again. It is probable that he had read Tolstoi whose *Confession* had appeared in 1882 and whose *Gospel in Brief* had been translated in Geneva in 1890. The pure, primitive Christianity of the Tolstoian teachings corresponded to his own views. Tolstoi, too, was an aristocrat who, converted by the sufferings of this life, had rebelled and been driven to renunciation and flight.

From Dunant's first two years in Heiden we possess a valuable correspondence which was recently published for the first time by René Sonderegger, the son of the teacher.

An uncontrollable inward excitement finds expression in these letters. He had still not found an equilibrium. His language alternates between the tearful complainings of an old man, apostolic wrath and clear purposeful soberness.

> They let me die of hunger.
>
> Let us destroy both infamies! The two great enemies of humanity are the church and the state, they are the intellectual and moral source of all slavery, two arbitrary and complimentary driving forces. One—brutal and Machiavellian, a hypocritical despotism. The other—callous and dishonest, swollen with pharasaical darkness, tyrannical and fanatical.
>
> You know that I hate state churches, the 'Reformed' as well as the Orthodox. But just as little do I love the Baptists, the Methodists, the Wesleyans, the Salutists, the Derbists, the Congregationalists and all the other 'ists' in the world. I am I, and that is enough. But till my last breath I shall strive to demoralize all your state trash. I shall all too soon have reached my end, but Christianity will have to pay for all the shames it has heaped up through the centuries. It is cowardly, mean and hateful to persecute conscience, as happens to-day in Russia, Spain and Switzerland . . .
>
> If you should ever write an obituary for me, please say that there are probably few men who have suffered as much as I from the malice of their enemies, from jealousy and envy, from the stupidity and cowardice of the Pharisees . . . I was the victim of those who deceived me. When I was completely ruined, I worked with the utmost energy and exertion for twenty years to pay my debts. I have known privation, lived the most miserable, obscure and parsimonious life, and often suffered hunger.

But my enemies have done everything to hinder me, to prevent my success, and to make me suspect everywhere by all kinds of slander. For years, in order to hurt me, they declared that I was not the real Dunant; they have charged me with crimes, have set well-meaning people against me, have ridiculed, annoyed, humiliated and insulted me. These are the thoughts that every night for hours on end rob me of my sleep with a kind of nervous fever. I have still so much to say . . .

We need social aristocrats! . . . A flock of blockheads find it easy to shout: Utopia! Utopia! We shall yet see whether they are not to blame, if through their own stupidity and blockheadedness, anarchy does not come. In any case, Europe is gravely ill. It is just these so-called moral doctors who are prescribing the poisoned medicine that must bring about its end. And civilization will seek out a new home. To a certain extent this has already begun. Australia, the United States, South Africa are the future centres of civilization.

Again and again, with the automatism of something thought over a thousand times, these maledictions, adjurations, prophecies, are repeated. At the same time, he clings to every hope. He considers William II the saviour of Europe, the Encyclical of Pope Leo is the dawn of a new world. His old optimism is instantly aroused, only to be plunged as swiftly by some new circumstance into abysmal despair. When a meaningless riot broke out at Tessin, he stormed upstairs to his friend Sonderegger late at night crying, 'The Apocalypse has begun!'

Like so many prophets, his sense of timing was poor.

Frau Sonderegger writes of this incident: ' I was terribly frightened and thought he had lost his mind. For at other times he always came up quietly and his whole person expressed distinction and restraint.' Another time he related very excitedly how two men had attacked and tried to kill him. It developed that two young lads were walking along the street behind him, joking and laughing. Dunant mistook them for 'enemies,' turned around and struck at them with his umbrella, whereupon they gave him something too.

Toward the end of 1891 Dunant's hosts moved to Lindenbuchl in Troyen, not far from Heiden, and Dunant went with them. Here at the foot of the Alpstein range he had a wonderful view across Lake Constance. But it was winter and the strong winds bothered him.

It had been a very troublesome removal. Dunant, single-handed had packed fifteen packages of varying sizes, for he would not let anybody touch his things. Father Sonderegger had to carry them down and Frau Sonderegger stood on the sidewalk 'to see that none of the packages fell into unbidden hands.'

With greater repose, the desire for organization came to him. In Heiden a relief society of the Red Cross was organized. Dunant accepted the honorary chairmanship and gave minute instructions as to how everything was best arranged. The organization of the little village group transported him to the time when he had helped so brilliantly to prepare the great Convention. He designed an envelope for the invitations—'pale lavender would be very nice, or even

light gray, pearl gray. I have not left enough white
space around the Red Cross, at top and bottom. The
word Heiden is somewhat too large in the rough
sketch.'

In this way Dunant sought to impart a little of his
propagandist wisdom to his students. 'Don't think I
am petty, remember, a famous man said that genius
is an infinite capacity for taking pains (assuming, of
course, that the pains are worth taking).' An an-
nouncement in the *Appenzeller Zeitung* he called
'that wretched little article which repeated a few
times will be worth more than a long speech.' He
outlined the program for a coming supper festival: he
recommended songs especially. 'You must neglect
nothing, and you must—excuse me for saying this—
completely eschew the petty and malicious small
town spirit.'

At the same time, Dunant was busy preparing a
new edition of the *Recollections of Solferino*. He sought
to influence his friend to attend the International
Conference which was held in Rome in 1892 and in
several letters the difficult problem of financing this
trip, which never took place, was discussed. But Sonderegger wrote a letter to the congress about Dunant
and his situation. The letter made a sensation. Dunant, to whom no man longer gave a thought, had
risen from the grave of oblivion!

But there was too much bitterness for them to ex-
tend to him the hand of reconciliation.

Things got worse and worse for Dunant at Linden-
buehl. The wind from the mountains set his nerves
on edge, and on nights when the storms howled

around the lonely house, lashed all the ghosts of the past through his dreams. For no reason at all he broke with his friend Sonderegger who had mislaid a sheet of manuscript, and now nobody might enter his room. The children, who used to pay him a visit on his birthday, 8 May, had to hang their wreaths on his locked door. He sat alone in the inferno of his torment, accustomed to having his hours pass like years, and his years like hours.

Presently they decided that some more basic care was essential for him. In 1892 the resort physician, Dr. Altherr, who treated him in a most friendly and devoted way, had him taken to the Hospice, at Heiden. For the last time, the boxes and little packages, the decorations and diplomas, the documents and outlines, wandered with him to a new roof. They were stored away tidily by the Deaconesses. Dunant never left this home for the poor again. And he still had eighteen years to live. Heiden's incumbent occupied Room Number 12. It was a clean, bright room with two windows. There was a bed, a desk, and between them, a sofa with a faded cover. There was a chest, two chairs and a table. The walls were covered with a cold lime-wash. There was no picture on them. Over the table was a little mirror such as is found in maids' rooms. Beside the bed hung a thermometer and on the door the house-regulations.

It was one of those cheerless barren rooms in which the world over old people wait for death, one of those old peoples' prisons in which the eyes grow blind and the ears grow deaf until the warmth of the grave brings release.

But to Dunant this cell was a haven from the rude tumult of the outer world, a place of boundless freedom where he could think and feel as he liked.

In his brown dressing-gown, from which his cuffs peeped out a little in faultless fashion, his black skullcap on his head, he sat silent and undisturbed, writing his recollections. Emperors and kings and ministers passed him by, and it was like a ghostly dance of death in which the mighty and the beggar paired.

Once more he looked into the eyes of countless faces from his life, impelled by the same suffering, the same hate, the same self-interest. There was hardly any boundary left between life and shadow. The great Napoleon and the poorest soldier of Solferino stood equally terrified against the wall of an irrational destiny.

When, very rarely, he permitted visitors across his threshold, for he was impatient of any incursion of their restlessness and officiousness into his peaceful realm, they found an old chevalier with a patriarchal beard, who spoke the polished French of the *haut monde*. His voice was mild, modulated, and a little high-pitched. But when he spoke of his work, it took on 'a sonorous and deep tonal color.'

Thus a Swiss journalist, Georges Bamberger, found him in 1895, and published a detailed account of his memorable meeting in the then much-read German periodical *Über Land und Meer*.

This article was the signal for the re-discovery of Henri Dunant. In those days people were talking a good deal about war. The Franco-Russian military agreement had become known, and Japan launched its first surprising raid on China, who succumbed without offering any real resistance, and, in the Peace of Shimonoseki, was forced to cede Korea and the harbour of Port Arthur on which Russia had designs. This war had grave consequences. It created the basis for the Russo-Japanese war of 1905, it led to the Anglo-Japanese alliance of 1902, and brought an unusually sharp protest from Germany which the Japanese remembered twenty years later, when demanding in the identical language that Germany evacuate Kiau Chow.

People recalled the legendary angel of peace from Geneva, and Baumberger's appeal for aid for the unfortunate Dunant met a wide response. Once more Dunant had found the shadows which had so disgracefully abandoned him. He read his name in the great newspapers of the European countries: The founder of the Red Cross is alive and in need!

The post brought him impressive documents. The most remote societies appointed him to honorary membership. The dowager Empress of Russia granted him a pension. The Samaritans of Rheims sent him a gold medal. His sixty-eighth birthday in 1896 took on the nature of a cultural event. 'Our Henri Dunant,' all Switzerland called him with pride. From Zürich came a splendid basket of white flowers among which bloomed a red cross. Pope Leo XIII sent him his picture with the inscription, '*Fiat pax in virtute tua Deus.*' And Cardinal Rampolla subscribed to these sentiments. The Archbishop of Rheims wrote: 'It pleases me to glorify to God this name which conceals itself, this name which the victims of war throughout the universe bless every day.' His picture was in all the illustrated papers. In St.Gal, they issued a Dunant-coin, on whose reverse 'was strikingly represented the moment when a severely wounded soldier in the tumult of battle is bandaged by a bearer of the international arm-band. Over this group hovers the genius of humanity, pointing to the Red Cross which is seen enhaloed.' The International Medical Congress in Moscow appointed him an honorary member, and the Swiss Diet awarded him a prize.

For Dunant there was nothing new in the martial music of fame. He might just as well have dreamed it all; he had already been through it, enjoyed it, despised it. With astonishment and wonder, he saw the alien splendour in his cell, and heard the voices that forced their way in, trying to right a wrong. Times were prosperous and once again magnanimous. business was picking up. In 1895 in every country there was an economic upswing such as had never been known before. It seemed as if the century wished to die in one last glamorous apotheosis before the curtain fell on this most tragic and most civilized age of human history, filled with so much inspired progress and so much goodwill, but also with so much old wickedness, and new.

Dunant knew that the nightmare of glory would again disappear and his name would again be left in darkness. The stigma of bankruptcy had been removed from him. It was a little late. He would be able to sleep better perhaps, hate less and need to worry less. Also he had written to the aged widow of his friend Basting, who had been one of the victims of Mons-Gemila. He had her reply in his hands:

I am sorry that you have suffered so much, and through a trouble, too, that you unwittingly caused your friends. But the work has prospered, God had chosen you to find and further it. It is to Him you must render an accounting for the ways you have gone. You are too old and too pious not to be truthful now. I am happy that I have written to you, and I hope we shall see one another again some day, there where so many dear ones have preceded us. God keep you.

The debt of debts was written off, and he could look forward with composure to meeting the Bastings in heaven. But was there not another, more burning, harder debt upon this earth of which he was not absolved? Solferino, Dueppel, Königgrätz, Sedan, the barricades of Paris, Plevna, Manchuria, and the foul abyss of endless wars to come, waiting to yawn open. Dunant saw his face in the narrow blinding mirror. Bare, worn, fragile, all but vanished. He had difficulty in swallowing and his swollen hands had lost their grip. But old men are tenacious and ungentle fighters. His fist was clenched again. There would be no reconciliation. There was still no peace. There was still work.

XX

The Nobel Prize

IN 1896 a visitor made a pilgrimage to Dunant's cell who far surpassed all others in importance—Bertha von Suttner. It was shortly before Alfred Nobel's death. The main features of the memorable will which turned the explosives millions over to the advancement of peace, and the international spirit of science, were already settled. Nobel's secretary, 'that tenacious dove of peace' as Theodor Wolff called her, the fighter for pacifism in whose veins flowed the blood of a warrior father, and who on her mother's side was descended from the singer of the German wars for freedom, Theodor Körner, had been issuing for several years in Vienna, the periodical *Lay Down Your Arms!* Its masthead borrowed the emphatic appeal of her world-famous book. The Genevese patrician and the Austrian aristocrat were cast in that same mould of enlightened and credulous Europeanism which made the century's enthusiasm for progress comprehensible. The lady who was able to transform the misanthropic and highly cultured explosives magnate into a posthumous idealist and philanthropist

was equally capable of tearing the embittered and re-
nunciatory Dunant from his hospice. She was deeply
moved by the sight of this fragile man whom fate had
destroyed and who had gone the opposite course from
friend of mankind to fearer of mankind:

' In the hospice of a little Swiss resort, in a tidy room
as bare as a prison cell, a man lives and works whose
description follows: sixty-eight years of age, long
white beard, gentle glance, the appearance of a
polished man of the world, full of *esprit*, voice
eloquent and warmhearted . . .'

And Dunant, who had traversed all the hells of
treason and desertion, over whom his later friends
had held a charming and pathetic necrology, this
feeble old man half buried beneath honours and diplomas, whom the slings and arrows of immortality
were robbing of his last breath, felt once more that he
was not alone. It was Bertha von Suttner's great
service that, at the end of his long and bewildered life,
restored Dunant to the front rank of those great
Europeans who constituted the rich harvest of that
century. For the first time, and all too late, he saw
himself and his instinct for the cause of goodness set
in that spiritual community of European humanitarianism, which transmuted the material blessings of
capitalism's glamorous age into human values.

There was Zola who, battling for the rights of an
individual, Captain Dreyfus, converted a world to
goodness. There was Anatole France, Tolstoi, Dosto-
evski, Björnson, Fontane, Conrad Ferdinand Meyer,
the Dane, Georg Brandes, the broad strophes of
Walt Whitman, the monist moral doctrine of Ernest

Haeckel. The youthful Thomas Mann began to write and to copy the mind and manners of his contemporaries. There was a great and living art called Naturalism and Impressionism. There was an imposing poetry and a classic body of critical and philosophic opinion which, even when it considered itself decadent, as in the case of Poe and Baudelaire, even when it was pessimistic and conscious of existing tensions as in Strindberg, and above all, Nietzsche, even when it was metaphysical as in Bergson, or aggressive and hostile to the age as in Richard Wagner, made up a thrillingly powerful consonance of the western mind.

Science was making revolutionary advances, and leaving behind the crumbling theorems of the past, was developing a practical knowledge for the practical needs of suffering men. Tyndall, Hertz, Pastour, Virchow, Koch and Darwin's theories were rooting out plagues, creating possibilities for technical aid and social development such as even the most boundless optimism had believed improbable. And in the wake of this cultural exuberance, the Utopian systems of humanity's well-wishers, the moral menders, the social reformers, expanded into broad movements of greater or less realism: Esperanto, vegetarianism, temperance, protection of animals, women's rights, Christian Science, free-thinking, monism, sex reform, land reform, clothing reform, physical culture.

'Culture' and 'education' were consumers' goods, on which the increased purchasing power of the masses flung itself. It is hardly strange that the hunger for cheap cultural commodities flooded the market with much trash, pseudo-art and pseudo-science.

The lexicon and the illustrated album were mass merchandise which brought the past closer. Automobiles, railroads, the new art of flying, photography, all made the distant world tangible, and styles were imposed one on another without selection or taste, forms were embellished and articles of use deformed. From ladles to gables, the world of commonplace things was fearfully and fantastically glorified. Useless things were invented with vast ingenuity. In the great apartment houses porcelain and plaster casts, chromos and crochet-work proliferated. People sent each other picture post-cards and collected souvenirs. They were titillated by the artificial and the novel from the housewife's paper flowers, and the gourmets' bananas, oranges and pineapples, to the greenish absinthe or drugs that tempted the pampered bourgeois with the joys of wickedness.

They prepared for the twentieth century as for a great artists' ball. It was a time which boasted of its realism like a child with a toy: they 'played' with the most serious things. There was misery, but they believed in trash-removal and civilization's sense of cleanliness which to-morrow would tidy it all up. Full of illusions were our fathers, the honoured protectors of our youth, with their moustaches and frock-coats. The socialists believed in the world revolution and the unity of the proletariat. The capitalists believed in the flawless perfection of their world-gospel. The politicians believed in the blessings of world imperialism, in the 'balance of power' and the 'concert of Europe.' And the masses as a whole almost believed in eternal peace.

Dunant rubbed the sleep out of his eyes. How willing we are to believe that when we are at the end we are also at the goal. With peace and anarchy in the balance, the balance seemed to incline toward peace. He did his last bit to tip the scales for peace. The cramped hand seized the pen again. Bertha von Suttner placed her magazine at his disposal. In the review *Lay Down Your Arms* appeared an appeal *To the Press; A Little Arsenal Against Militarism,* and *A Little Arsenal Against War.* The *Monthly Supplement for Freedom, Peace and Progress* published his *Word of Fire.*

He dreamed of a 'great international party for the maintenance of the social order,' of a 'Women's Welfare League,' under the leadership of the princesses, 'to exercise the twin dangers that threaten our race, anarchy and world war.' He planned a 'Bureau for the Protection of Women,' whose emblem would be a 'green cross on a white shield with purple edges.' 'The ladies of the green cross' would provide legal protection, spiritual and material aid for all persons socially stranded or jeopardized, above all 'in the great and perilous centres of population.'

But most important was his struggle against war, and those were truly prophetic words which the hermit of Heiden addressed to a lost world in 1897:

Ah, war is not yet dead! If it has changed its form, it is only to become—more terrible. Everything that makes up the pride of our civilization will be at the service of war. Your electric railroads, your dirigibles, your submarines and flying bridges, your snap-shot photography, your telegraphs, telephones, photophones, and so many other wonderful inventions, will perform splendid service for war side by side with the instruments of human murder. What does not man invent to make death quicker and surer! So quick of hand and heart are the 'humane' when it comes to shedding the blood of their fellow men.

Train your noble race-horses for battle. Train your innocent doves to be messengers of destruction. Train swallows for your birds of war. Use horses, mules, oxen, elephants, camels and dromedaries for military transport, and to be your fellows in the field! Use the whole creation for your slaughter! Drive all together with you to the blood-bath! But be quick, so that everyone will be ready for the great day of the slaughter! Spur on your ingenious inventors who perfect their destructive weapons with such joy and such enthusiasm! Heap honours on them, cram them with gold! Vie with each other in destroying the most beautiful masterpieces, the pride of civilization—palaces and castles, embankments, and harbours, viaducts, buildings and monuments of all kinds! But do not forget that then this civilization, on which you prided yourselves so much, will infallibly lie in ruins, and with it will go your welfare, your trade, your industry, your agriculture, and perhaps also your national freedom and your domestic happiness!

This was in 1897! Europe had begun slowly but inevitably to move toward the great tragedy, and the clouds were concentrated at three danger-points, in the Balkans and around the Berlin-to-Bagdad railroad, in Morocco, and in the North Sea where the German fleet was growing.

William II had begun as a 'social' ruler, and his break with Bismarck was caused by his liberal labour policies. When the Social-Democrats emerged in 1893 as the strongest party in the Reichstag, the social policies of the Empire had already turned reactionary, and the Subversion Law of 1895, and the Penal Law of 1899, aimed sharp exceptional legislation against the socialists. William II began as a prince of peace, and in a few years German policy was a standing threat to peace. He began as a friend of England: the exchange of Zanzibar for Heligoland was effected in 1890, the Russian 'reinsurance' treaty was not renewed. A few years later, he developed a violent friendship for Russia and an incurable resentment toward England to which he first gave expression during the Boer War, in 1896, in his message to President Krueger of the Transvaal. William constantly felt himself an absolute monarch by the grace of God, but he was lacking in the wisdom of his grandfather. He was ungoverned, fitful, brilliant, poorly advised and obsessed with an imperialist ambition which represented the specific German mixture of sober realism and romantic speculation. In 1897 the forces were mustered for the voyage to grief. Admiral von Tirpitz became Minister of Marine and announced the first naval building program. Buelow became Foreign Minister and in 1900 Imperial Chancellor. Kiaochow was occupied in China, Germany had acquired an important naval base in the Far East. Shortly afterwards, Russia occupied Port Arthur in order to insure a warm-water port in the Pacific.

England celebrated Victoria's Jubilee while still completely under the sway of that 'splendid isolation' which had assured her rise since the Congress of Vienna. But Russia's menacing expansion in the East made preventive steps essential, and there began in

1898 a series of efforts at *rapprochement* with Berlin which were consistently rebuffed and finally led to the Triple Alliance against Germany.

The Emperor developed his unfortunate love for speeches which were always the prelude to a diplomatic catastrophe. On a pilgrimage to Jerusalem he proclaimed himself the Defender of the Mohammedans, thereby arousing France and England.

From May until June 1899 the Peace Conference met in The Hague: it had been called by the youthful Nicholas II who had occupied the Russian throne for the past few years.

The conference was enthusiastically hailed by all friends of peace, but its sole result was to sharpen the feeling for war. To be sure, on England's urging and against Germany's opposition, the organization of The Hague Tribunal was resolved, but the Emperor made it known that he would not depend upon courts of arbitration, but upon his own sharp sword. Germany categorically rejected all proposals to disarm.

Before the conference, Dunant published a long article: *The Proposal of His Majesty the Emperor Nicholas II*. It was his last attempt to change the course of events with his failing voice.

The Red Cross societies were the first land-mark of brotherly *rapprochement* in the field of the highest and noblest philanthropy. The Red Cross and the Geneva Convention have shown the way for the accomplishment of other great work. To-day there exists an agreement where material interests are concerned between all the civilized nations. This has led to a common course of conduct on certain definite points. This common conduct has been made effective through the International Postal Union, the International Telegraphic Union, the International Bureau for Weights and Measures, international unions for the protection of industrial, artistic and literary property, the Bureau for the Publication of Tariffs, the International Union for Transport and Railways. Nobody had any idea of all this fifty years ago . . . May this Conference too be a favourable portent of the coming century. May it unite in a mighty league the efforts of all countries which are sincerely striving for the triumph of the great idea of world peace over the elements of strife and discord. May it seal the joint consecration of those principles of law and justice on which the security of states and the welfare of nations rests.

It was a far hail from international harmony in the question of weights and measures to the international harmony of men, and nothing indicates that our barbarous century, which the departing Dunant greeted, will see it through to the end.

The discovery had just been made in the state factory at Dum Dum, near Calcutta, that the effectiveness of the modern steel-jacketed bullet could be increased devastatingly by exposing the lead nose, and a skirmish among the Indian border tribes at Chitra brilliantly confirmed the experiment. In the *German Revue*, the famous surgeon Dr.F.von Esmarch, the founder of the German Samaritan Union (1882), proposed in an 'open circular letter' that this type of bullet, 'which may perhaps be excusable in a fight with fanatical barbarians,' be forbidden for European use, as explosive projectiles under 400gr. had been prohibited by a general agreement in 1864. There was no discussion of gases, hand-grenades or incendiary bombs at this congress.

Hardly had the delegates returned to their homes than the last and most violent of the Boer Wars, that of 1899, broke out and ended with the formation of the Union of South Africa. William II went to London and returned empty-handed. The new century began with the Boxer Rebellion in China. A German Consul was murdered, resulting in an international punitive expedition to the unhappy country, which since its 'opening up,' had become a bone of contention among foreign business interests.

Queen Victoria died at the beginning of 1901. Edward VII became King of England. The sun of 'splendid isolation' set upon the island empire, and a new sun arose darkened by a web of alliances, *ententes* and European troubles and military agreements.

After the Boxer Rebellion Germany had for the third time rejected the advances of England. The result was the Anglo-Japanese Alliance of 1902. Its object was the safeguarding of England against Russia in Asia. But its effects went much farther and led to the stabilization of the groups of powers as they confronted each other at the outbreak of the World War in 1914.

In 1901 Tolstoi was excommunicated. In 1901 Andrew Carnegie, defeated in the struggle of his steel works against the banking-house of Morgan, retired and decided to devote his fortune of several hundred million dollars to philanthropic ends. In 1901 the Nobel Prize was awarded for the first time. The peace prize was divided between two old men, one half to the seventy-nine-year-old Frédéric Passy, founder of the French Union for Peace and President of the French Association for Arbitration between Nations —the other half to the seventy-three-year-old Henri Dunant.

The award of the prize to Dunant was passionately opposed by a few radical pacifists because the Red Cross was not an organization for furthering peace. They did not do themselves very much credit thereby and showed that blind fanaticism can disfigure even the cause of peace. If ever anyone deserved the prize it was Dunant. A hater of war since the day of Solferino, his whole life became nothing but a reflection of those few terrible hours, while by an unparalleled tenacity and capacity for suffering, he had more and more clearly come to recognize the sin of war, and more and more decisively and definitely fought against it. He wanted the Red Cross of the battlefields to become the Red Cross of peace! The honour of the first Nobel Peace Prize, which the enfeebled Dunant had achieved at the end of his road, was a comfort and a hope to him: it created an obligation to keep alive his work, the union of Red Cross societies, the idea of peace—and in his spirit. 'I was never understood!!!' he complains in one of his letters. At last he was understood.

The sudden wealth in the stiff hands of the aged Dunant was one of the tragic ironies with which his life was strewn. It seemed as if heaven could not bear to see the son of Geneva patricians go poor into eternity. But poverty had become too loyal a friend and companion for him to give it up. He had long been a

monk of his own persuasion. He never left his call
again, or laid aside the robes of poverty. If there was
one thing he need fear in this life it was money. He
bequeathed the prize to philanthropic societies. Nine
years of the new century passed, looking very alien
and suspicious to his weary eye. In those last years of
Dunant's life the battle-lines were drawn for the
World War. The means of spiritual and material
communication, with which the achievements of the
nineteenth century had endowed the world, succumbed before the arms and the selfish interests of
nations: they turned against civilization. The world
was partitioned according to the laws of boldness and
of chance. But the lava masses of mankind grew and
grew as the result of a biological anarchy from which
the ordering hand of the cultivator was lacking.
Birth control was still an idea. The leadership of
states was bound up with historical traditions and
political concepts of honour which, although they no
longer corresponded to the state of civilization and
its revolutionary possibilities, left the free will of
feeble men no room. There resulted a Strindbergian
situation of tortured suspense, a shackling together of
bodies and souls in love and hate from which there
was no escape but by dynamite and tragedy.

After every effort at alliance between England and
Germany had failed, a decisive turn was made in
British policy. Edward VII made a trip in 1903 which
took him to Lisbon, Rome, Vienna and Paris. The result was the Anglo-French *entente* of 1904, after the
Italians had already sabotaged the Triple Alliance by
a secret treaty of neutrality (1902) upon France's

promise to allow them a free hand in Tripoli. Spain was similarly promised a slice of Morocco. France's only rival in Morocco was Germany. In March 1895 the Emperor's yacht arrived at Tangiers, and he made his unfortunate speech promising to uphold an independent Morocco. Germany demanded an international conference. Delcassé, the French Foreign Minister, opposed this and was compelled to resign. The Emperor appeared to have won an important diplomatic victory.

Meanwhile Russia had occupied Manchuria, and the Russo-Japanese War had broken out in February 1904. The Russian people under the dull and bigoted rule of Tsar Nicholas were in the hands of corrupt favourites and reactionaries. It was an imperialism of defective rails and poor cannon. Contrary to all expectations the war resulted in a decisive defeat for Russia. On 22 January 1905 the factory workers, led by Father Gapon, marched to the Winter Palace to hand the Tsar a petition requesting constitutional rights for the people. They were shot down. Terror rose against terror. Lenin's shadow was lengthening over Russia. The army was destroyed at Mukden, the fleet at Tsushima. A sham parliament was convoked, the *Duma*. The Peace of Portsmouth on 9 May 1905 gave Japan Korea, Manchuria and Port Arthur.

On July of the same year there was a mysterious rendezvous at Björko between William II, inspired by the demonic intriguer Holstein, and his friend and cousin, Nicholas. There a secret alliance between the two countries was concluded 'before God Who hears our vows.' It was immediately revoked, for it still seemed insane in 1905 that two monarchs of such absolute authority should bargain away the fate of their nations *en tête à tête*. Russia received from France the greatest loan in history. Witte, who now ruled in Russia, saw with concern and vexation the development of the German *Bagdadbahn* and William II's arming of Turkey. In 1907, after Germany's defeat at the Algeciras Conference, came the Anglo-Russian *entente*. The 'encirclement' of Central Europe was complete.

The second Peace Conference met in The Hague in 1907. It was in fact no more than an overture to World War, for it made pointedly clear how much the critical state of Europe had changed for the worse in seven years. A request of England to Germany to limit naval armaments to reasonable proportions was rejected. A new and extensive naval building program was begun and rushed forward. In 1908 William II gave the *Daily Telegraph* an unhappy interview in which he stressed the belligerence—which simply did not exist—of the German people against England. His repeated and astounding political attacks intensified the atmosphere of embitterment and distrust. In 1909 Germany began the construction of nine dreadnoughts; England built eighteen.

In 1908 began those final discords in the Balkans that caused severe Austro-Russian tension. The magyarizing of the Hungarian Serbs resulted in a violent and immoderate counter-agitation in free Serbia, where since the murder in 1903 of the last Obrenovitch, the government of King Peter, and especially the overheated chauvinism of the Crown Prince

George, led to a dangerous worsening of relations with Austria.

In Turkey there was a revolution of the 'Young Turks' under Enver Bey. On 5 October 1908 Bulgaria threw off all Turkish control, and Prince Ferdinand proclaimed himself Tsar of an independent kingdom. On 7 October Austria-Hungary announced the definite annexation of Bosnia and Hercegovina, which it had occupied since 1778. The inhabitants of Bosnia and Hercegovina belonged ethnologically and linguistically to the Serbian nation, and their separation caused a deep bitterness which was intensified by the mistakes of the Austrian Foreign Minister Aehrenthal, and a back-stairs political affair with forged documents. But under pressure of an ultimatum from Von Buelow, the Russian government of Isvolsky gave up its support of the Serbs, and by 1909 the crisis seemed to be settled. But a mounting hatred remained. Russia could not forget the defeat which she, as protector of Pan-Slavia, had suffered with Germany's help. Serbian irredentism could never be stopped by official efforts and was becoming more and more intolerable to Austria. When in 1910 a Yugo-Slav student made an unsuccessful attempt on the life of the Governor of Bosnia, he cried before he killed himself: 'I leave to Greater Serbia the duty of avenging me!' Such were the watchwords that the youth of Europe gladly followed and for which they gave their lives.

XXI

Death

DUNANT was silent. With half-closed eyes he dreamed through the long winter-sleep of the last few days, and his white hair lay on his wrinkled face like snow. Mists rose from Lake Constance and slowly the landscape of reposeful and home-like peace began to fade from before his narrow cell. Once, far away, like a delusion of blindness, he saw a monstrous shadow gleam through the clouds: it was Count Zeppelin's dirigible.

The great names of 1914 were at their posts, waiting for their cues to be called. Everywhere reigned a boundless well-being ruffled only by the growing struggle of the workers for a share in the social security. The budget of the Liberal government in England, with its inheritance and unearned increment taxes, its old-age pension and state social insurance plans, was violently contested and affords a good insight into the pressures which were forcing capital and business out of their private capacity and loading them with social obligations. Economy had been internationalized to a high degree and loans from the great powers financed the smaller and less civilized states; vast lots of North American securities were in European hands and vice versa, while machines and commodities circulated through space and created an international standard of desires and satisfactions to which the masses quickly adapted themselves. In a few minutes the cable could conclude stupendous deals between the hemispheres.

In January 1910 Edward VII died. George V came to the throne. Edward VII, a man of the world, had during his reign performed the heavy task of breeching the Chinese wall of isolation and leading England back into world politics. It did not happen voluntarily. Germany's flourishing imperial economic system and the United States compelled it. Sir Edward Grey, Balfour, Asquith, Lloyd George were in office. In France, Clemenceau, Poincaré, Briand dominated the political scene. In Germany Bethmann-Hollweg was trying in vain to correct the mistakes of Von Buelow's policies. The superiority of German goods was capturing market after market despite protective tariffs of all kinds. But German policy was not geared to the difficult role of a successful competitor. Bridge after bridge was burned.

Only a few historical moments were left before the coming of the 'great times:' the sending of the Panther to Agadir, the Italo-Turkish War with its occupation of Tripoli, the defeat of Turkey by the Balkan Alliance, the shot at Sarajevo. In 1910 Carnegie endowed a Peace Foundation with ten million dollars.

The world's munitions works were working day and

night. The 'balance of power' rested upon alliances and threats, following no natural law and no rational perception, but springing from private imaginations, resentments, feudal traditions and concepts, money interests, inertias, and the lack of any notion of the future. Between the powerful and the humane there was an unbridgeable gulf. There was no group, from the most radical socialists to the most ingrained conservatives, that took its humanitarian phrases seriously. The few honest men abandoned politics. It was a betrayal on all sides—less from wickedness than from stupidity and the power of suggestion. The worst failure was the International's, because it had been the most blatant in its promises of action. On 25 July 1914 the leading committee of the German Social-Democracy proclaimed: 'Danger ahead! A World War is threatening! The ruling classes that beat, despise and exploit you in peace time now want you for cannon-fodder . . . Down with war! Long live the international brotherhood of all peoples!' A few days later the shouters voted the war credits—almost unanimously. And the socialists in all other countries behaved much the same.

Peace and class struggle are two ideas of very different spirit. International repulsion proved stronger than international cohesion. Four years of war destroyed the constructive work of centuries—what had seemed to be the almost inevitable advance of the spiritual and material unity of the world. There was not much humanitarianism to be seen on the battlefields. Private life and property were not spared, treaties were not respected, destructive weapons were not restricted. And the Red Cross, technically imposing, like everything else in this war, and devoted to its work, stood powerless before the moral dissolution. Humanitarianism was the unknown soldier, over whose mouldering limbs the eternal fire of remorse now burns.

But a gracious destiny closed the eyes of the great friends of peace of the preceding century before they could see the horror. Clara Barton died on Easter morning 1912. Frédéric Passy died in 1912. Bertha von Suttner died in June 1914. Jaurès was assassinated in August 1914. Tolstoi died on 20 November 1910, on his flight from the world to solitude—the railway station at Astapovo. This great disciple of Christ opened and closed his eyes at the same time as his less articulate brother, Dunant—1828–1910.

Dunant died at Heiden on 30 October 1910. He was eighty-five. On his eightieth birthday the sound of voices had once more broken in on him, and the burden of good wishes.

But he stood beyond the glory or disgrace of life, which he had tasted in such excess. His testament was written:

'I wish to be carried to my grave like a dog without a single one of your ceremonies which I do not recognize. I trust to your goodness faithfully to respect my last earthly request. I count upon your friendship that it shall be so. Amen. I am a disciple of Christ as in the first century, and nothing more.'

This savage message from Dunant on his death-bed was the last to find its way from the cell into which life had banished him. He asked for himself the great freedom of the animals, to return unwept and unconsecrated, to nothingness.

Most men leave this world with the rigidity of old age and the unaltered prejudices of their youth. Dunant's old age brought him youth and radicalism and the transformation of his prejudices into a clear and simple verdict.

The world he could not change. But he could change himself. He was no dictator of humanity. He created humanity and goodness under an irresistible compulsion, the same compulsion that moved the saints and martyrs, and which is the last hope of a suffering humanity.

His grave is in Zürich.

XXII

The Future of the Red Cross

A MAN'S fate is inextricably bound up with the historical space through which his life makes its way. Be he as deaf and insensitive as possible to the tone of his time, still the sum of the events he lives through is part of the heritage of his generation, and his own image is stamped with the image of the world about him. Hardly anything, from hair-cut to *weltanschauung* is entirely dependent on his free will.

But it is one of fate's incivilities that a man can never quite grasp or scrutinize the reality he belongs to. Man is the mirror and cannot see himself. Only the succeeding world knows what was right and can determine the place where a man belonged. For while we are living, we often do not recognize our closest brothers or our surest comrades. The street of to-day is more difficult to appraise than yesterday's hundred years.

It is the biographer's task to set a life in its context, to diagnose justly and scrupulously the symptoms of its existence. One must proceed like a physician, carefully writing the case history of an illness.

Any attempt at completeness is out of the question. For every newspaper headline bears on the final stage of our life just as every tiniest trauma bears on the final stage of an illness. But even half an attempt must repay itself.

The usages of contemporary biography require a life to read like a novel. Since the discovery that the course of destiny strives toward a condition of drama, the reader has been trained to look for the spiritual and 'private' background of historical facts. He wants to know his hero in everyday dress, how he ate, what he wore, how he made love. He knows that great deeds are enclosed in little sorrows and that the sum total of physical and psychic functions determines a life.

But suppose a life is so veiled that it has left none, or only insufficient, documentation of its private sphere? Then invention begins. Speeches are invented that were never uttered. The emphasis of event and character is arbitrarily shifted. Conflicts and situations are fabricated and described as they never happened.

Such procedure is criminal and not to be distinguished from the irresponsible reporting of a scandal-sheet: it is forgery and slander. A life is too serious and inviolable a thing for it to bear the loose touch of such treatment. The legacy of fault and merit may not be changed, if history is to retain its meaning. Every false word and every false statement is a sacrilege against a defenceless man.

Concerning the private life of Dunant, there is nothing, as far as is known, which we have not related here. There are no friends, no women, no confidences, no observations by contemporaries. The reader will feel this lack as the author has already regretfully felt it. But if a life so long, so active and so significant, is reflected so little in others, this silence of men concerning Dunant is itself an acute symptom of his personality and we may not alter it.

There are human beings whose destiny is identical with their work to the point of inhumanity, in whom the every-day alternations of desire and pain by which we all live, are profoundly replaced by an unflagging effort toward some definite end. Dunant was such a man.

Handwriting experts and psycho-analysts may find many motives and explanations for the private anonymity of a world-famous man. But those are uninteresting, if not impermissible and shameless.

The life of Dunant was framed in a century of human history. It was a century very closely related to us, in the course of which we, or our parents, were born. We feel its breath and its movements clearly enough. Capitalism, Marxism, nationalism, militarism are movements of the nineteenth century. They grew up with us and have only just reached maturity. Yet humanitarianism, which seemed to us healthier than any of these, is sickly and languishing. What has happened?

Let us confront the barbarism of to-day with the humanitarianism of yesterday. In 1882 Moynier gave a comprehensive account of the development of the Red Cross since its founding.

Finally, let us mention the use of this Convention, in 1864, during the Carlist uprising in Spain. It was the only civil war in which the Convention was respected by both parties. Although it was a fierce struggle, there were no atrocities. The opponents who faced each other in arms did not fail to recognize—either on one side or the other—the obligation to brotherhood which the fate of the wounded laid upon them: they mutually respected the doctors and nurses. The wounded prisoners were well treated and received careful attention. The government even gave the wounded insurgents who reached Pamplona, their freedom . . . This chivalrous example deserves to be emphasized and recommended for imitation in every country where a similar situation may arise.

To this may be added—although the analogy is not perfect—the example which the Japanese—strangers to the Geneva Convention—gave in 1814 on the eve of a war with China. The military practices of the Celestial Empire are still strongly tinged with barbarism. Nevertheless the Japanese received instructions from their government which sound as if they had been drawn up by the philanthropists of Europe. It is very interesting to observe in a nation of peasants the sprouting of that moral seed which their representatives had discovered only a year before at Geneva.

Historical parallels are a thankless and dangerous pastime, but no one can object that the conditions and the times in this case are different. Yes, the times were different! But the nations are the same that are fighting in 1938. Again there is a civil war in Spain. Again there is a Japanese invasion of China. Only a generation lies between. A generation over which floats the white flag with the Red Cross. Yet to-day in Spain, thousands of prisoners are massacred, hospitals and infirmaries are bombed, crowds of women and children murdered. And in China—in Shanghai and Nanking—the prisoners were executed in such long lines that the sluggish rivers were red with the blood of the slain. Abandoned infants, half-dead under debris, incendiary bombs dropped on defenceless cities—these are the pictures that the news-reels unroll before our horrified eyes.

On 1 July 1911 Germany sent the gunboat Panther to the south Moroccan harbour of Agadir 'to protect German interests and subjects there.' Dissensions had broken out in Morocco between two brothers who were fighting for the sultanate. There was a commotion in the world and the Panther stole away again. To-day, twenty-six years later, in wars which are never declared, ships of neutral powers appear and sink the ships of other neutral powers, are bombed and in reprisal shell unfortified cities. The American gunboat Panay is sunk in a country with which the United States is at peace by another power which has not declared war on the first country. In the nineteenth century, inheritances, successions, unpaid debts, the shot of some crazy fanatic were occasions for war. In the twentieth century, kings are murdered in foreign lands, goods are confiscated, countries are annexed or occupied with troops, invasions are financed and equipped, ships sunk and populations incited to revolt—and we act as if it were a matter of course. And not because the wrong will be investigated and restitution made, but because might is always right. In the nineteenth century a newspaper article, Zola's *J'accuse*, shook the globe, revolutionized the conscience of a country and restored its laws. In the twentieth century thousands of people are sentenced, imprisoned or exiled without judgment or even a public hearing—and nothing happens.

What happened to mankind in those few years? What can explain this dreadful change?

We can attempt this cultural and political diagnosis only with the reservation that we too share the common bewilderment, injury and guilt.

The volcanic eruption of the World War fractured our material, spiritual and civilized life into a thousand atoms, and the 'Peace' was only a false and shabby patch-work. It has got us into several of the grotesque dilemmas that we see to-day. Technology has given us a surplus of potential freedom, but actually it has robbed us of our individual freedom. It hampers us in the event of personal defence or attack and delivers us over to countless alien influences and interferences in our lives from which escape is hardly possible anywhere. A uniformity of ideas and life results, in a constantly shrinking world, so that the need for freedom rebels, as in a family circle that is too close and narrow, and hate, rivalry and resentment are engendered. Hence the reaction to the greatly enhanced opportunities for understanding in our times expresses itself in a feeling of dislike and misunderstanding, in the creation of arbitrary boundaries, separations and peculiarities. Countless new nations and groups, crowded closely together on similar geographic and historical ground, retreat into tiny 'autarchic' cells, incapable of supporting life, and hate their neighbours.

But even in these microscopic units there is duality. Behind the cage-like frontiers, the unregulated flood of population heaves and presses constantly. The great emigrations have almost ceased. There is no way in and no way out. The passport has been promoted from a political and technical device to a symbol of the century's agony. And the immovable and defenceless human herd is trained through all the instruments of propaganda, the radio, the motion pictures and the newspapers, to mass reactions of obedience. The world's economy, with its practical and theoretical bases shattered by the war, was confronted with entirely new, and in part, entirely unsuitable economic entities. Imaginary war debts and imaginary reparations, giant industries which had become irrational in peace times, completely changed markets, and the newly partitioned centres of strength, all had to be organized again. One whole section of the world works and produces under Marxism. The international credit system was shattered. Co-operation in the division of raw materials, provisions, and even labour power was no longer possible. Struggles over labour, wages, standards of living broke out in the cellular units. Free enterprise was obstructed by necessary state interference. Common burdens had to be borne in common. This further intensified the feeling of segregation from, and hostility toward, the outer world. And it made it possible to foist upon the threatened masses, with their lack of education and freedom, every kind of political theory from the socialist class state to the national socialist commonwealth.

Europe had blown herself up suicidally. The mud of the shell-holes not only ate away the necessary bonds of understanding and goodwill; what is far worse, it damaged incalculably the bases of western culture. The world's centre of gravity was displaced from Europe to the American continent and to Asia. 'The balance of cultures' was definitely destroyed. Distant lands cover with the outward forms of European civilization the fragments of their own high cultures, but the spiritual traditions of the West are lacking in them—the humaneness of the Christian and the Ancient Worlds, the great ideal of human freedom that was once created and revered in Europe.

The renunciation of this ideal of Christian and ancient humanity means a real suicide for Europe. It was the unique moral reserve of European history. Strength and authority for the European individual, strength and authority for every European people streamed for centuries from this source, justified the vehemence of Europe's rise, yes, even the aggressions and the coercions which were practiced in its name. All this has been denied and lost. The 'revolt of the masses' has given the power into the hands of those who neither know nor care for the traditions and ideals of culture, and who are stirred by no yearning for knowledge. They live in a prehistoric and barbarous state, having outwardly assimilated the complicated weapons of civilization only in order to misuse them. It is a deceptive change which they are initiating. In word and deed, the pyres of their revolutions have already consumed the moral world of antiquity, the humanity of Christendom, and the freedom of the individual. Tyrants move the masses according to a technically perfected apparatus and by watchwords whose mysticism goes back to the most primitive condition of pre-logical thinking, such as before the downfall we used to study only among the savage races of the aboriginal jungles.

This explains a little of the terrifying change in a generation, our generation, and the cheerless outlook for humanitarianism in the twentieth century. It was aggravated by an irrational and unjust peace, which began with the promises of Wilson's Fourteen Points and ended in an orgy of revenge and stupidity in the Treaty of Versailles.

If the totalitarian war, whose primitive form we experienced in 1918, has demonstrated anything, it is that a great nation cannot be conquered. Armies can be defeated, and it is indicative that it was the armies that were built according to Clausewitz' plans, unrestrained and uncontaminated by parliamentary control, the armies of Russia, Germany and Austria, which were defeated. Clausewitz' theory of merciless attack by a totalitarian power can only be successful as long as the adversary is unprepared and is not resolved on desperate totalitarian defence. The offensive wars of our day with their frightful destructive means teach us that the totalitarian war strengthens the defence, and that nature resists the extirpation of the peaceful by the violent part of the human race. And since the peaceful man is biologically healthier and more valuable than the criminal man, force will never triumph in this struggle!

But this struggle between men who recognize humanity, and men who no longer, or do not yet, recognize it, must be fought out to the end.

There has been the League of Nations, and its tragic corridors still stand in Geneva. In The Hague are the proud ruins of the Peace Palace whose tasks were reconstructed in 1919 as a Permanent International Tribunal. The League of Nations has produced great and noble documents for the safeguarding of peace: the Geneva Protocol of 1924 for the outlawing of war and security against peace-violators; in 1925, the Locarno Pact, for the safeguarding of peace in Western Europe; in 1928, the Kellogg Pact for mutual outlawing of war; the numerous disarmament conferences. Article eight of the League of Nations reads: 'The members of the League recognize that the maintenance of peace demands the limitation of national armaments.'

But the League of Nations has missed every opportunity to take action against crying injustice. It has let slip every possibility voluntarily to correct the impossible consequences of the peace treaty. It has let aggressors go unpunished and has never protected a victim. It is an intriguing microcosm of highly paid diplomats, functionaries and their secretaries who, in their frivolous way, further the pre-war games of diplomacy, and a contempt for their own decisions. It devotes itself to the opium traffic and to combating white slavery, and publishes distinguished medical works on hygienic problems and questions of international nutrition. But in every serious conflict it has failed mankind.

After the war there were the beginnings of a powerful and influential peace movement: The International Women's League for Peace and Freedom, the League of Nations Society; the revolutionary pacifists. There was a very successful and distinguished literature of peace: Barbusse, Latzko, Leonard Frank, Romain Rolland, Remarque, H.G.Wells. Part of it has been burned, part is literary history.

In 1922 Pope Pius XI issued his peace bulls, *Pax Christi in regno Christi*, and *Ubi arcano*. In 1914 the Protestant churches formed a World Union for Friendship among the Churches, and in 1919 an International Reconciliation Union.

The Hague Conference of 1907 forbade the use of poison gas. The poison gas protocol of 1925, signed by thirty-three nations, renewed the ban. To-day every European will soon own his own gas-mask, and the children learn to use them at school. There are agreements prohibiting the bombardment of unfortified cities, prohibiting bombing with explosives and gas from airplanes. No man in his right mind expects these agreements to be carried out.

The features of the war of to-morrow have been described too often and too impressively to require repetition. It will be a war of super-tanks with a speed of ninety miles an hour, of thermite incendiary bombs, of 'flying fortresses.' In the World War, the heaviest bomb weighed ninety pounds; those of to-day two thousand. There will be death-rays and death-centrifuges that fire 33,000 shots a minute;

bacteria swarms to infect continents, and motorized divisions.

The League of Nations Armaments Book for 1937 lists, while referring to the withholding of numerous armament figures, these minimum estimates: standing armies of 8,500,000 as against 6,000,000 in 1913; total armaments expenditures of the world 7,100,-000,000 on the old gold basis (12,000,000,000 on the devaluated basis) against 2,500,000,000 in 1913. Of the expenditures, 63.4% are for Europe as against 30% in 1932. Between 1932 and 1937, the military budgets of the European countries rose about 80%, that of the United States only 50%, Japan's more than 100%, Russia's around 200% (quoted from the *New York Times*, 14 December 1937).

This is what the world looks like twenty-seven years after Dunant's death: it squanders its riches, with which it could create a paradise, on a gigantic armaments machine that is set in ever more furious vibrations. Its economy, which could provide bread for all, is going to pieces as the result of an unnatural partition. Its social need is mounting and with that its social unrest. In politics and in international law anarchy reigns. There have been powerful voices against the evil, the voice of the late Thomas Masaryk, the voice of President Roosevelt which gives no respite, even Eden's vast self-control may be mentioned.

But we, at the end of our wanderings through the life of little, unpretentious Monsieur Dunant, can no longer cry, 'Lay Down Your Arms!' We do not wish to have this cry die in our throats before the great holocaust to come, as did Bertha von Suttner and her friends. We wish to survive it in order to rescue the voice of humanity at a time when the old doctrines of salvation and freedom can be proclaimed as a new redemption to the masses who to-day despise them, and to the youth which has never heard them.

On what did the humanitarianism of Dunant and his generation go to pieces? On their weakness, their non-political position, their wishy-washy emotions, their unscientific methods, their lack of radicalism.

> Nothing will expose us to the danger of a war quicker than unclear and superficial pacifism. If we are not prepared to sacrifice sectarianism, parties, sentimental and patriotic loyalties, financial interests, to subordinate race pride and race prejudice to this greater end, in order to elevate it into a law and a standard not only of our political, but our social life, then our friendly intentions will all have been in vain. (H.G.Wells.)

Dunant needed the martyrdom of a long and unhappy life in order finally to recognize the enemy, the author of the cry of Solferino—and then it was too late, he was mute and broken, and the more his touching, childlike and earnest form began to lapse into the shadows, the shriller and swifter was the rush of events toward disaster.

Dunant's fate looms before us as a warning. One may feel a conviction, but an objective has to be thought out. The nineteenth century reversed these things: it developed certain convictions, but had no idea how to put into effect the objectives for which it nebulously yearned.

Humanitarianism, to succeed and to be effective, must be bold, well thought out, unsentimental, politically alert, radical in morality and scientific in methods.

But does the Red Cross really have a choice?

The Red Cross is the work of Henri Dunant and is a part of the sum of his ideas. He thought this idea through to the end, and at the end stood the word Peace! It was not granted him to guide his work to this same end, but it is bound up organically and indissolubly with his spirit and his fate. Dunant's sacrifice, the years of suffering and of solitude, was a sacrifice for the Red Cross.

What is required is to strengthen this organization and animate the spirit of its founder in every branch.

The Red Cross to-day consists of fifty-seven national societies. The International Committee of the Red Cross has its seat at Geneva, and consists of at most twenty-five Swiss citizens. It serves as a kind of umpire for the national societies and is the political court of review for the international agreements of the Convention.

In addition, since 1919 there has been the League of Red Cross Societies in Paris. It is concerned with the tasks of the organization in peace time—the care of the sick, help in catastrophes, and the Junior Red Cross.

The national representatives and the representatives of the societies meet in the International Conference in Geneva.

To-day the Red Cross is the only international organization of an official and semi-political character that survived the War and the post-War period without disintegration and compromise. In the League and at the International Conferences, the representatives of the Soviet state still sit beside those of the fascist and democratic countries.

Does it owe this unique position to its humanitarian activity, its diplomatic shrewdness or its humanitarian passivity? It is a difficult question to answer. Probably to all three.

The Red Cross has been in existence seventy-five years. A thousand times it has brilliantly demonstrated its capacity for work and readiness for action. It has never interrupted its services to humanity, and it has performed them despite growing difficulties in principle and of an organizational kind.

But one is compelled to ask with concern how long this will still be possible? Is the Red Cross adequately prepared to meet the horrors of the coming war? Is it sufficiently energetic in safeguarding its contract against all violations? Does it not feel the necessity of striving for the prevention of inhumanities, does it not believe that it must take an active part in the struggle for peace, for the prevention and the abolition of war?

Is the Red Cross a pacifist organization, or not? Is its help on the battlefield like that of the doctor, the enemy of disease, who never abandons his patient, or does it help like the Samaritan who binds the wounds of the antagonists after a fight so that they will be better able to attack each other again? Both are necessary activities, but one is a social duty and the other is a professional obligation without moral gain.

Among the thirty-seven organizations, of a religious, cultural, political and pedagogic kind that make up the National Peace Conference in the United States, the Red Cross is missing.

But if with justifiable prudence it wishes to avoid even the appearance of infringing its neutrality, must it not insist the more rigidly on the observation of the agreements of the Geneva Convention, which form the basis of its existence?

Under present-day conditions of warfare, will the hospitals be protected and respected according to Article One of the Geneva Convention? No, they will be shelled.

Will the inhabitants who come to the aid of the wounded be spared and left free in accordance with Article Five? No, they will be tortured and murdered.

Will the prisoners who are found unfit for labour be returned to their homes? No, they will be imprisoned.

The excuse has been urged that modern totalitarian war, which mechanically annihilates its unseen enemies from a cowardly distance, cannot distinguish between hospitals and barracks, between children and generals. But is not the inevitable consequence, then, that a blind rage must drive men to fight these weapons of destruction with more effective means than with treaties which everybody knows will not be respected? Is it not timely once more to consider Dunant's proposal of 1870, recommending the creation of neutral protective areas for wounded and noncombatants? Then, if they were bombed, it would at least be a startling and unmistakable violation of humanity. And should not the dramatic findings of the Nye Committee, the special committee of the U.S. Senate, which investigated the munitions industry, give the Red Cross an opportunity to come out for a nationalization of the munitions industry in all countries, as has now been done in France, so that some limits may be set at least to the private world of irresponsibility and lack of conscience?

These are only examples. The Red Cross, which heals wounds, must also prevent wounds. The Red Cross, which in our desolate present remains one of the few havens of humanitarianism, will also be one of the few sources from which humanitarianism may once more water the parched and ruined earth. It will if it resolutely and radically declares for the party of peace, stimulate the enthusiastic co-operation of an awakened youth, which is no longer deaf to the brazen voice of humanity as it has been formed forever by the Bible and Antiquity.

The work and the life of Henri Dunant will have become one on that day when all that remains is the Red Cross of Peace!

Dunant's Principal Works

(Extracted from Alexis François: '*Henri Dunant, un grand humanitarian*,' *Revue Internationale de la Croix Rouge*, Geneva, vol.III, March 1928.)

Notice sur la Régence de Tunis, Geneva, 1858.

L'Empire de Charlemagne rétabli ou le Saint-Empire romain reconstitué par Napoleon III, Geneva, 1859.

Mémorandum au sujet de la Société financière et industrielle des Moulins de Mons-Djemila en Algérie, Paris, n.d. [1859.]

Un Souvenir de Solférino, Geneva, 1862.

L'Esclavage chez les Musulmans et aux États-Unis d'Amérique, Geneva, 1863.

La charité sur les champs de bataille, Geneva, 1864.

Projet de Société internationale pour la rénovation de l'Orient, n.p.n.d. [Paris,1866.]

Les prisonniers de guerre, Paris, 1867.

Bibliothèque internationale universelle, Paris, 1867.

Société internationale de prévoyance en faveur des citoyens sous les armes, auxiliaire de la Société internationale de secours aux blessés des armées de terre et de mer. [Program and statutes, without author's name.] Paris, 1870.

A proposal for introducing uniformity into the condition of prisoners of war. [Paper read at a meeting of the National Association for the Promotion of Social Science, 6 August 1872,] London, 1872.

[A letter on the necessity of establishing an international court of arbitration, presented to the Social Science Congress at Plymouth, 1872], the *Globe*, London, 13 September 1872.

International Society for the protection of prisoners of war. [Lecture at Brighton, 15 September 1873.] London, 1873.

'*An die Presse.*' *Die Waffen Nieder!*, No.9, pp.327–31, Vienna, 1896.

'*Kleines Arsenal gegen den Militarismus.*' *Die Waffen Nieder!*, Nos.5,6,8–9, pp.161–6, 208–10, 310–14, Vienna, 1897.

'*Kleines Arsenal gegen den Krieg.*' *Die Waffen Nieder!*, No.10, pp.366–7, Vienna, 1897.

La proposition de Sa Majesté l'empereur Nicolas II, n.p.l.d. Heiden, 1898.

Works Consulted

Adams, J.T., The Epic of America, Boston, 1934.

Appia, Louis, *Le chirurgien à l'ambulance*, Geneva, 1859.

Barton, Clara, The Red Cross, Washington, 1898.

Beard, Charles A. and Mary, The Rise of American Civilization, New York, 1927.

Berthcrand, A., *Campagne d'Italie de 1859*, Paris, 1860.

Boardman, Mabel T., Under the Red Cross Flag at Home and Abroad, Philadelphia, 1915.

Buckle, H.T., History of Civilization in England, London, 1882.

Bülow, Fürst, *Erinnerungen*, Berlin, 1931.

Cazenove, Léonce de, *La Guerre et l'humanité au dix-neuvième siècle*, Paris, n.d. [1870.]

Channing, E., History of the United States, New York, 1921–6.

Cushing, H., From a Surgeon's Journal, Boston, 1936.

Davison, H.P., The American Red Cross in the Great War, New York, 1919.

Du Camp, Maxime, *La Croix Rouge en France*, Zürich, 1918.

Dunant, J.H., *Les debuts de la Croix Rouge en France*, Zürich, 1918.

Engelbrecht, H.C., Revolt Against War, New York, 1937.

Epler, Percy H., Life of Clara Barton, New York, 1915.

François, Alexis, *Le berceau de la Croix Rouge*, Geneva, 1918.

Gooch, G.P., History of Modern Europe, London, 1924.

Grant, A.J., and Temperley, H., Europe in the Nineteenth and Twentieth Century, London, 1934.

Gretton, R.H., Modern History of the English People, London, 1913.

Guedalla, Phillip, The Hundred Years, New York, 1937.

—The Second Empire, New York, 1928.

Haje, C., and Simon, J.M., *Les origines de la Croix Rouge*, Amsterdam, 1902.

Howe, M.A. De Wolfe, Causes and Their Champions, Boston, 1926.

Kautsky, K., *Sozialisten und Krieg*, Prague, 1937.

Ludwig, Emil, *Kaiser Wilhelm II*, Berlin, 1926.

Lueder, C., *Die Genfer Konvention*, Erlangen, 1876.

Mannheim, K., *Mass und Wert*, Zürich, 1937.

Mottram, R.H., *Wesen und Geschichte der Finanzspekulation*, Leipzig, 1932.

Moynier, G., *Les dix premières années de la Croix Rouge*, Geneva, 1873.

—*Ce que c'est la Croix Rouge*, Geneva, 1874.

Moynier, G., *La fondation de la Croix Rouge*, Geneva, 1903.

—*La Croix Rouge, son passé et son avenir*, Paris, 1882.

Muir, Ramsay, Expansion of Europe, London, 1922.

Müller, R., *Entstehungs Geschichte des Roten Kreuzes und der Genfer Konvention, mit Unterstützung ihres Begründers J.H.Dunant*, Stuttgart, 1897.

Page, Kirby, Must we go to War?, New York, 1937.

Pauli, Hertha, *Nur eine Frau: Bertha von Suttner*, Vienna, 1937.

Poplimont, C., *Lettres sur la campagne d'Italie*, Brussels, 1860.

Revue Internationale de la Croix Rouge, Geneva, 1869– [date].

Sombart, W., *Sozialismus und soziale Bewegung*, Jena, 1905.

Sonderegger, René, *Jean Henri Dunant, Revolutionär*, Zürich, n.d.

Strachey, L., Eminent Victorians, London, 1918.

Thayer, W.R., Cavour, Boston, 1911.

Vagts, A., History of Militarism, New York, 1937.

Vial, J. and C., *Histoire abrégée des campagnes modernes*, Paris, 1910.

Weber, A., *Kulturgeschichte als Kultursoziologie*, Leyden, 1935.

Woodward, E.L., Great Britain and the German Navy, Oxford, 1935.

Young, C.S., Clara Barton, Boston, 1922.